Studying Education

# Studying Education

## AN INTRODUCTION TO THE KEY DISCIPLINES IN EDUCATION STUDIES

*Edited by Barry Dufour and Will Curtis*

 Open University Press

Open University Press
McGraw-Hill Education
McGraw-Hill House
Shoppenhangers Road
Maidenhead
Berkshire
England
SL6 2QL

email: enquiries@openup.co.uk
world wide web: www.openup.co.uk

and Two Penn Plaza, New York, NY 10121-2289, USA


First published 2011

A catalogue record of this book is available from the British Library

ISBN-13: 978-0-33-524105-7 (pb) 978-0-33-524106-4 (hb)
ISBN-10: 0-33-524105-0 (pb) 0-33-524106-9 (hb)
eISBN: 9780335241071


*Library of Congress Cataloging-in-Publication Data*
CIP data applied for

Typesetting and e-book compilations by
RefineCatch Limited, Bungay, Suffolk
Printed and bound by CPI Group (UK) Ltd, CR0 4YY.

The **McGraw·Hill** Companies

# Contents

# List of figures

# Acknowledgements

We would like to acknowledge our gratitude to a number of people. First, to our contributors (Clyde Chitty, Rebecca Allen, Richard Waller, Diahann Gallard, Angie Garden and Deborah Le Play), who endured our constant requests for small modifications, additional information and clarification right up to the final stages in the preparation of the book. Second, to our families for their forbearance during sometimes intense editorial activity. Third, to our invariably enquiring and hard-working students at De Montfort University, who acted as a stimulus for us and are a pleasure to teach. And last, but not least, to our publisher at Open University Press, Fiona Richman, and her editorial assistant, Stephanie Frosch, who both provided the most unbelievable and patient support and advice during the preparation of our book.

*Barry Dufour*
*Will Curtis*

# Contributors

**Dr Rebecca Allen**
Rebecca is Senior Lecturer in Economics of Education at the Institute of Education, University of London. She is the course leader for the MA/MSc in Economics of Education, a course designed for policy-makers and teachers from all over the world. Her research interests include secondary school admissions policies, parental choice of school, quasi-market reforms to education, measuring segregation and estimating school effectiveness. Her research is predominantly quantitative, using large-scale datasets, such as the National Pupil Database in England, to analyse the effects of policy reforms.

**Professor Clyde Chitty**
Clyde Chitty is currently Visiting Professor at the University of London Institute of Education and was, until recently, Goldsmiths Professor of Policy and Management in Education at Goldsmiths College, University of London. He was Head of the Department of Educational Studies at Goldsmiths from 1998 to 2006. Prior to joining the department in 1998, he was Reader in the Modern History of Education at the University of Birmingham. His teaching career began in London in 1966 where he taught English and history in a number of comprehensive schools for over a decade before moving to Leicestershire in 1977 to become Senior Vice Principal, and later Principal, of the newly established Earl Shilton Community College, a pioneering community school that attracted visitors from all over the world. He is the author, co-author or editor of over 30 books and reports on education, including *Thirty Years On* (1996), a large-scale study of the British comprehensive school, co-authored with the late Caroline Benn.

His most recent books include *Education Policy in Britain* and *Eugenics, 'Race' and Intelligence in Education.* He is Editor of the campaigning journal, *Forum: For Promoting 3–19 Comprehensive Education.*

**Dr Will Curtis**
Will Curtis is Subject Leader and Principal Lecturer in Education at De Montfort University, Leicester. He began working in education as an FE lecturer in the south-west, teaching on programmes in Philosophy and Sociology. After completing his

doctorate, an ethnographic study of learning cultures in 16–19 education, he taught on the PGCE for lecturers in the post-compulsory sector. He has developed Education Studies modules on Philosophy of Education, Radical Educations, Cultural and Educational Transformations, and Learners and Learning, and supervises research students in a variety of educational fields. Will is a member of the executive committee of the British Education Studies Association and is on the editorial board of the journal *Educational Futures*. A Teacher Fellow, Will established and now edits *Gateway Papers*, a journal for pedagogic research in higher education at De Montfort University. He has previously co-written two Education Studies undergraduate texts, entitled *Learning in Contemporary Culture* (2009) and *Education Studies Reflective Reader* (2010).

**Barry Dufour**
Barry Dufour is Visiting Senior Research Fellow in Education at De Montfort University, Leicester. He has taught on undergraduate and postgraduate education courses at the School of Education University of Leicester and at the School of Sport and Exercise Sciences at Loughborough University. Since the 1960s, he has pioneered the teaching of the social sciences and humanities in schools, working on early pilots of GCE sociology and contributing to the development of the first A level GCE in Anthropology. He has written many books and articles, and his most recent publication is *Developing Citizens: A Comprehensive Introduction to Effective Citizenship Education in the Secondary School*, edited with Tony Breslin (Hodder Murray, 2006). He is currently working on several books on his other main interests, including disruptive behaviour in schools, and outstanding schools around the world. Beyond the university sector, he has been an education inspector and a consultant to inner-city schools. He was a founder member of the Association for the Teaching of the Social Sciences in the 1960s, holds several fellowships and vice presidencies with national education organisations, and serves on their committees.

**Diahann Gallard**
Diahann Gallard is Senior Lecturer in Early Years Education at Liverpool John Moores University. She currently leads modules on Education Studies, Early Childhood Studies and Primary Education QTS programmes, teaches on the PGCE Early Years course and is the route leader for the Primary Education with Early Years (QTS) course. Diahann is also a Liaison Tutor for teacher training school placements and consultant for Primary school creative partnerships. Diahann has contributed to a number of education studies books and she has reviewed various educational text books including *The Psychology of Education* (2010). Her particular research interests are educational psychology, the early years of education and educational anthrozoology.

**Angela Garden**
Angie Garden is Senior Lecturer in Education Studies and Early Years and Early Childhood Studies at Liverpool John Moores University. Prior to this she held the post of Lecturer in Psychology at Edge Hill University and has worked directly with children in a range of settings including special needs schools and with Barnardo's Charity undertaking a consultative report on supporting siblings of children with

special needs. Her module leadership responsibilities currently include the examination of atypical development and the understanding of how children learn, and she supervises independent studies at undergraduate levels. Angie's research work addresses emotional and behavioural difficulties in childhood. She is currently undertaking a Masters in Advanced Educational Practice specializing in dyslexia, working on a one-on-one basis with children in mainstream settings utilizing specific reading and comprehension techniques.

**Debbie Le Play**
Debbie is Head of Quality in the Faculty of Art, Design and Humanities at De Montfort University, Leicester. She taught at secondary and post-compulsory levels in France for eight years, and began her career in higher education teaching French and French Studies in 1990. Her module leadership responsibilities currently include an undergraduate module that studies education systems and educational issues in Europe from a comparative perspective, and a further module that combines theory and practice in the context of Teaching English as an Additional Language to Young Learners. She is undertaking doctoral research on the student experience in Higher Education focusing specifically on student expectations and implications for retention and engagement, and drawing on Pierre Bourdieu's 'thinking tools' to conceptualize and analyse these phenomena.

**Dr Richard Waller**
Richard Waller is Director of Lifelong Learning and Principal Lecturer in Education at the University of the West of England. He has taught in further and higher education since 1994. As well as teaching sociology of education modules, he trains teachers in the adult education sector, manages a number of Masters degree courses, and supervises postgraduate students. Richard's doctoral research was on the experiences of adults returning to formal education, and he has presented and published widely on this topic. His other research interests focus upon the intersection of identity, social class and education, including widening participation and student experience, and qualitative research methods. Richard is co-convenor for the British Sociological Association's Education Study Group and reviews editor for the *International Journal of Lifelong Education*.

# Introduction

## *Barry Dufour and Will Curtis*

The intention of this book is to provide an accessible overview of the basic or 'foundation' education disciplines, in one handy volume, for the ever-increasing population of undergraduates on Education Studies courses. It is also of relevance to students on Postgraduate Certificate in Education (PGCE) courses and other education courses. The background to the book is twofold. First, there has been a fundamental change in the professional training of teachers in recent years, with an increase in the focus on the National Curriculum and how to teach it, and a decrease and gradual removal of theory-based academic courses on the basic education disciplines surveyed in our book. This decline has been well documented by Furlong and Lawn (2010), who claim that 'the education disciplines' are more accepted in Europe and the USA than they are in the UK. They also assert the current and future relevance of the education disciplines in spite of their relative demise in teacher training. The Education Act of 2011 is likely to remove 'theory' even more from PGCE courses with the creation of Teaching Schools within outstanding schools, thus handing over the teacher training function to these proposed new schools.

Second, and by contrast, non-professional undergraduate courses on education, usually called 'Education Studies', have spread throughout the new universities and into many traditional universities. Students have become attracted to a three-year academic, analytical and non-professional course that allows them to enter any career afterwards or to move onto a PGCE course, having gained a wide and deep knowledge of education and educational issues from their undergraduate studies.

It is often difficult for any student of education to make sense of the vast and complex disciplines that underpin it. It was therefore our intention to provide a general overview of each subject, each written by an experienced scholar in the specialism. At the same time, we have tried to ensure that the chapters are written in easy-to-understand language, with any difficult concepts or ideas carefully explained. While each chapter borrows in style from the disciplines it outlines, there are a number of features they all share. These common features have been designed with the intention of enabling readers to explore each discipline (and aspects within each discipline) in greater depth. As such, each chapter is grouped around a number of 'key themes'. Each also incorporates boxes that identify key research, researchers and publications within the field. Chapters conclude by identifying books, websites and journals that are at the forefront of their discipline, and provide the reader with suggestions for further independent study.

In Chapter 1, Barry Dufour offers an extended introduction to the history of education, focusing on nine key topics or themes. In Chapter 2 Clyde Chitty explores the constant government policy changes in education in the context of changing political, economic and social contexts. Will Curtis, in Chapter 3, on the philosophy of education, considers the fundamental ideas at the heart of any debates about education, beginning with the Greek philosophers and taking us forward in time to today by looking at the influential educational ideas of Freire, Illich and Neill. Rebecca Allen, in Chapter 4, contributes a highly original survey of the increasingly important area of economics of education. In Chapter 5, Richard Waller looks at some of the main sociological perspectives and landmark research on education to be found in the sociology of education. Chapter 6, by Diahann Gallard and Angie Garden, is a summary of three major areas of focus and research in the psychology of education – behaviour, learning and intelligence. Finally, in Chapter 7, Debbie Le Play surveys the world scene by presenting an overview of the important area of comparative education, where we learn that, by looking at various countries through the prism of research on comparative education, we can place our own education system in context.

We hope you find this overview of the education disciplines both enlightening and a spur to further study.

## Reference

Furlong, J. and Lawn, M. (eds) (2010) *Disciplines of Education: Their Role in the Future of Education Research*. Abingdon: Routledge.

# 1

## BARRY DUFOUR
## The History of Education

---

### Learning outcomes

By the end of this chapter, you should be able to:

- understand the history of education as a discipline;
- draw on research and writings to outline and assess key themes in the history of education;
- identify the main historical trends in education from the 19th century to the present day;
- assess the role of individuals and social movements in bringing about educational change.

---

## Introduction

To study the history of education in any country with a formal state education system involves engaging with and unlocking the particular interplay of social, cultural, economic and political forces at work at any given time. Over the centuries, in the gradual transition from piecemeal voluntary provision to universal state schooling in the UK, many processes are apparent, especially in the form of major movements such as industrialization and globalization. We can also observe the operation of progressive campaigning groups that wish to broaden educational opportunity or, conversely, the actions of entrenched special interest groups that wish to preserve educational structures and class inequalities. But equally prominent, as we shall see later, are the examples of determined, enlightened and pioneering individuals who have made a distinctive historical mark in their efforts to reform, improve and extend educational provision for ever-widening sections of society.

## Overview of the discipline: what is 'history of education'?

The subject and discipline that analyses all of these trends is history of education. Historians of education have their own methods of research and theoretical perspectives. In relation to research methods, much of their effort is directed at the study of primary and secondary sources of information, including the perusal of original documents such as archive material, letters, diaries, books, pamphlets, newspapers, journals, biographies, autobiographies and now the World Wide Web. The themes they explore are considerable, including researching influential educationalists, government policy, changes in schooling and teaching, and access to education; many of these areas are explored below in this chapter. Major contributions to the history of education in the UK are from a wide range of scholars, including Roy Lowe, Brian Simon, Richard Aldrich, Peter Gordon, Gary McCulloch, Jane Martin and many more.

Theoretical perspectives have ranged from straight descriptive, conservative or liberal accounts of the growth of aspects of education, often politically complacent, to the more openly Marxist critiques especially from Brian Simon who charted the dominance of inequality and social class in the educational story, particularly in his magisterial four-volume history, *Studies in the History of Education*, researched and published between the 1950s and the 1990s, and stretching in scope from 1780 to 1990 (Simon 1960, 1965, 1974, 1991). Furthermore, in his essay *The History of Education: Its Importance for Understanding* (Simon 1994), he surveys key epochs in the development of state education and links it with the general advance of educational theory, suggesting a cyclical trend, for example, at the end of the 19th century with the development of the higher grade schools, and the 1960s that witnessed a flowering in Britain of expansion in higher education and progressive changes in schools. These periods, he demonstrates, were followed by retrenchment. Gary McCulloch (2011) also traces these changing fortunes in a recent important overview of history of education as a university subject. Simon argues that it is the job of the historian of education to analyse these changes for the greater enlightenment of trainee teachers, teachers and students of education in general.

### Key figure: Brian Simon (1915–2002)

Brian Simon has been the most influential historian of education in the UK, with his research in this field and many others, such as the nature of teaching and learning, spanning several decades. His seminal work of scholarship, the four-volume *Studies in the History of Education*, was researched and written over a period of 40 years. Although from an aristocratic background, he was, like his parents, passionately involved in education and, politically, on the Left. Throughout his life, he not only researched and wrote about education, he took an active political and campaigning role in promoting comprehensive schools and state education. He played a key part, in the 1950s, with Robin Pedley and Stewart Mason, in the setting up of the famous Leicestershire Plan for comprehensive education (still thriving today but with some emerging modifications). He was also a founder of the influential education journal,

*Forum*, still flourishing today, with its commitment to reclaiming the radical tradition in state education for 3–19 year olds through comprehensive education. His abiding attachment was to the concept of human educability – to a belief in the potential of all children.

If you google *Brian Simon* you will find many sites, including the Wikipedia entry on him, and you can read his own account of his life in his autobiography, *A Life in Education* (Simon 1998).

**Key figures: Institute of Education, University of London**

Several of the key researchers and writers on the history of education have been based at the Institute. These include Emeritus Professor Richard Aldrich, who has produced hundreds of articles and important books in his long career; Professor Jane Martin, who has written several key books on women and education; and Professor Gary McCulloch, who holds the title of the Brian Simon Professor of History of Education. Gary has produced many key books, including the Routledge reader in the history of education cited in the Further Reading list at the end of this chapter. If you google their names at the Institute (www.ioe.ac.uk), you will find details of their publications.

The following nine themes will largely cover the period from the late 19th century to today. The topics chosen include some of the most important areas of interest and scholarship, but they are just a selection. The intention is to provide a very basic introductory overview of each topic but with key references to further specialist sources so that you can investigate in more depth.

## Key theme 1: the growth of state education – elementary and primary education

### The 19th century

In the 19th century, a whole range of voluntary and private schools existed for the few, there being no state education until 1870. Children were still working long hours in the factories and the mines so the idea of going to school was a benefit most did not experience. The charitable and fee-paying schools, often for the younger age ranges, provided what was then called an 'elementary' education, which today we would call 'primary school education'. There were charity schools endowed by wealthy people, 'ragged schools' for the very poor, industry schools for learning a trade, and monitor schools run by the educational pioneer, Joseph Lancaster, where older pupils would teach younger ones. There was often a clear distinction in the curriculum for boys and girls, with girls learning household skills such as cooking and sewing and boys learning practical skills and a trade. The major emphasis for all was on the three Rs – reading, writing and arithmetic, but two others Rs were also to the fore – the teaching of religion and 'respect', the inculcation of obedience and good behaviour. There were also many Sunday schools because children only had Sunday off from work.

**Key figure: Robert Owen (1771–1858)**

Robert Owen was an early socialist pioneer who provided a school for the children of workers at his cotton mill factory in New Lanark, Scotland. He helped to pioneer infant schools and community schooling as well as having an impact on the Cooperative movement. His ideas are also relevant to the progress made in our understanding of working conditions and the provision of childcare and healthcare.

If you search for 'New Lanark Robert Owen' thousands of websites become available, including a Wikipedia entry on this great philanthropist. You can download a considerable amount of information about his school, his ideas, the mill and the village that has been restored – and you can visit. The visitor centre runs events including the re-enactment of being a pupil in a 19th-century school. New Lanark is now a World Heritage Site and tourists from all over the world visit this very special place to see the mill and the school. The official web address is www.newlanark.org.

As the 19th century wore on, there was increasing pressure from many quarters for a state-provided compulsory system of elementary schools. There were sound economic reasons for a universal school system given that increasing industrialization and the growth of factories and towns were going to require a skilled workforce who, at least, could read. The campaign for educational reform came from many sources including from working-class people through their trades unions, radical middle-class groups, the churches (although concerned about their influence on religious instruction in a possibly secular system), and from key politicians such as William Forster, Henry Bruce and Earl de Grey. These three used their long-term friendship in careful collaboration as they guided the 1870 Elementary Education Act into law (Baker 2001). The Act is often referred to as the Forster Education Act, in recognition of William Forster's key role.

Democratically elected School Boards (the forerunners of the Local Education Authorities) were set up to run the schools and to build them by levying a local rate (a local tax), with some funding from central government, although the church schools did not receive a local rate. Furthermore, school boards could allow their schools to choose no religious instruction or, alternatively, non-denominational teaching from the Bible. The school leaving age was gradually raised, to 13 in 1899.

**Activity: 19th-century school buildings**

Depending on where you live, see if you can find a primary school built in the 19th century. Maybe you could ask to visit.

## The 20th century

The 1902 Education Act abolished the school boards and made the new local education authorities (LEAs) responsible for elementary and secondary schools. School
meals and medical examinations were gradually introduced. Schools continued to
stress the three Rs (or the five Rs if we include respect and religion). Desks were in
rows and there was iron discipline enforced by corporal punishment (the cane).
Teaching methods were usually strict and formal right into the 20th century, often
with the use of rote learning. The education was rudimentary because children would
leave to start work at the age of 13, later 14. Class sizes were large, often 40 or more.
This pattern continued through into the Second World War. However, the 1944
Education Act, passed near the end of the war in preparation for the post-war world,
had a major impact on primary schools, formalizing the three sectors of primary,
secondary (grammar, modern or technical) and further education, but with the 11+
examination used to filter so-called able children (the minority) into grammar schools
and the majority into secondary modern schools (few technical schools were built).
Many primary schools now began to stream pupils so that the top stream could reach
appropriate levels in English and arithmetic in order to pass the 11+ exam.

It was not until the 1960s and 1970s, especially following the radical Plowden
Report of 1967, that more child-centred and progressive methods were championed,
with many primary schools freed from the pressure of the 11+ because many LEAs
had abolished selection as they developed non-selective comprehensive secondary
schools. But this period of relative freedom and autonomy for the teachers and pupils
did not last long. By the 1980s, there was a political backlash against the so-called
progressive methods, partly influenced by right-wing Conservatives with their Black
Papers on education that appeared in the late 1960s and early 1970s (Cox and Dyson
1971). The Conservative government's 1988 Education Reform Act brought in the
centrally imposed and prescriptive National Curriculum of ten subjects plus Religious
Education and heralded in SATs (Standard Assessment Tests) and league tables:
what some people have called the era of tests, targets, tick lists and tables (league
tables) that is still with us today, certainly in England (Wales and Scotland do not have
SATs and league tables).

## The 21st century

The New Labour government, from 1997 onwards, continued with these Conservative
arrangements but added several National Strategies, especially the Numeracy Hour
and Literacy Hour for each day in primary schools, as additional responsibilities. The
aim of the Conservative and New Labour reforms was to generate higher standards
for the pupils in primary schools to achieve, but the reforms also placed a stranglehold on the curriculum and teaching methods and were surrounded by constant criticisms from many sections of the education community.

Revisions to the National Curriculum were made at various times, including
in 2000 with the advent of the new subject of Citizenship, but potentially the
biggest changes were recommended in 2009 with the publication of two major
reviews of primary education, the government-initiated Independent Primary Review

(Rose 2009) and the independently sponsored Cambridge Primary Review (Alexander 2010), with 75 recommendations including the abolition of SATs. Neither of the reviews was implemented because the coalition government, elected in May 2010, decided on its own Review of the National Curriculum for 2011. It will be interesting to see the outcome of this beyond 2011 as a result of any recommendations. But it is important to note that changes in primary schools go far beyond just the curriculum and include debates about how the schools are run, all of which were addressed in the landmark Cambridge Primary Review, the most comprehensive enquiry into English primary education for 40 years.

## Key theme 2: secondary education – a long divisive history

The development of secondary education in the UK has been a history of selection, elitism and social class prejudice, admittedly alongside real progress, refinement and success. Compulsory secondary education for all children in the UK did not arrive until the 20th century but it could have flourished in the 19th century if a key reform were allowed to expand.

### The 19th century

In the late 19th century, after the 1870 Elementary Education Act, the only secondary schools that could call themselves 'secondary' were the grammar schools, attended by a minority of pupils, largely from middle-class backgrounds. Many elementary schools, where children left at 12 or later 13, were allowing pupils to stay on at school into 'higher grades'. In addition, special purpose-built 'higher grade schools' were being created by the local school boards in many cities in the UK, including in Bristol, Manchester, Birmingham and London. Working-class children were attending these schools. The schools were teaching a broad curriculum to boys and girls but were also strong on science. The education provided by these schools was seen as an excellent preparation for a wide range of commercial careers and skilled trades. Many people considered them to be an alternative form of secondary education to the grammar school. But various entrenched interests in the Tory Party and the established churches took the view that they were a threat to the grammar schools. In 1902, with a Conservative landslide in the election, the higher grade schools were abolished by act of parliament. You can read a full account of their rise and fall in Meriel Vlaeminke's landmark study, *The English Higher Grade Schools* (2000).

### The 20th century

Right from the start of the 20th century, following the 1902 Education Act and the championing of the grammar schools as the only form of education entitled to name itself 'secondary', the seeds were sown for a diverse and divisive secondary system of education. The grammar schools continued, while new names were found for the other post-elementary schools, such as 'higher elementary', 'central schools' and 'junior technical schools'. All of these schools offered a practical curriculum geared towards the commercial or industrial world. Gradually, the idea developed that there should be a clear primary and secondary education, with a selective examination at the age of 11 (the 11+) to allocate pupils to grammar schools (for the minority) or secondary modern or technical schools. All of this was consolidated in the 1944 Education Act, sometimes known as the Butler Act (after R.A. Butler, the minister who guided it).

The exception to these trends was the growing interest throughout the 20th century in the idea of a non-selective secondary school for all – the comprehensive school. The London County Council (LCC) had been thinking about this since the 1930s and, after the Second World War ended in 1945, was among many LEAs proposing to create comprehensive schools. In fact, the LCC did create England's first purpose-built comprehensive school in 1954, Kidbrooke School in south London. The UK's first comprehensive school was in Wales, Holyhead High, on the island of Anglesey, opened in 1949. Wales still has a fully comprehensive system today.

The spread of comprehensive schools was unstoppable from the 1960s (see Benn and Simon 1970) to the 1990s, with most LEAs reorganizing along comprehensive lines and with support from Labour governments and opposition from Conservative governments, especially under prime minister Margaret Thatcher from 1979 to 1990. By the late 1970s, most children were being educated in comprehensive schools. One of the most interesting schemes was the Leicestershire Plan, a system of 11–14 high schools (the converted secondary modern schools), and 14–18 upper schools and community colleges, converted from grammar schools (see Mason 1960; Fairbairn 1980). This was a simple but bold idea in a very conservative county, and involved support and advocacy from a number of key people including Stewart Mason, Leicestershire's director of education, and two ardent advocates of comprehensive schools, both lecturers at the University of Leicester School of Education, Robin Pedley (see Pedley 1963) and Brian Simon (see Rubinstein and Simon 1969). In 1970, the system was completed with the opening of a purpose-built school, Countesthorpe College (see Watts 1977; Chessum 2011), possibly the most radical and progressive state comprehensive school in the UK at that time, and with Brian Simon heavily involved in its creation and as a governor, and with the writer of this chapter as a part-time teacher there and at the University of Leicester School of Education as an academic under the direction of Brian Simon. The Leicestershire Plan still thrives today with only a few modifications.

## The 21st century

Following the election of the New Labour government in 1997, yet more experiments in secondary education were unleashed. The term 'comprehensive school' was hardly ever used by New Labour. The government certainly was not against comprehensive schools but wanted to 'modernize' and diversify the secondary sector to address the issue of lower standards of achievement in many schools. The approach was to be a typical New Labour one – combining public funding with private funding – thus leading to accusations from critics that schools were being semi-privatized.

New Labour introduced many reforms but three can be selected in relation to the structure and provision of secondary education. One was the audacious Building Schools for the Future (BSF) progamme that committed the government and local authorities to rebuild or replace every secondary school in England. Many schools did benefit before the coalition government cancelled the programme on grounds of cost in July 2010.

The second major reform was to extend the number of schools with a specialist status, started under a previous Conservative administration. This was to be done partly by widening the range of specialisms to offer more choice and attraction. For example, a school could call itself a specialist 'sports school' or a specialist 'arts school' – later they were called 'colleges'. Nearly all secondary schools now have a specialist designation.

The third and most controversial reform was to develop city academies, later just called 'academies', in deprived areas and where the standards of pupil achievement were often comparatively low in 'failing' schools. Private sponsorship was required, often in the region of £2 million and the government would then build the academy, sometimes costing around £25 million. The academies programme has been immensely controversial, with opposition and campaigns whenever and wherever they are proposed. Many teachers, parents and educationalists oppose the programme because they argue it is undemocratic as it introduces rich sponsors who can have an influence on the curriculum and on the pay and conditions of teachers. Some are sponsored by faith organizations thus raising questions about the lack of diversity in these schools. Research into academies has suggested mixed success in improving the achievement of pupils (see *Management in Education* 23(3), 2009) and some of the new buildings have been criticized as either being badly constructed or inappropriate as school environments. Academies are still in the minority in the supply of secondary schools but the numbers are increasing, and the coalition government elected in May 2010 proposed extending the status to those schools designated as 'outstanding' by Ofsted, thus totally reversing the aim of New Labour's academies that were intended for struggling or failing schools.

A final development, before we leave the story of secondary education, was the coalition government's proposal for 'free' schools that could be set up by anyone. These can be primary or secondary and will be similar to academies, with a high degree of independence but publicly funded. Another idea has been the creation of 'university technical colleges'. There are now over a dozen different types of secondary school, including the survival of the 166 grammar schools across several Conservative LEAs, leading to the question of whether the schooling system is now more confusing, diverse and complex than that in earlier parts of the 19th and 20th centuries.

### Activity: academies

Consult the websites cited here to find two very different perspectives on the academies programme:

- www.ssatrust.org.uk: this is the website of the Specialist Schools and Academies Trust. This organization promotes and supports these two types of school.
- www.antiacademies.org.uk: this organization, the Anti-Academies Alliance, campaigns against academies and features key information on current developments.

---

**Activity: trades unions in education**

Via a web search engine, visit the major teacher union websites to discover their views on recent developments in education. The unions also commission their own research so they are a useful source of opinion and analysis on all aspects of education. The unions include:

- The National Union of Teachers (NUT);
- The National Association of Schoolmasters and Union of Women Teachers (NASUWT);
- The Association of Teachers and Lecturers (ATL);
- Voice – formerly The Professional Association of Teachers (PAT);
- Educational Institute of Scotland (EIS);
- The National Association of Head Teachers (NAHT);
- The Association of School and College leaders (ASCL);
- University and College Union (UCU).

---

## Key theme 3: technical and vocational education

### The 19th century

The debates about education and training or, more often, education versus training, stretch back hundreds of years – and today are still far from being resolved.

Adam Smith, in *The Wealth of Nations* published in 1776, argued that factory production and enterprise in general would be best served by an educated and skilled workforce. But one of the central features of the entire history of education in England has been the unequal nature of educational provision, and the way social class and vested interests have influenced this, with a historic split between academic and vocational education. The education provided in the grammar schools, then and now, and in historic public schools such as Eton and Harrow, was decidedly not technical or vocational but academic and liberal, with the assumption that the pupils, invariably, would be entering universities and the professions. In contrast, the success of the English higher grade schools, at the end of the 19th century, was that they provided a rounded education for working-class children (in the main) but with a strong technical, commercial and vocational bias – thus providing a foundation for entry to artisan trades and clerical occupations.

### The 20th century

After the decline of the English higher grade schools, their successor secondary schools continued to provide a practical education. From the First until the Second World War, the tripartite secondary school pattern developed, with the three types of secondary school. The secondary modern schools, for the majority of pupils, were supposed to provide them with an adequate and sufficient education for their entry into trades – presumably where they could use their hands rather than their brains! The timetables included lessons in metalwork, woodwork, technical drawing, and sometimes gardening, for the boys – and cookery/domestic science for the girls. It is yet to be discovered why the education system assumed boys should not go near the cooker and girls should avoid the garden! Where technical schools were built, they did provide a rounded education but with a technical bias. Meanwhile, the grammar schools were resolutely committed to an academic curriculum including the teaching of the classics.

The further education (FE) sector for post-16 education, via FE colleges, throughout the 20th century and today, has provided a vast range of technical and vocational education, along with second-chance opportunities for students to study for GCSE and A levels. It has continued to play a vital role. FE colleges exist in all major towns and in many counties. There is not the space to cover this major specialist sector here except to say that its role will continue to grow as reforms are made in the provision of vocational education.

Throughout the history of education in the UK, employers and business leaders have constantly bemoaned the lack of skills and education of their workforces, putting pressure on governments to influence schooling so that literacy, numeracy and technical skills are adequate for the needs of industry. Various strategies were tried in the 1970s and 1980s including the Youth Opportunities Programme, or YOPs, in 1977 and, in 1982, the Technical and Vocational Initiative (TVEI) to encourage innovative teaching with a vocational bias. But, oddly, the 1988 Education Reform Act made no provision for vocational education in the new National Curriculum (see Cultural Studies 1991).

The 1990s were dominated by the difficult implementation of the overcrowded National Curriculum. But there were alternatives such as GNVQs (General National Vocational Qualifications) in a wide range of vocational subjects, such as Business Studies, although many schools were reluctant to introduce them into the curriculum for fear of dilution of academic standards, preferring the more traditional and academic GCSE for 14–16 year olds.

## The 21st century

With New Labour in power from 1997 onwards, various government committees and groups looked at 14–19 education, addressing the ongoing dichotomy of academic versus vocational education, piecemeal provision and the issues of quality. In 2004, the Tomlinson Report recommended the gradual abolition of GCSEs and A levels and the creation of a points-based unified baccalaureate system of academic and vocational subjects based on diplomas. Diplomas were introduced in 2008 but the A level GCE was retained. In 2009, the final report was published of Professor Richard Pring's six-year independent review of 14–19 education and skills, funded by the Nuffield Foundation. It was highly critical of the provision, arguing that the education, targets and forms of assessment for 14–19 year olds were still inappropriate. Among many other recommendations, it asserted, like the Tomlinson Report, the importance of a more coherent and unified system. This key report is available in book form (Pring et al. 2009).

Apart from Tomlinson and Pring, two other relevant interventions on vocational and technical education include the work of the charity, Edge, an independent education foundation committed to raising the status of practical, technical and vocational educa-tion. It has helped to produce a film and fund key projects (see www.edge.co.uk).

And, second, the Review of Vocational Education was chaired by Professor Alison Wolf and published in 2011 (Wolf 2011). Commissioned by the coalition govern-ment, it contains many observations and recommendations, including the suggestion that there are too many low-level vocational qualifications, and that subjects and skills such as English and Mathematics must be given a prime role in any restructured vocational provision. It has dramatic implications for schools, further education colleges and employers, and may begin to address the problem of the one million young people (aged 16–24) labelled as NEETs – not in employment, education or training – in 2011. It will be interesting to see whether the coalition government's Wolf Review and its Review of the National Curriculum in 2011 will make a vital contribu-tion to change and improvement.

---

**Activity: Edge Foundation**

Go online to the website of Edge Foundation – www.edge.co.uk. Explore and make a note of the many different activities and projects that Edge is involved in.

---

## Key theme 4: higher education – the universities

### The 19th century

It may surprise you to know that the only universities in England at the start of the 19th century were Oxford and Cambridge, both with some of their constituent colleges dating from the Middle Ages, and with ways of working that were equally medieval, for example only allowing members of the Anglican Church to graduate, and offering only a narrow range of subjects, with a strong bias towards the classics. But, during the 19th century, they both gradually modernized their curricula to include science and other areas. Although they guarded their autonomy fiercely, they eventually bowed to government pressure to widen their intake from a broader range of applicants and not just those from the wealthy upper classes, partly by offering more open scholarships, and they abolished religious tests for undergraduate entry into the universities at the beginning of the 20th century. But the requirement to have a qualification in Latin for entry was not abolished until the second half of the 20th century. New colleges were added and efforts were made to allow the entrance of women, in part by setting up new colleges (see below under Women and Education).

Durham University was founded in the 19th century along with some of the colleges in London that eventually became part of the University of London. The London colleges reflected a desire from many sections of the community, including industrialists, secularists and non-Anglicans, for a curriculum that included more science and where there was no religious test or religious teaching. The University of London also pioneered the awarding of external degrees allowing non-resident students, and students from colleges that would later become universities, to receive degrees.

Scotland has distinguished itself by having several universities before the 19th century and now has nearly two dozen for just over five million people, but its student population is not entirely Scottish-born – it is also made up of students from other parts of the UK and an increasing number of overseas students.

## The 20th century

The English provincial universities were founded in the 20th century, usually following historic bequests from rich philanthropic individuals and considerable lobbying from civic dignitaries in the local area. Many of these had their origins as colleges in the 19th century – these include Leeds, Manchester, Sheffield, Liverpool, Nottingham, Bristol, Birmingham, Reading and the Welsh colleges. Other universities received their charters in the mid-1950s; these include Leicester, Exeter, Southampton and Hull.

But with increasing demand from suitably qualified school leavers and the belief in governments and industry that Britain needed ever-increasing supplies of university-trained technologists, scientists, people for the professions and other specialists, yet more new universities were created in the 1960s, following the report by Lord Robbins on higher education. These included Sussex, York (based on a collegiate system similar to Oxford and Cambridge), East Anglia, Kent, Essex, Warwick, Lancaster and Keele. The final dramatic expansion came in 1992, following the Conservative government's Further and Higher Education Act, when the polytechnics, largely concerned with technical and vocational degrees, were allowed to designate themselves as 'universities', as were many colleges of higher education – some of these had a teacher education function and continue with this. This new group is often referred to as 'the post-1992 universities'.

There are now 115 universities and 165 higher education colleges in the UK.

The higher education colleges and the schools of education and departments of education at universities that teach the PGCE courses (Postgraduate Certificate in Education) now provide extensive undergraduate and postgraduate education and training in education and in the preparation of teachers. A growing pattern has been the three-year Education Studies undergraduate degree course (now over 100 courses in the UK mainly at the 'newer' universities) followed by the one-year PGCE training to become a teacher.

With increasing pressure on universities from applicants from a wide range of social class backgrounds, the scholarship system became more widespread so that able young people from poorer backgrounds could obtain free places. All of the universities needed ever-increasing grant aid from central government and this was administered by the University Grants Committee for many decades until the Higher Education Funding Council for England replaced it in 1992: Wales and Scotland also have their own funding councils but Northern Ireland is funded directly by its own Department of Employment.

## The 21st century

The higher education sector experienced dramatic and significant changes under New Labour from 1997 to 2010 in terms of management, financing, teaching, learning and accountability. The universities have increasingly been pressured into a competitive market system as part of the neo-liberal project that has swept across the globe since the 1980s. This has involved the universities in an extension of public accountability and scrutiny to an unprecedented intensity, with the annual publication of league tables of all universities and departments in the national press and scrutiny from the Quality Assurance Agency for Higher Education (QAA), set up in 1997, to safeguard quality and standards and to report on how well universities and colleges are meeting their responsibilities. (You can read about QAA's role and read reviews of each university and each subject by going to its website: www.qaa.ac.uk.)

Furthermore, the three higher education funding councils conduct a Research Assessment Exercise every five years that evaluates the quality of research in each institution and this then influences the allocation of central funds to each university. These rankings are publicly available, and become league tables, but of course they do not give the whole picture of each university and the process has been heavily criticized. In addition, internally, all institutions and departments are also now constantly undertaking their own internal quality monitoring and review. A different perspective is offered, however, by the confidential National Student Survey conducted annually amongst third-year undergraduates who report on their levels of satisfaction with the teaching and learning in their own subject areas.

But students have been at the sharp end of changes in university funding. While students paid a means-tested contribution towards tuition fees from 1998 onwards, in 2004 the highly controversial top-up fees were passed into law by only a five-vote majority in the House of Commons for the New Labour Government, even though in the 2001 Election Manifesto New Labour had promised not to introduce them. Students can obtain a loan from the Student Loan Company but they leave university with significant debts. They are therefore 'customers' as well as students and have a right to demand the best-quality treatment and teaching. Currently, universities in Scotland do not require tuition fees.

Along with debates about quality and the increasing number of students attending university – reaching 40 per cent of the age range under New Labour – issues of finance will continue to dominate the higher education sector, as the coalition government manages the financial problems in the UK economy by swingeing cuts to university budgets, and imposes dramatic increases in tuition fees for students.

---

**Activity: higher education**

When studying recent history and current issues in higher education, it is important to consider a range of interests and perspectives. Go to the three websites below and compare their different views on changes in higher education.

**Universities UK** is the representative body for the executive heads of UK universities – vice-chancellors of universities and principals of colleges of higher education. This organization represents the management view: www.universitiesuk.ac.uk

**UCU (University and College Union)** is the key trades union for academics and related staff working in further (FE colleges) and higher education: www.ucu.org.uk

**HEPI (The Higher Education Policy Institute)** is based in Oxford and is one of the key research centres on higher education. HEPI's website contains details of current research and issues in higher education: www.hepi.ac.uk

## Key theme 5: women and education

The struggle to achieve an education for girls and women, at school and at university, is one of the most gripping and emotionally moving narratives in the history of education. Their history recounts the life stories and successes of groups of women and individual pioneers such as Emily Davies, Elizabeth Garrett Anderson, Francis Beale, Dorothea Buss, and many more, to create equal rights to an education.

Although much of the campaigning was conducted in the 19th and 20th centuries, the starting point must be Mary Wollstonecraft's *Vindication of the Rights of Women* published in 1792, a major treatise on educational and sexual inequality, still widely read today, which asserts that general equality between the sexes and educational equality cannot be separated. Many women, in the 19th century, believed that the education of men and women must be the same. Emily Davies, who helped to found Girton College, Cambridge (a college for women only until the late 1970s), argued that women's education would be judged less favourably if it were not identical to men's education.

### The 19th century

In the 19th century, a basic social assumption, certainly among men, was that women were inferior to men. This was demonstrated by social class and gender inequalities. For many working-class women, their lives were characterized by domestic drudgery, with children to raise and with home-based work, such as sewing and laundry, used to supplement the man's income. Large numbers of working-class women worked in the factories so they also experienced employment drudgery. There was a more genteel domestic life for middle-class women, many of whom were not expected to be educated. Generally speaking, women suffered social repression and political exclusion.

After the 1870 Act, domestic subjects such as cooking, laundry, sewing and general housewifery, became a key feature of the education for girls. The scholarship system for entry to grammar schools in the later 19th century favoured boys, and few working-class girls were fortunate enough to gain admission. Many middle-class girls were educated at home by governesses, at day schools and at boarding schools. On the whole, girls were mainly required to become good wives and mothers.

As a response, a women's education reform movement began to develop spurred on by campaigns for women's rights from the suffragettes and also because there were new roles opening up for women in office work and in teaching. Much of this was associated with the efforts of brave and determined women to open up new schools and university colleges for women. You can read about Miss Buss and Miss Beale in the box below.

In higher education, the setting-up of women-only colleges was associated with Emily Davies who, in 1873, founded Girton College, Cambridge; Anne Clough, the first principal of Newnham College, Cambridge, opened in 1875; and Dorothea Beale who founded St Hilda's College, Oxford, in 1893. Many of these women knew one another and had links with the women's suffrage movement (see Robinson 2010).

---

### Activity: Miss Buss and Miss Beale

Research the lives and achievements of these two pioneers: Miss Frances Buss (1827–1894) and Miss Dorothea Beale (1831–1906). These two pioneering women are held in great affection by students of the history of education, mainly because of their determined work in the furtherance of women's education but partly because of the short popular poem that gently poked fun at them at the time because they were not married and were totally dedicated to their activities promoting education for women and girls:

> Miss Buss and Miss Beale,
> Cupid's darts do not feel.
> How different from us,
> Miss Beale and Miss Buss

Miss Buss was the principal, from 1850, at her parents' private school, North London Collegiate School, in Camden, north London. She made it an outstanding school for girls and it is still a successful school today, with a small archive room that includes documents linked to Miss Buss. As a suffragette, she also campaigned generally for a greater presence for girls in public examinations and universities, where they were hardly represented at the time.

Miss Beale is known for her pioneering work on extending and improving the education of girls, especially linked with her headship, from 1858, of the private school, Cheltenham Ladies' College, which still thrives to this day. She was also active in the suffragette movement and contributed to the foundation of the women's college, St Hilda's, at Oxford University, even though women were not eligible for Oxford degrees until 1920, long after the death of Miss Beale. In 2008, St Hilda's lost its single-sex status when men were admitted as undergraduates for the first time, although it still retains a strong attraction for female applicants.

---

## The 20th century

Well into the 20th century, society was still deeply unequal, especially for women, many of whom were now supporting the suffragette movement and campaigning for votes for women, which they did not achieve until 1928, following their campaigns and their mass employment during the First World War in fields and factories, transport and armaments manufacture, all of which proved their equal worth to men.

In education, for much of the early half of the 20th century, the curriculum and education for girls still assumed differences in gender requirements, with domestic science for girls but not for boys. However, academic subjects were increasingly seen as normal for girls as is illustrated in Summerfield's fascinating detailed research on two girls' secondary schools in Lancashire from 1900 to 1950 (cited in Hunt 1987). In fact, in these schools, the teachers and the girls appear to have viewed domestic science subjects as very low level compared with their academic studies, with higher education and a career in teaching as a key objective. But making sure the girls were 'ladylike' and 'feminine' was still important. Beyond this, there is very little published historical research on girls' education in the second half of the 20th century, although this will no doubt be remedied soon.

Many of the education reports in the 20th century, such as Norwood's, *Curriculum and Examinations in Secondary Schools*, in 1943, assumed that girls' education should still be about homemaking, among other pursuits, but by the time of the Crowther Report in 1959 more egalitarian attitudes were expressed and there were now more mixed schools (both sexes), especially with the later building of comprehensive schools in the 1960s and 1970s. However, in spite of the second wave of women's liberation in the 1970s, there was still selection at 11+ when girls were not entering grammar schools in appropriate numbers except where there were girls' grammar schools – and the 1975 Sex Discrimination Act did not apply to education so there could be no radical legal attention to unequal chances. There was also the issue of the overcrowding of the curriculum for girls, expected to follow the same curriculum as boys but also to engage with subjects and interests assumed to relate to girls. However, the 1988 National Curriculum is seen as a landmark in levelling out access and subjects, imposing a legally required range of subjects that all pupils would follow, boys and girls.

## The 21st century

Although the change began in the 1990s, by the early part of the 21st century girls were outperforming boys at all levels of education, including in GCSE, A level results and in higher education. This change is carefully analysed by Francis and Skelton in *Reassessing Gender and Achievement* (2005). The concern now is about the performance of white working-class boys and black boys. As for the girls and women, after their education, they still have an uphill struggle in the work–life balance, compared with men, and to attain a more equal share of the top positions in employment.

## Key theme 6: race, ethnicity and education

The backdrop to any consideration of this important and sensitive area must be located deep in the history of Britain's involvement in the slave trade and its colonial encounters with large parts of the globe. This history has a bearing on patterns of immigration, the make-up of the school population today and on a wide range of education issues.

## The 19th century

Much of the historical literature on immigration and settlement in the UK in the 19th century highlights the increasing numbers of three key groups in Britain's growing industrial nation. Especially linked to the slave trade and its aftermath, and the growth of new steamship lines, black people were arriving in the UK from the United States, the West Indies and West Africa. Irish people were coming to England, especially following the Irish famine of the 1840s that killed thousands. And Jewish people from eastern Europe, mainly poor and from working-class backgrounds, were also settling, particularly in the latter part of the 19th century. All of these groups were being pushed to leave their countries by poverty or persecution but also were being pulled to the UK with the hope of a more prosperous life. The major cities were the main focus of settlement, especially London, and particularly the East End of London.

There is very little historical data on how the children of minority groups integrated into school following the 1870 Elementary Education Act that heralded universal elementary education, but we do know that religion and faith were especially important and that some of these groups made every effort to maintain their faith, through attending Catholic schools in the case of the Irish, but this did not necessarily preserve or promote their Irish heritage, language or culture in the curriculum. There were some Jewish schools in the big cities, including the Jews' Free School in Spitalfields, London, which was founded in 1817. You can read a detailed account of the history of settlement in the UK in Panayi's book, *An Immigration History of Britain* (Panayi 2010).

It is also the case that blacks, the Irish and the Jews were at the receiving end of racism and discrimination, which was fairly widespread at the time.

---

**Activity: the history of ethnic minority settlement**

Visit the *Moving Here* website, where you can trace the history of settlement of any of the ethnic minority groups. It is an attractive, wide-ranging and constantly updated website run by the National Archives in Kew, Surrey. It includes information and personal oral histories of the four main ethnic communities in the UK: the Caribbean, Irish, Jewish and South Asian communities. The web address is: www.movinghere.org.uk

---

## The 20th century

People and groups from all parts of the globe continued to settle in the UK throughout the 20th century, arriving especially from the former colonial territories such as the old Commonwealth (e.g. Australia, Canada and New Zealand) and the new Commonwealth (the West Indies, South Asia and Africa), with the famous arrival after the Second World War of the ship, *Empire Windrush*, bringing African-Caribbean people in 1948, that included men who were ex-servicemen and who had been part of the British armed forces. They had been invited because of Britain's severe labour shortage after the war. In the early 1970s, Asian immigrants came to the UK from

Kenya and Uganda to escape persecution and banishment from those countries, with many settling in Leicester.

It was really in the 1960s that schools began to develop educational programmes that took account of the presence of different minority communities and here lie the beginnings of multicultural education in schools. There has been a standard historical model to analyse the reaction of education to the changing ethnic composition of the schools and of society, moving through four main phases of multicultural education, from the 1950s to recent times.

1. The assimilationist phase covers the 1950s to the mid-1960s when the main aim was to absorb Commonwealth immigrant children, teach them English and help them become absorbed into British society.

2. The integrationist phase, roughly from 1965 to the early 1970s, was characterized by a move away from often racist and superior stances to a policy that placed more emphasis on equality of opportunity, and an attempt in schools to learn about and celebrate ethnic minority cultures. Various government funding streams were also opened up for inner-city multicultural and English language initiatives. And Race Relations Acts in 1965 and 1968 represented an attempt to combat racism in society.

3. The cultural pluralism phase from the early 1970s into the early 1980s involved a move away from preferences about a culturally unified society towards an acceptance that different ethnic groups and cultures could be distinctive without having to fully integrate.

4. Anti-racist education became more widespread from the early 1980s onwards as schools and LEA initiatives began to feature coverage of race and racism as an issue, along with broader issues of disadvantage and inequality. Black educationalists and parents were lobbying for a fairer and more non-discriminatory system for their children. The Swan Report in 1985 promoted the notion of 'education for all' (DES 1985). Anti-racist education essentially comprises a range of aims and practices relating to professional, curriculum and institutional development that promote and enhance cultural diversity in school and society, while also identifying and combating racism and discrimination.

## The 21st century

Five key elements are still part of the overall focus for researchers, policy-makers, teachers, parents and governors.

1. Analysing and tackling racism and discrimination in school and society.
2. Issues relating to ethnic minority experience and cultures, including religion.
3. Issues of language – the English language and minority languages.
4. The curriculum – the extent to which it should reflect diversity.
5. Education and schooling in general, in terms of whole-school policies on multicultural education and anti-racist education.

Two of the key issues for the 21st century revolve around the relative rates of achievement in school of different ethnic groups, with Chinese and south-east Asian pupils being among the most successful and African-Caribbean boys being among the least successful, thus leading to various research and intervention programmes such as the Ethnic Minority Achievement Programme (see the DES website). The other area concerns the issue of 'Britishness', partly a response to Islamic terrorism in the world and in the UK, such as the London bombings in 2005, and worries that some elements of some ethnic communities are not sufficiently 'integrated'. Thus two new policy areas for schools from the New Labour government (1997–2010) involved a new element in the Citizenship curriculum – Identity and Diversity – and a requirement from 2006 that schools must actively promote 'community cohesion' (see Dufour 2009). The extent to which the coalition government will take these reforms forward remains to be seen.

## Key theme 7: social class and inequality in education

Debates about equality, fair access and equality of opportunity in the British education system have been continuous since the 19th century, with Conservatives, Liberals, Labour and socialist opinion usually in disagreement about whether achieving equality is possible or whether even trying to create a more level playing field in terms of equality of opportunity, a more modest ambition, is alternatively more achievable or desirable. Education has been at the forefront of competing views about society because schooling and education are seen as the key levers offering increased opportunities in work and life for all children, regardless of family background. The history of education in the UK tells a story of constant struggle by different groups and classes to either improve their chances in education (women, working-class people, ethnic minorities) or to maintain and enhance their relatively comfortable position (middle and upper classes). This is the case through the 19th century and into the 20th century – and is still a key part of the reform agenda in 21st-century education in the UK.

### The 19th century

We have seen already how schooling in the 19th century was a hit-and-miss affair, largely funded by private and voluntary sources, and with most children unschooled, until the 1870 Act legislated for a state-funded system of elementary (primary) education for all children. But, as we discussed earlier, this did not include a natural right to a secondary education. The extension of the grade system in elementary schools and the building of stand-alone higher grade schools in some cities were attempts to provide a secondary education for ordinary children, but this was ended by the Conservative Party's 1902 Education Act, abolishing these schools partly because they were a threat to the middle-class-dominated grammar schools, which were exclusively deemed 'secondary'.

### The 20th century

By 1903, Local Education Authorities (LEAs) were established (formed after the School Boards were abolished in the 1902 Act) and the progressive ones were beginning to set up new 'municipal secondary schools', similar to the higher grade schools. Other measures to promote more fairness in some LEAs included free school meals for very poor children, and school medical services. In 1907, an Education Act required that 25 per cent of the intake into secondary and grammar schools should be from elementary schools (as opposed to being from private schools). A Free Place system meant that by passing a test (the beginnings of the later 11+) – a scholarship system – elementary children could go to the grammar school.

Gradually, other kinds of secondary school developed that spread opportunities further. These included 'central schools', selective to begin with, but later open to all, and technical schools with a selective entry for 13 year olds. The developing tri-partite system of secondary schools – modern schools, technical schools and grammar schools – continued throughout the inter-war years. The 1944 Education Act enshrined the system, arguing that there was 'parity of esteem' between these schools – equal but different. Very few believed this as the grammar schools continued largely as a preserve of the middle class and with access to the better jobs, economic prospects and life chances.

Research from sociologists in the 1950s and 1960 focused on access to grammar schools by different classes of people, and more recent research has focused on how the middle classes continue to secure places at the best schools.

The major strategy for creating a more equal secondary school system was the development of comprehensive schools. These were continuing to spread so that by the 1970s, most pupils were in non-selective schools, but these of course varied depending on their quality, their intake and catchment area, so some could be oversubscribed and, in some senses, 'selective'. But grammar schools continued to exist in a minority of LEAs and the private schools continued to flourish, so in spite of all the changes and experiments towards a fairer and more equal provision, especially at the secondary school level, hierarchies, inequalities and privileges remained. Furthermore, the experiments with schooling under the Conservative governments from 1979 to 1997 created a market system and competition between schools that began to highlight differences in achievement levels and inequalities between schools, even though by then most schools were theoretically comprehensive at the secondary level.

## The 21st century

New Labour (1997–2010) developed many new policies to combat social exclusion but continued with and extended Conservative policies on competition, encouraging the setting-up of academies that were partly privately funded, initially by millionaire benefactors, and located mainly in deprived areas. Although the nature and level of success for academies is still debated, they have been an attempt to address inequalities, deprivation and underachievement in parts of our cities.

In 21st-century Britain, while issues related to access to secondary, technical and higher education are even more to the fore, wider debates, beyond schooling, have been addressing the link between poverty, inequality and educational opportunity, and even extending to a focus on well-being. Wilkinson and Pickett's (2010) study of inequality in the UK and other countries, including of educational achievement, has raised many questions with their argument and evidence that more equal societies are happier.

There are debates about the role of private education in helping students to secure around 50 per cent of places at Oxbridge, with Alan Milburn's (2009) study revealing how senior post holders across many public and private organizations in the UK come from a very selective group, having been educated at independent schools and Oxbridge.

And in terms of the well-being debate, UNICEF's report in 2007 chronicles the four million children in the UK still living in poverty, one in three of all children, while describing the impact of this on poor children's lack of educational resources including books, dictionaries, calculators, computers and space to work (UNICEF 2007). Richard Layard and Judy Dunn (2009), in their analysis of childhood in the UK, include material on the effects of poverty on children and its impact on achievement at school. Much other research also points up continuing inequalities in education – see the box below about the Sutton Trust. It remains to be seen how these circumstances will change over the next few years.

---

**Activity: Sutton Trust**

Visit the website of the Sutton Trust to check its latest research reports. The Sutton Trust is a research organization that investigates inequality in education. Through its research and publicity, it is dedicated to improving educational opportunities for young people from non-privileged backgrounds and to increasing social mobility. The web address is: www.sutton-trust.com

---

## Key theme 8: the role of the churches and the issue of faith schools today

The churches and religion have occupied a key role in the development of education in the UK, often with humanitarian intent, with a desire to see greater equity and social justice, but sometimes driven by motives that can only be described as narrow and self-serving in order to protect and promote their own vested interests. The defence and promotion of their role in education has especially been the case with the Church of England, the Established Church and the Roman Catholic Church, while the smaller non-conformist churches have invariably supported liberal movements to ensure less selection and wider participation in education. Religious education as a required element in the curriculum of all state schools has, over the years, experienced varying fortunes – being a legal requirement at some points of history but with choice and freedom at others. In more recent times, intense debates have occurred about the role of faith schools in the overall provision of schooling.

### The 19th century

Until the 1870 Education Act, schools were provided by charities and religious denominations, with the Church of England especially prominent in the running of parish schools. Bitter arguments occurred about funding and freedom to worship, with all groups including the Roman Catholic Church and Dissenters advancing the merits of their own position. The 1870 Act reached a compromise when it introduced state-funded education for all by enacting that only Bible stories would be taught in religious instruction and that there could be no denominational teaching representing any particular church or religious persuasion. Voluntary-aided schools such as Roman Catholic schools did not have to follow this injunction.

With attempts to develop secondary education, bitter disputes between church and state really became apparent, especially in relation to the creation of the English higher grade schools, discussed earlier, at the end of the 19th century. Much church opinion (Catholic and Anglican), with sympathy from the Tory Party (later called the Conservative Party), was concerned about the growth of the higher grade schools because they were competing with – and threatening the existence of – the endowed grammar schools and voluntary-aided church grammar schools. Also, church schools, which still provided for most children, were coming under pressure from School Board schools, which were better funded and becoming increasingly popular. So when a Tory government was elected in 1895, the church schools saw their chance to gain more funding – and they did. The conflict in many local areas between the School Board schools and the church schools was mounting because many Boards were often progressive and represented secularization and radicalism. A good example was Birmingham where Joseph Chamberlain and the Liberals had been busy creating higher grade schools.

## The 20th century

During the 20th century, debates continued in relation to the teaching of religious education in schools and in relation to the Dual System – secular state schools (often called 'provided schools') and the church schools, called 'non-provided' or voluntary, in terms of government financing. But there is space here to review only two of the major highlight education acts that had a central bearing on these issues. One was the 1944 Education Act and the other is the 1988 Education Reform Act.

The background to the Butler Act – R.A. Butler was the President of the Board of Education – is recounted in two books. Marjorie Cruickshank, in her account, *Church and State in English Education* (1963), describes the tortuous consultations with all interested religious and political groups that lasted the entire period of the Second World War, and eventually led to the 1944 Act's provisions on the status and variable state funding of the voluntary church schools and the enactment of compulsory religious education, based on locally set Agreed Syllabuses made up of panels representing a variety of interest groups, and the requirement for a compulsory daily act of worship, of a non-denominational character, in all schools. This would be of a Christian nature. It seems a missed opportunity that the only pronouncement on any kind of curriculum subject in the 1944 Act was on religion and religious education.

The 1988 Education Reform Act and its clauses took these requirements even further by specific referral to the Christian faith. It declared that each school must have a daily act of collective worship for all pupils and that it must be wholly or mainly of a broadly Christian character, and that religious education 'shall reflect the fact that the religious traditions in Great Britain are in the main Christian whilst taking account of the teaching and practices of the other principal religions represented in Great Britain' (ERA 1988: 6). These clauses created controversy at the time but their enactment is still legally required. It would be logical to argue that they are inappropriate in a multi-faith and multi-ethnic society as the UK now is in the 21st century. Priscilla Chadwick has explored some of the issues surrounding the religious components of the 1988 Education Reform Act in her book, *Shifting Alliances: Church and State in English Education* (1997).

## The 21st century

One of the central debates in recent years has been to do with the growth of faith schools and therefore with the continuing influence of religion on education. It is now estimated that one-third of all schools, including primary and secondary, are faith-based schools.

The two major churches in the UK, the Roman Catholic Church and the Church of England, continue to hold sway but with an ever-increasing number of Islamic schools. There are also Jewish schools and Sikh schools. They are variously state-funded or semi-state funded, such as the voluntary schools, while many are private.

In addition, the Church of England is set to become the biggest sponsor of the academies programme, while many other Christian charities, such as the United Learning Trust, are also active in their sponsorship of academies. Supporters, including parents, argue that, quite apart from their promotion of religious faith, the faith schools offer a better ethos, better pupil behaviour and higher levels of achievement, although, in terms of pupil academic success, research has suggested this has been exaggerated, in primary education at least, and that any advantage here, which is very small, is down to family background, the status of the schools and admission procedures and that, therefore, the pupils are not a 'typical' cross-section (Gibbons and Silva 2007).

Opponents of faith schools, such as the National Secular Society, claim that with church attendance at its lowest ever for the Church of England, the expansion of their academies and the high number of church schools is a way of winning converts and cementing the Church's survival. And nearly all the finance is at the taxpayer's expense.

However, it is also true that most academies are jointly sponsored, usually by the Church of England, which sponsors most academies, but with non-religious interested benefactors. For example, the Samworth Academy in Leicester is jointly sponsored by the Church of England and a food company, Samworth Brothers Limited. As yet there are no multi-faith academies, although Samworth has pupils from all faiths and none.

It has to be said that the extensive self-interest of the churches and other faiths in seeking to consolidate their own relatively partial view of life in the schools flies in the face of other trends in modern Britain such as the promotion of diversity and the celebration of all faiths, and those without faith, in our society and in our schools, which are increasingly multi-ethnic and multi-faith.

---

**Activity: faith schooling**

To consider opposing views on the issue of faith schools today, google any of the main religious faiths and their academies in order to find out the detail of where they are and what their aims and principles are. For example, a search for 'Church of England academies' brings up a number of relevant sites including the Church of England Academy Services Ltd (CASL), an organization set up in 2007 following Tony Blair's encouragement for more faith-based schools including academies, before he stood down as Prime Minister – see the website: www.churchacademies.org.uk

You can also access, as a contrast, the website of the National Secular Society, which was founded in 1866 in order to resist the influence of religion, to end the link between Church and State, and to promote the views and interests of non-religious people. It also campaigns today against faith schools. Website: www.secularism.org.uk

---

## Key theme 9: teaching, learning and the curriculum

We have come a long way since the 19th century, when many pupils were in overcrowded classrooms or tiered lecture rooms, controlled by iron discipline, punished severely for transgressions, taught by strict teachers using talk and chalk, and offered a narrow curriculum based on the three Rs – reading, writing and arithmetic. Most of today's classrooms could not be more different, although some very traditional secondary schools have certain similarities in their adoption of formal styles. But overall, there have been dramatic changes in teaching, in conceptions of how children learn, in the curriculum, and in the nature of resources for teaching and learning.

### The 19th century

In the 19th century, as now, there were good teachers and bad and by no means were all of them represented by the caricatures of the regulated Victorian classrooms in Charles Dickens' novels. Aldrich (1996) reports on the views of 19th-century educationalists such as James Kay-Shuttleworth on what constitutes good teaching, and suggests that the qualities identified are not so different from modern writings on effective teaching; however, Kay-Shuttleworth's ideas were theories and did not necessarily represent actual practice. There was very little individualization in learning for pupils then, with the beginnings of mass schooling in 1870 very much geared to the needs of mass manufacture in the factories. Towards the end of the 19th century, the basic school curriculum was becoming more defined but there were some differences between the subjects for boys and those for girls, with needlework, cooking, cleaning and laundry work for the latter. At the secondary level, the grammar schools offered a classic curriculum while the developing English higher grade schools attempted to mount a broad curriculum for both sexes including science and vocational subjects.

## The 20th century

Space does not allow us to trawl through all major developments in teaching, learning and the curriculum in the 20th century but two dates stand out, representing official attempts to prescribe what children should learn at school. In 1904, regulations were set down that defined the curriculum for maintained secondary schools but not until 1988 was another major official ruling made on the school curriculum. Richard Aldrich (1996) has set out a list (Table 1.1) revealing that the grammar-school style secondary curriculum in the regulations of 1904 was little different from the 1988 list of National Curriculum subjects.

**Table 1.1** The curriculum in 1904 and in 1988

| 1904 | 1988 |
| --- | --- |
| English | English |
| Mathematics | Mathematics |
| Science | Science |
| Foreign language | Foreign language |
| Geography | Geography |
| History | History |
| Drawing | Art |
| Physical exercise | Physical education |
| Manual work/housewifery | Technology |
| [Music] | Music |

In 1988, the required subjects for all children to be taught, from 5 to 16, were set down as part of the Education Reform Act of that year. The new system has had a profound impact on the very nature of teaching and learning, on the curriculum and on education in general, basically instituting central government direction of the curriculum and assessment, and, in effect, telling teachers and schools what to teach, when to teach it and how to teach. The famous (or infamous) SATs (Standard Assessment Tests) were introduced as the core of this. Some of the intentions of this whole new structure were noble – to raise standards and levels of achievement – and they were continued by the successor New Labour governments up to May 2010. But the price to pay has been a substantial reduction in teacher autonomy and their professionalism, as the 'culture of performativity' characterized by the four Ts – tables (league tables), tick lists, tests and targets – has continued unheeded, although widely opposed.

Various modifications were made to the unwieldy National Curriculum such as in 1995, following the Dearing Review of 1994 (Dearing 1994). A letter to the *Guardian* newspaper by an anonymous writer characterized the National Curriculum as being 'conceived by Kafka, designed by Dali and administered by Stalin'. Broader studies, such as the cross-curricular issues dealing with such areas as environmental education, were added but these were an afterthought, outside the legislation and never made statutory (see Dufour 1990).

The creation of Ofsted, a semi-privatized inspection system, in 1993, had, argu-ably, a democratic effect on ensuring a standardized curriculum and assessment system but, in its early form, it was a policing and monitoring system concerned with 'compliance', which risked having a negative effect on styles of teaching and learning, as teachers taught to the content and were cautious about conducting more adventurous teaching, especially when inspectors were present. But it might also be the case that teachers carried on as normal using their professional skills and judge-ment in interpreting how they would deliver the National Curriculum.

From 1997 onwards, with New Labour in power, there was a continuation with the emphasis on raising standards of achievement and a rigorous effort to improve literacy and numeracy in primary schools by adding the required daily Literacy Hour and Numeracy Hour. Along with the pressure on schools to reveal success in the SATs, these initiatives had the potential to engender a somewhat dampening effect on teaching and learning styles. Similarly, with the Key Stage Three Strategy for 11–14 year olds, extensive guidance was provided by the QCA and the DfES websites on 'good teaching'. That often boiled down to safe teaching via the three-part lesson – introduction by the teacher, pupils working on the tasks set, and then the plenary for pulling together and reviewing learning.

## The 21st century

At the start of the new millennium, the New Labour government introduced a revised National Curriculum that included a statement of principles, modifications to content and the introduction of Citizenship as a new subject, although it was more than a subject because it followed the ideas in the Crick Report (QCA 1998) and included a curriculum specification for key stages 1–4, suggestions about pupil democracy (involvement in the running of the school, school councils and skills such as debating) and community engagement. A fourth strand was added in 2008 for secondary school pupils, dealing with issues related to multi-ethnic Britain, diversity and identity. A Review of the National Curriculum was set up by the coalition government in January 2011 so more changes can be expected.

---

**Activity: Ofsted**

Go to the Ofsted website: www.ofsted.gov.uk

1.  Search for an Ofsted report of a school near where you live (they are arranged by education sector, e.g. secondary schools) or a school you attended. Look at what it says about teaching and learning.
2.  Search for the latest Annual Report by HMCI (Her Majesty's Chief Inspector) and read its overall summaries on the quality of teaching and learning in various education sectors.

## Conclusion

There are amazing educational opportunities for teachers and pupils in British schools in the 21st century. The use of information and communications technology is now part of every classroom and school library, allowing for types of flexible learning, communication and investigation unknown and unimagined in previous times. Many schools, through the academies programme and *Building Schools for the Future*, have had their physical environments totally transformed, even if some of the gleaming palaces may not always look like schools. Teachers can now draw on a vast range of teaching and learning styles, ranging from the traditional taught instructional lesson to resource-based pupil-centred enquiry. They also have the support and help of 'teaching assistants', greatly expanded in primary and secondary classrooms following the Workforce Agreement of 2003 in order to tackle teacher workload and contribute to raising achievement. Textbooks from publishers and learning materials are now attractive, with most printed in colour. Many schools, especially in the primary sector, have a happy and informal ethos. And Ofsted annual reports from HMCI routinely confirm the general competence and success of most pupils, most teachers, most school leaders and most schools.

The downside is the constant attempt of every government to over-prescribe the curriculum from the centre and to tell teachers how to teach, leading to a serious erosion in teacher professionalism and autonomy. The constant experiments with school structures, by Conservative, New Labour and coalition governments, has led to a complex secondary school system, possibly more fragmented now than in the 19th and first half of the 20th century. In addition, the increasing erosion of state education by privatization under all governments since 1979 has become a major trend and yet has only recently begun to be seriously chronicled by academic research (see Ball 2007). It affects all levels, from the outsourcing of central and local government services to the procurement procedures that schools now have to indulge in to buy in commercial services that were previously provided by local or central government.

The continuing drive by all governments since 1979 to raise pupils' standards of achievement has led to previously unmatched levels of stress for pupils, teachers and school leaders within a competitive market of league tables and scores, described by one educationalist as 'the tyranny of testing' and 'education by numbers' (Mansell 2007). And the Education Act of 2011 from the coalition government extends the pressure even more with changes to league tables, examinations and much more. The coalition government has also instituted wide-ranging and deep cuts in education budgets, including the abolition of the funding for sixth formers through the EMA (Education Maintenance Allowance) for 16–19 year olds in schools and colleges, unprecedented cuts in university funding, with 80 per cent of the teaching budget axed, but to be replaced by the trebling of university tuition fees paid by students. There is a real risk that all of these measures may undermine the ambition of the coalition government to raise standards even more in relation to improving the UK position in world league tables for achievement in schools and universities. In the light of all of this, it remains a stark contrast and irony that the country normally at the top of world league tables for school and university success, Finland, achieves this by generous spending on schools and universities, with no university fees, and without an all-embracing system of accountability in schools – with no school inspections, no league tables, no national testing, no targets, no uniforms, no streaming and no selection.

---

**Further research**

Choose **one** of the nine key themes surveyed above and explore it in greater depth by consulting the suggested reading and visiting appropriate websites. Focus especially on why changes were proposed and why they were resisted. Explore the role played by prominent individuals and key organizations.

---

## Key readings

### Books

McCulloch, G. (ed.) (2005) *The RoutledgeFalmer Reader in History of Education*, Abingdon: Routledge. This is the most recent and wide-ranging overview of key themes and research in history of education with contributions from leading specialists.

Simon, B. *Studies in the History of Education*, a four-volume series, published by Lawrence and Wishart:

- *The Two Nations and the Educational Structure 1780–1870* (published 1960 with a paperback edition in 1981);
- *Education and the Labour Movement 1870–1920* (published 1965);
- *The Politics of Educational Reform 1920–1940* (published 1974);
- *Education and the Social Order 1940–1990* (published 1991 with a paperback printing in 1999).

These four books were researched and written from the 1950s until 1990 and together constitute a major academic achievement in history of education. Apart from the scholarship, their special contribution is the analysis of the contribution to educational reform that came from working-class movements, the trades unions and radical thinkers hitherto neglected in previous traditional histories of education. The four volumes are available in university libraries and for second-hand purchase on the internet. There are plans by Lawrence and Wishart to re-publish them through a digital process in 2011.

### Additional reading

#### Primary education

Arthur, J. and Cremin, T. (eds) (2010) *Learning to Teach in the Primary School*. Abingdon: Routledge.

#### Secondary education

Vlaeminke, M. (2000) *The English Higher Grade Schools: A Lost Opportunity*. London: Woburn Press.

#### Technical and vocational education

Bosch, G. and Charest, J. (2010) *Vocational Training: International Perspectives*. Abingdon: Routledge.

### Higher education

Tight, M. (2009) *The Development of Higher Education in the United Kingdom since 1945*. Maidenhead: Open University Press.

### Women and education

Robinson, J. (2010) *Bluestockings: The Remarkable Story of the First Women to Fight for an Education*. London: Penguin.

### Race, ethnicity and education

Banks, J.A. (ed.) (2009) *The Routledge International Companion to Multicultural Education*. Abingdon: Routledge. (Note especially, Chapter 8 by Professor Sally Tomlinson, on Multicultural Education in the United Kingdom.)

Ladson-Billings, G. and Gillborn, D. (eds) (2004) *The RoutledgeFalmer Reader in Multicultural Education: Critical Perspectives on Race, Racism and Education*. Abingdon: Routledge.

### Social class and inequality in education

Wilkinson, R. and Pickett, K. (2010) *The Spirit Level: Why Equality is Better for Everyone*. London: Penguin.

### The role of the churches and the issue of faith schools today

Lawton, D., Gardner, R. and Cairns, J. (2004) *Faith Schools: Consensus or Conflict*. Abingdon: Routledge.

### Teaching, learning and the curriculum

Ofsted *Annual Report* from Her Majesty's Chief Inspector, accessed via the Ofsted website: www.ofsted.gov.uk

## Journals

*History of Education*. This journal is a leading international forum. It has been running since 1972 and is published six times a year. It covers all aspects of educational history from around the world. It is published by Taylor & Francis and is available for a modest subscription and accessible in all good university education libraries.

## Websites

Campaign for State Education: www.campaignforstateeducation.org.uk
*Guardian* Education: www.guardian.co.uk/education
*Times Educational Supplement*: www.tes.co.uk

## Acknowledgements

1. This chapter is partly based on Barry Dufour's undergraduate and postgraduate lectures on the history and politics of education for the Education Studies degree course at De Montfort University, Leicester, from 2003–2011.
2. The chapter draws on the work of Brian Simon and is dedicated, with affection and respect, to his scholarship and memory.

3. I would like to acknowledge the advice of a colleague, Dr Lorna Chessum, in the drafting of parts of this chapter, although the final version is entirely my responsibility and I am responsible for any mistakes or misinterpretations.
4. Finally, I would like to acknowledge the kind help and support of staff at the University of Leicester David Wilson Library, who helpfully administered all of my book requests during the writing and research for this chapter.

## References

Aldrich, R. (1996) *Education for the Nation*. London: Cassell.

Alexander, R. (ed.) (2009) *Children, Their World, Their Education* (Final Report and Recommendations of the Cambridge Primary Review). London: Routledge.

Baker, G. (2001) The romantic and radical nature of the 1870 Act. *History of Education*, 30(3): 211–32.

Ball, S.J. (2007) *Education plc*. Abingdon: Routledge.

Benn, C. and Simon, B. (1970) *Half Way There (Report on the British Comprehensive School Reform)*. Maidenhead: McGraw-Hill.

Breslin, T. and Dufour, B. (eds) (2006) *Developing Citizens: A Comprehensive Introduction to Effective Citizenship Education in the Secondary School*. London: Hodder and Murray.

Chadwick, P. (1997) *Shifting Alliances: Church and State in English Education*. London: Cassell.

Chessum, L. (2011) *Revisiting Radical Education: Learning from Countesthorpe College 1970–1990*. London: Continuum.

Cox, C.B. and Dyson, A.E. (eds) (1971) *The Black Papers on Education*. London: Davis-Poynter.

Cruickshank, M. (1963) *Church and State in English Education*. London: Macmillan.

Cultural Studies, Birmingham (1991) *Education Limited: Schooling, Training and the New Right in England since 1979*. London: Unwin Hyman.

Dearing, R. (1994) *The National Curriculum and its Assessment*. London: School Curriculum and Assessment Authority.

DfES (2004) *14–19 Curriculum and Qualifications Reform. Final Report of the Working Group on 14–19 Reform*, chaired by Mike Tomlinson. London: DfES.

Dufour, B. (ed.) (1990) *The New Social Curriculum: A Guide to Cross-curricular Themes*. Cambridge: Cambridge University Press.

Fairbairn, A.N. (ed.) (1980) *The Leicestershire Plan*. London: Heinemann Educational Books.

Francis, B. and Skelton, C. (2005) *Reassessing Gender and Achievement*. Abingdon: Routledge.

Gibbons, S. and Silva, O. (2007) *Faith Primary Schools: Better Schools or Better Pupils*, Discussion Paper No 72, Centre for the Economics of Education (CEE). London: London School of Economics and Political Science

Layard, R. and Dunn, J. (2009) *A Good Childhood: Searching for Values in a Competitive Age*. London: Penguin.

Mansell, W. (2007) *Education by Numbers: The Tyranny of Testing*. London: Politico's.

Mason, S. (1960) *The Leicester Experiment and Plan*. London: Councils and Education Press.

Mason, S. (1970) *In Our Experience*. London: Longman.

McCulloch, G. (2011) *The Struggle for the History of Education*. Abingdon: Routledge.

Milburn, A. (2009) *Unleashing Aspiration: The Final Report of the Panel on Fair Access to the Professions*. London: Cabinet Office.

Panayi, P. (2010) *An Immigration History of Britain: Multicultural Racism since 1800*. London: Longman.

Pedley, R. (1963) *The Comprehensive School*. Harmondsworth: Penguin.

Plowden Report (1967) *Children and Their Primary Schools*. A Report of the Central Advisory Council for Education (England). London: HMSO.

Pring, R. et al. (2009) *Education for All: The Future of Education and Training for 14–19 Year Olds*. Abingdon: Routledge.

Qualifications and Curriculum Authority (QCA) (1998) *Education for Citizenship and the Teaching of Democracy in Schools: Final Report of the Advisory Group on Citizenship* (the Crick Report). London: QCA.

Robinson, J. (2010) *Bluestockings: The Remarkable Story of the First Women to Fight for an Education*. London: Penguin.

Rose, J. (2009) *Independent Review of the Primary Curriculum: Final Report*. London: DCSF.

Rubinstein, D. and Simon, B. (1969) *The Evolution of the Comprehensive School 1926–1966*. London: Routledge.

Simon, B. (1960) *The Two Nations and the Educational Structure 1780–1870*. London: Lawrence and Wishart.

Simon, B. (1965) *Education and the Labour Movement 1870–1920*. London: Lawrence and Wishart.

Simon, B. (1974) *The Politics of Educational Reform 1920–1940*. London: Lawrence and Wishart.

Simon, B. (1991) *Education and the Social Order 1940–1990*. London: Lawrence and Wishart.

Simon, B. (1994) *The State and Educational Change (Essays in the History of Education and Pedagogy)*. London: Lawrence and Wishart.

Simon, B. (1998) *A Life in Education*. London: Lawrence and Wishart.

Summerfield, P. (1987) Cultural reproduction in the education of girls: a study of girls' secondary schooling in two Lancashire towns. In F. Hunt (ed.) *Lessons for Life: The Schooling of Girls and Women 1850–1950*. Oxford: Blackwell.

UNICEF (2007) *Child Poverty in Perspective: An Overview of Child Well-being in Rich Countries. A comprehensive assessment of the lives and well-being of children and adolescents in the economically advanced nations*. Florence: UNICEF Innocenti Research Centre. Available online at: www.unicef-irc.org/publications/pdf/rc7_eng.pdf

Vlaeminke, M. (2000) *The English Higher Grade Schools: A Lost Opportunity*. London: Woburn Press.

Watts, J. (ed.) (1977) *The Countesthorpe Experience*. London: George Allen & Unwin.

Wilkinson, R. and Pickett, K. (2010) *The Spirit Level: Why Equality is Better for Everyone*. London: Penguin.

# 2

## CLYDE CHITTY
## The Politics of Education

---

**Learning outcomes**

By the end of this chapter, you should be able to:

- describe some of the key areas of focus in the politics of education;
- understand that education policy in Britain and elsewhere largely reflects the views of the dominant groups in society at any particular time;
- appreciate that even decisions about the content of the school curriculum are essentially political ones, with central government and opposition groups determined to influence what goes on in the classroom;
- outline and assess some of the theory and ideology behind everyday developments in education policy and practice.

---

### Introduction: overview of the discipline

Educational change never happens in a vacuum. It is widely understood that education reflects the dominant politics of a society's institutions and therefore has a powerful role to play in sustaining and perpetuating the existing social order. Schools exist, in part at least, to serve the interests of the political elites in society, but this is not their only function and educational reform can have unforeseen consequences. It seems clear that, by their very nature, modern education systems are an area where the objectives of different social classes and political groups meet and very often clash. The historical record shows us that, in this problematic situation, there is always scope for a variety of outcomes and that the success of any of these depends on the balance of political forces at any particular time. That being said, and accepting that education systems possess a degree of autonomy, it is, of course, true that educational choices can never be taken out of the realm of political debate because any political party's views as to what constitutes a desirable education system will always be determined by its views about the sort of society it wants to create.

## Key theme 1: six decades of political change – an overview

### The post-war welfare capitalist consensus

Amid all the turmoil and suffering of the Second World War (1939–45), it was generally agreed that a better world must be created for the next generation of children. In the words of historian Brian Simon, there must be no going back to 'the stagnant, class-ridden depressing society of the 1930s' (Simon 1991). The 1944 Education Act (which you will have read about in the previous chapter) came to be regarded as a cornerstone of the new welfare state, with secondary education for all pupils becoming an integral part of an education system now viewed as a continuous process – ranging from the primary sector through to further education. The Act was, in fact, seen by many as a sort of manifesto for a better society and R.A. Butler (since 1941, President of the Board of Education) argued that it would be a means of welding the people of Britain into one nation – a way of bringing an end to the 'two nations between whom there is no intercourse and no sympathy' that the 19th-century Conservative Prime Minister, Benjamin Disraeli, had talked about in his 1845 novel, *Sybil*.

In his important book, *The Unprincipled Society: New Demands and Old Politics*, Professor David Marquand (1988) argues that, from the mid-1940s until the mid-1970s, most of Britain's political class shared a tacit governing philosophy that can be called 'Keynesian social democracy'. It did not cover the whole spectrum of political opinion nor did it prevent vigorous party conflict. The two main parties (Conservative and Labour) often differed fiercely about specific details of policy, particularly where education was concerned; and on a deeper level, their conceptions of political authority and social justice differed even more. But they differed within a structure of generally accepted values and assumptions. Both front benches in the House of Commons were determined to banish the misery and hardships of the inter-war years (1919–39) and to make sure that the conflicts those hardships had caused did not return. And their views were shared by most of the members of what might be called 'the establishment': senior civil servants, the leaders of the most powerful trades unions, heads of nationalized industries, heads of large private-sector companies, and influential commentators in the quality and popular press. In Professor Marquand's view, the post-war settlement involved a three-fold commitment: to full employment, to the new welfare state, and to the harmonious co-existence of large public and private sectors in the economy.

### Division and conflict

Where the organization of the education system was concerned, the post-war consensus involved a broad commitment to 'a national system, locally administered'.

The two main parties might differ strongly about the arguments supporting the reorganization of secondary education along comprehensive lines, but the role of local education authorities went largely unquestioned. When the comprehensive reform became national policy in 1965, the Labour government sent out Circular 10/65, requesting all 163 local education authorities in England and Wales to submit viable plans for reorganizing their secondary schools along comprehensive lines.

All this was to begin to fall apart in the mid-1970s, when Keynesian social democracy could not cope with the economic shocks and adjustment problems occasioned by the major world recession that erupted in 1973–74. The post-war consensus collapsed during the period of the Wilson/Callaghan Labour government of 1974–79, amid mounting inflation, swelling balance of payments deficits, unprecedented currency depreciation, bitter industrial conflicts and what seemed to many on the Right of British politics to be ebbing governability. At one point during the summer of 1976, Chancellor of the Exchequer Denis Healey had to turn round at Heathrow Airport and cancel a proposed trip abroad in order to apply for a massive loan from the International Monetary Fund.

It was during this period that the New Right began to put forward radical new ideas for the organization of the education service. And their significance can be judged by the way in which the nature of the contributions to the Black Papers changed between 1969 and 1977. The five Black Papers represented an attempt by the Right to mount an intellectual critique of the educational proposals of the Left. The contributors to the first of these Black Papers, published in 1969 and 1970, were seen as simply wanting to turn back the clock: to the halcyon days of 'formal' teaching methods in primary schools; of tough academic standards associated with a grammar-school education; and of well-motivated, hardworking and essentially conservative university students. The articles they produced were largely devoid of radical, forward-looking ideas; theirs was clearly the voice of the past. But all this had changed by the time the last two Black Papers were published, in 1975 and 1977.

The Editors of these 1975 and 1977 Papers urged experimentation with various forms of privatization, including the education voucher, a scheme by which all parents would be issued with a free basic coupon, to be cashed in at a school of their choice and fixed at the average cost of the schools in the local authority area. The new emphasis was to be on choice and competition and parental control of schools. The powers of the local education authorities were to be steadily whittled away. From being on the defensive at the end of the 1960s, the Right was preparing itself to go on the offensive, with the floating of radical new ideas for the future organization of the education service.

The period 1976 to 1997 was one of genuine political conflict between the two main parties at Westminster – and this was particularly true of the years from 1979 to 1990, during the three Conservative administrations of Margaret Thatcher. While the Conservative leadership turned towards a new, updated version of the classical market liberalism of the 19th century, the Labour Leadership stuck to a version of right-wing Labourism, which, while it could hardly be described as Socialism, did at least observe the basic tenets of Social Democracy, including the traditional view that society was made up of a number of important and often conflicting interests, all of which deserved to be respected.

Where education was concerned, the Labour Party tried to respond to the right-wing agenda of choice, diversity and privatization by building a new consensus around more central control of the school curriculum, greater teacher accountability and the more direct subordination of secondary education to the perceived needs of the economy. These were the themes taken up by Prime Minister, James Callaghan, during the so-called Great Debate of 1776–77, following his famous Ruskin speech in 1976. As we shall see in a later section, the Labour opposition rejected most of the provisions of the 1988 Education Act, but felt unable to stop the onward thrust of the right-wing juggernaut. This period of educational policy is covered very well by Ken Jones (1988) and by Christopher Knight (1990).

## Choice, diversity and privatization

By the time New Labour had secured a landslide victory in the general election of May 1997, a new consensus had developed between the two main parties on education policy, and this time it was a consensus largely on the Right's terms. Prime Minister, Tony Blair, and Education Secretary, David Blunkett, were anxious to jettison many of the Labour Party's traditional commitments, particularly with regard to the future of 11+ selection (which several LEAs still used as part of their selective system for secondary schools), and, in their place, to embrace the fashionable dogmas of parental choice and diversity of secondary school provision. Education would be allowed to continue as a market commodity driven by consumer demands, with parental choice of schools being facilitated by greater teacher accountability and the publication of test and examination results.

Many of those reviewing an edited collection of essays published in 1999, with the title *State Schools: New Labour and the Conservative Legacy* (Chitty and Dunford 1999), drew particular attention to the cartoon, specially drawn for the book's cover by the *Guardian* and *Times Educational Supplement* cartoonist Martin Rowson, which seemed to neatly summarize the basic message of all the book's contributors. A gowned and mortar-boarded headteacher (unmistakably Margaret Thatcher) is shown handing a prize to a beaming, blazered student (unmistakably Tony Blair). The prize is a neat scroll of Conservative education policies.

In March 2000, David Blunkett launched a programme of academies (originally known as city academies) as 'a radical new approach' to 'breaking the cycle of underperformance and low expectations' in inner-city schools by introducing the idea of private sponsorship of schools. In a speech delivered to the right-wing Social Market Foundation, he announced that these new academies would 'replace seriously failing schools', and would be 'built and managed by partnerships involving the government, voluntary, church and business sponsors'. And this was a speech by the Education Secretary of a party that had been so vociferous in its opposition to the Conservatives City Technology Colleges Project dating from 1986, upon which the new Academies Programme was based!

> **Activity: the Local Education Authority**
>
> Think back to where you received your secondary education. What was the local LEA? What kind of school did you attend in terms of its status or designation – secondary modern, grammar, technical, comprehensive, voluntary-aided faith school, academy, CTC or private. Were you aware of the local LEA system at the time? What did you think about your school and the system? If you are not too sure about the local system, try to do some research on it – ask family members or go online to a search engine to find out about your LEA and its history,

## Key theme 2: changing patterns of policy-making

As we touched upon briefly in the last section, administratively, the system of educational policy-making established in England and Wales as part of the 1945 post-war settlement involved a commitment to what was described as a national system, locally administered. Until the late 1970s, the role of the local education authorities seemed unassailable, and the system involved the continuing operation of a more or less benign partnership between central government, local government and individual schools and colleges. The same model of partnership, implying a genuine dispersion of power and responsibility, also existed in Scotland, and here right-wing attempts to undermine the powers of local authorities have taken longer to take root.

For a period of at least 30 years, the formulation of education policy was largely in the hands of government ministers, top civil servants, local education authorities and a select group of union leaders. And, as we have already seen, this was also a period that many have come to view as a high point of the consensus on education, when most of Britain's political class shared a tacit governing philosophy that might be called 'Keynesian Social Democracy'.

The system began to break down from the mid-1970s onwards, when the influential role of civil servants and local authorities, and even of cabinet government itself, were to fall victim to increasing prime ministerial power, particularly as wielded by Margaret Thatcher and Tony Blair. And of special significance in this regard was the setting-up of the Downing Street Policy Unit in 1974.

### The Downing Street Policy Unit

It is generally accepted that the nature of policy formulation – across a whole range of subjects – changed irreversibly with the creation of the Downing Street Policy Unit in March 1974. This new body was established shortly after the Labour Party's narrow victory in the February 1974 election, and was described by Peter Hennessy, Professor of Contemporary History at Queen Mary College, University of London, in his 1986 book, *Cabinet* (1986), as 'Harold Wilson's most important and durable innovation' (p. 82). Under the strong leadership, from 1974 to 1979, of Dr Bernard (later Lord) Donoughue, a political scientist from the London School of Economics, it soon became, in Professor Hennessy's words, 'a prime-ministerial cabinet in all but name'.

According to a press release on the new Policy Unit issued from Downing Street in 1974, it was intended that this new body would 'assist in the development of the whole range of policies contained in the Labour government's programme, and especially those arising in the short and medium term'. This was a clear attempt to distinguish it from the Central Policy Review Staff (CPRS), which had been created by Conservative Prime Minister Edward Heath on taking office in 1970 and was more, although not exclusively, orientated to longer-term policy horizons.

Bernard Donoughue played a large part in determining the style and content of Prime Minister James Callaghan's contributions to the so-called Great Debate of 1976–77, and, in so doing, provoked considerable resentment on the part of Education Secretary, Shirley Williams, and her officials at the Department of Education and Science. This was, after all, a period when civil servants did not expect political advisers to play a significant role in the shaping of education policy.

Somewhat paradoxically in the light of later developments, it was Margaret Thatcher's initial inclination, on replacing James Callaghan as Prime Minister in 1979, to rely for political advice on her newly appointed ministers, and, by implication, for policy advice on their departments. She reduced the number and seniority of her political aides at Number Ten and also cut down the size of the Policy Unit.

Over the period of her term in office, however, she came to revise this earlier judgement; and it seems to have been the (from her point of view) debilitating experience of working with a predominantly cautious set of ministers that caused her to change her style and gather round her a set of keen, like-minded individuals.

**Key figure: Denis Lawton**

A key figure for understanding the politics of education, and particularly the politics of the school curriculum, is Professor Denis Lawton, who was Director of the Institute of Education, University of London, from 1983 to 1989.

In his books, *Social Change, Educational Theory and Curriculum Planning* (1973) and *Class, Culture and the Curriculum* (1975), he argued that comprehensive schools had not done enough to re-think the school curriculum and plan a programme that could be appropriate for universal secondary education. He defined 'curriculum' as 'a selection from the culture of a society' and proposed that comprehensive schools should adopt 'a common culture curriculum'.

In his 1980 book *The Politics of the School Curriculum*, and in a lecture delivered to the British Educational Management and Administration Society in 1983, which became his 1984 Institute of Education Bedford Way Paper *The Tightening Grip: Growth of Central Control of the School Curriculum* (1984), he identified three competing groups within the central authority in the education system of England and Wales.

**Table 2.1** Three ideologies in the education system in the 1980s

|  | Beliefs | Values | Tastes |
|---|---|---|---|
| (a) Politicos (ministers and political advisers) | Market | Freedom of choice | Independent schools fees |
| (b) Bureaucrats (DES officials and civil servants) | Good administration | Efficiency | Central control examinations standard tests |
| (c) Professional (HMI) | Professionalism | Quality education | Impressionistic evaluation of schools |

Source: Lawton (1984).

In Table 2.1, the political advisers and members of the Downing Street Policy Unit (described as 'politicos') were seen as being supporters of a 'market' in education and therefore keen to experiment with new forms of 'privatization' – Oliver Letwin held the education portfolio in the Policy Unit from 1983 to 1986 and wrote a book called *Privatising the World*, published in 1988 (Letwin 1988). The officials and civil servants of the Department of Education and Science (described as 'bureaucrats') were concerned with efficiency and teacher accountability. And members of Her Majesty's Inspectorate (described as 'professionals'), a body that had been created back in 1839 to inspect and advise schools, was concerned with professional standards.

Where the curriculum was concerned, Her Majesty's Inspectorate published a 1977 *Red Book* where children's learning was based on eight 'areas of experience': the aesthetic and creative, the ethical, the linguistic, the mathematical, the physical, the scientific, the social and political, and the spiritual. The civil servants of the DES, on the other hand, believed in a rigid and outdated subject-based model for the curriculum, which eventually became the National Curriculum outlined in a 1987 consultation document and consisting of ten subjects: English, Maths, Science, a modern foreign language (except in primary schools), Technology, History, Geography, Art, Music and Physical Education.

We can now move on to see how the divisions within Professor Lawton's model of the Central Authority are obvious if we look at the tensions and difficulties caused by the drafting of the government's 1987 Great Education Reform Bill (that many educationalists called 'Gerbil' for short), which became the 1988 Education Reform Act.

## The 1988 Education Reform Act

While most of the provisions of the 1988 Education Act (to be looked at in more detail in the next section) were inspired by the thinking of Mrs Thatcher's political advisers, the National Curriculum was seen by these same advisers as an essentially alien concept imposed on them by Education Secretary, Kenneth Baker, and the civil servants of the DES. Interviewed by the author of this Chapter on 24 November

1995, Stuart Sexton, one of the Prime Minister's principal advisers, saw the curriculum proposals in the Act as constituting a quite separate and unnecessary piece of legislation, serving merely to divert attention from all the laudable free-market objectives that he and other members of the Policy Unit had been working towards. This is what he said:

> Well, in our view, that Great Reform Act ... was really two Acts of Parliament. Now one of these Acts of Parliament that the Policy Unit and I had been working on in the latter days of Keith Joseph for the better Management and Financing of schools – and there you will find the grant-maintained schools and all the rest of it – well, that was the part of the Act that we really cared about. The second Act of Parliament ... which got pushed in at the last minute ... was all to do with central control over the school curriculum, and I claim no credit for that, and neither do all the others who were working with me in the time of Keith.
>
> (Interview with the author, 24 November 1995)

## The role of advisers under New Labour (1997 onwards)

The Policy Unit retained much of its power and influence after the Labour Party's landslide victory in the 1997 general election. In order to have a knowledgeable and respected academic to head the Unit, the new Prime Minister turned to the young David Miliband, who had been drafted in from the IPPR (Institute for Public Policy Research) to work with Tony Blair at the time of the Labour Party leadership election following the untimely death of John Smith in May 1994. David Miliband became the MP for South Shields in 2001 and then, at the age of 36, a minister of state in the Department for Education and Science (DfES) in a reshuffle occasioned by the resignation of Stephen Byers. His successor as Head of the Policy Unit was Andrew Adonis, who took a keen interest in education policy but was viewed with some suspicion among the more traditional elements within the Party on account of his lack of Labour credentials and his known opposition to comprehensive education. He is, in fact, often credited with initiating and promoting the new government's Academies Programme. Following New Labour's victory in the 2005 general election, he was given a peerage and became a junior schools minister under Ruth Kelly.

In recent years, the Policy Unit has been merged with the Prime Minister's Private Office to create the 'Policy Directorate', working on both short- and medium-term policy, and this would seem to be a further important development in the process of moving away from collective to presidential government. Furthermore, an important recent publication confirms the pivotal role in education policy of the personal wishes of prime ministers along with their non-elected advisers. In *Instinct or Reason: How Education Policy Is Made and How We Might Make it Better*, Perry and colleagues (2010) demonstrate that since the 1970s, much education policy has been influenced less by the results of educational research, and more by political ideology, prime ministerial likes and dislikes and the views of political advisers.

---

**Activity: educational advisers**

Since the 1970s, all of the governments – Conservative and Labour – have increasingly relied on unelected and unaccountable education advisers, often bypassing the Permanent Secretary for Education (the most senior civil servant) at the Department for Education and the Cabinet.

1. What is your view about this?
2. Google any of the advisers mentioned in this chapter and find out more about their careers, roles and influence.

---

## Key theme 3: the Conservative governments and education from 1979 to 1997

### Margaret Thatcher's three administrations, 1979–1990

Margaret Thatcher, who replaced Edward Heath as leader of the Conservative Party in February 1975 and became Prime Minister in May 1979, made little secret of her fundamental desire to undermine and eventually destroy both the comprehensive system of secondary schooling and the concept of 'a national system of education, *locally* administered'. Indeed, the new Prime Minister felt a profound sense of shame that she had done so little, during her time as Edward Heath's Education Secretary (1970–74), to impede the process of comprehensive reorganization. In an interview with the Editor of the *Daily Mail* on 13 May 1987, she explained that she had been up against powerful forces in the education establishment. These were her words:

> This universal comprehensive thing started with Tony Crosland's Circular 10/65 in 1965 when all the local education authorities were asked to submit plans in which secondary schools were to go totally comprehensive. And when I was Secretary of State for Education in the Heath Government … this great rollercoaster of an idea was moving, and I found it difficult, if not impossible, to move it.

Bearing in mind the strong radical instincts of the new Prime Minister and the scope of the education reforms being prepared by her fervent admirers in the Policy Unit, it is surprising that the first two Thatcher administrations (1979–87) achieved comparatively little as far as radical educational change was concerned. Indeed there had been nothing in the 1979 Conservative election manifesto to suggest that a significant alteration of the structure of education was intended, with plans to maintain and improve educational standards being subsumed as part of a broader section with the title 'Helping the Family'.

Mrs Thatcher's first Education Secretary was Mark Carlisle (1979–81), a middle-of-the-road figure, who simply did not understand the arguments in favour of privatizing the system. The one radical measure introduced during his time in office was the Assisted Places Scheme, designed, in the words of the 1979 manifesto, to 'enable less well-off parents to claim all or part of the fees at certain independent schools from a special government fund'. It was broadly conceived as a form of 'scholarship ladder' that would benefit 'bright' children from 'poor homes' who would otherwise be 'inadequately stretched' at their local 'under-achieving' comprehensive school. In the event, it was soon discovered that the majority of the children who gained 'assisted places' were, in fact, from homes with 'educationally advantaged' parents. An influential research study on the Assisted Places Scheme was carried out by Tony Edwards and colleagues (1989). The Labour Party pledged to abolish the scheme if it came to power, and this actually happened in 1997.

It was widely anticipated that the right-wing Keith Joseph, Mark Carlisle's successor as Education Secretary (1981–86), would be the minister who could be relied upon to implement the Thatcherite agenda for the education system, but he failed to find a way of introducing the education voucher (already referred to in an earlier section) and it was left to his pragmatic and opportunistic successor, Kenneth Baker, to pilot through Parliament the most far-reaching education legislation of the Thatcher years. The central purpose of the 1988 Education Act was that power should be gathered to the centre and, at the same time, devolved on to schools and parents, both processes being at the expense of mediating bureaucracies, whether elected or not. Writing in the *Independent* on 11 June 1987, the day of the 1987 general election, education journalist Peter Wilby had forecast: 'The election of a Conservative government today will mean the break-up of the state education system that has existed since 1944.'

We have already seen that the main centralizing feature of the 1988 Act was the introduction of a national curriculum for all state schools. This provision upset all the neo-liberals among Mrs Thatcher's supporters, but Kenneth Baker was able to argue that such a curriculum would serve as justification for a massive programme of national testing at 7, 11, 14 and 16, which would, in turn, provide the raw data for the publication of league tables providing evidence to parents of the desirability or otherwise of individual schools.

The second main feature of the Act was the introduction of a new system of school management, known as LMS (Local Management of Schools), whereby the new delegated budget to schools would be determined by a formula largely reflecting the number of pupils on the school roll. At the same time, there would be significant changes to admissions regulations, obliging all schools in future to admit pupils to their full capacity.

And the third major change involved the creation of a new tier of schooling, particularly at the secondary level, comprising City Technology Colleges and grant-maintained (or GM) Schools. This new tier was absolutely central to the Conservatives' plans to create more choice and diversity in the system and deserves closer attention.

The CTC Project was actually announced by Kenneth Baker shortly after his appointment as Education Secretary in a speech he delivered to the 1986 Conservative Party Conference. These new colleges for 11 to 18 year olds – around 20 in number and situated largely in inner-city areas – would be financed partly by the private sector and would be completely independent of local education authority control. Grant-maintained schools – the second component of the new tier of schooling – would be those schools, both secondary and large primaries, where a requisite proportion of parents voted to take the school out of local authority control and the school would then receive direct funding from central government. In the event, neither project was an unqualified success. It proved impossible to find enough sponsors or suitable sites for the new CTCs, and when the last college was authorized in April 1991, it brought the grand total to just 15. And by the beginning of 1992, schools wanting to opt out of local authority control were concentrated in just 12 of the 117 education authorities in England and Wales.

## Choice and diversity under John Major, 1990–97

It was now the task of Education Secretary, John Patten, who acquired the portfolio in April 1992, to experiment with new ways of re-introducing forms of secondary selection without returning to the days of the tripartite secondary system (grammar, technical and secondary modern schools). And the new idea was to be 'selection by specialization'. In an article that Patten wrote for the *New Statesman and Society*, published on 17 July 1992, the new Education Secretary argued that Socialists must now 'come to terms with the concept of Specialisation'. This is what he wrote:

> Selection is not, and should not be, a great issue of the 1990s, as it was in the 1960s. The new S-word for Socialists to come to terms with is Specialisation. The fact is that children excel at different things; it is foolish to ignore it, and some schools may wish specifically to cater for these differences. Specialisation, under-pinned, of course, by the National Curriculum, will be the answer for some – though not all – children, driven by aptitude and interest, as much as by ability.

The White Paper *Choice and Diversity* (HMSO 1992) attacked the comprehensive system for 'presupposing that children are all basically the same and that all local communities have essentially the same educational needs' (p. 3). And the idea that all children would benefit from a much greater variety of schools, particularly at the secondary level, was clearly articulated in a 1996 White Paper, *Self-government for Schools* (HMSO 1996), published during Gillian Shephard's period as Education Secretary (1994–97).

By the time the Conservatives were defeated in the 1997 election, there were still 163 grammar schools in England and Wales, concentrated in many of the larger conurbations, and in English counties such as Buckinghamshire, Kent and Lincolnshire. At the same time, there were about 1100 grant-maintained schools, accounting for almost one in five of all pupils at secondary school; in addition, there were 196 specialist schools and colleges, comprising 15 City Technology Colleges, 151 new technology colleges and 30 language colleges. It was confidently expected by many that a new Labour government would try to make the secondary system fairer and easier to understand but, as things turned out, nothing could be further from the truth.

Two key books on the Thatcher and Major years include *Conservative Party Education Policies 1976–1997: The Influence of Politics and Personality*, by Daniel Callaghan (2006), a book that contains a large number of interviews with key figures of the period, and *Education Answers Back: Critical Responses to Government Policy*, edited by Clyde Chitty and Brian Simon (1993), a book that brings together a number of speeches and essays by prominent educationalists hostile to the Conservative government's agenda.

---

**Activity: 'Choice and Diversity' or 'Chaos and Perversity'?**

Professor Denis Lawton, referred to the White Paper, *Choice and Diversity*, by a different name – 'Chaos and Perversity'! Do you think this is fair? What is your view of the Conservative attempts to diversify secondary education, bringing in competition and wider selection, thus rowing back on previous decades of development and growth in comprehensive schools?

---

## Key theme 4: New Labour and education from May 1997 to May 2010

### Continuity and change

New Labour came to power at the beginning of May 1997 after a landslide general election victory bringing to an end 18 years of Conservative rule in Britain. Securing 43 per cent of the national vote, the election of 419 New Labour MPs gave Tony Blair's Party a House of Commons majority over all other parties, of 179. With only 165 MPs and just 31 per cent of the national vote, the Conservative Party had suffered its most crushing election defeat since the general election of January 1906.

The Conservative governments of Margaret Thatcher and John Major had passed some 30 Education Acts between 1979 and 1997, covering every aspect of education, from early years to higher education, and particularly affecting the structure of the secondary system. Tony Blair's pre-election slogan had been 'education, education, education', and it was soon pretty obvious that there was to be no lull, brief or otherwise, in the avalanche of education acts, policy initiatives and school reforms. The first education White Paper of the new administration, with the title *Excellence in Schools*, was published in July 1997, just 67 days after the election. The early abolition of the Conservatives' Assisted Places Scheme led some commentators to assume that there would now be a radical break with the past but, as we have already seen, there was to be much evidence, right from the outset, of an essential continuity with the policies of the outgoing Conservative government.

It had been emphasized by Tony Blair even before the election that, in the event of a New Labour victory, several key personnel would retain their jobs heading the country's major education quangos. Those involved included Andrea Millett at the TTA (Teacher Training Agency), Nicholas Tate at the QCA (Qualifications and Curriculum Authority), and Chris Woodhead at Ofsted (Office for Standards in Education), an independent body that had been set up by John Major's government in 1992 with responsibility for contracting independent teams to inspect all primary and secondary schools. Woodhead was a particularly controversial figure, largely on account of his thinly disguised contempt for most classroom teachers and his eugenic belief in the limited capabilities of working-class children in inner-city areas.

Under New Labour, there was to be a preoccupation with the culture of 'targets' and a commitment to a rigid standards agenda for schools that required an enormous amount of assessment and testing, and centralized control of both teachers and the curriculum. This standards agenda included the setting-up of a new Standards and Effectiveness Unit in the DfEE (Department for Education and Employment), headed in the early years by Professor Michael Barber; a Standards Task Force (STF); Literacy and Numeracy Task Forces to oversee the daily Literacy and Numeracy Hours to be in place in all primary schools by September 1999; a New Deal Task Force and Advisory Group to oversee policies for youth and unemployment; and a Continuing Education Advisory Group. The role of Ofsted was to be steadily enhanced, with inspection of LEAs and the identification of 'successful' and 'failing' schools part of the remit from 1998 and an Adult Learning Inspectorate created in 2000. The enthusiastic introduction of performance-related pay and the publication in the media of league tables of examination results school by school was further designed to exert pressure on teachers and thereby raise standards.

Where secondary selection was concerned, there was to be no unequivocal support for comprehensive schooling; and a Labour Party document published in 1995 had also made it clear that a future Labour government would not deal with the remaining grammar schools as a matter of national policy. In the words of *Diversity and Excellence: A New Partnership for Schools*:

> While we have never supported the grammar schools in their exclusion of children by examination, change can come only through local agreement. Such a change in the character of a school could follow only a clear demonstration of support by the parents affected by such a decision.

Shadow Education Secretary, David Blunkett, found it very difficult to defend this curious formula at the October 1995 Labour Party Conference. Accordingly, in his reply to the somewhat acrimonious education debate, he said: 'Read my lips. No selection, either by examination or by interview, under a Labour government.' The strategy seemed to work and the delegates went home satisfied that the remaining grammar schools would indeed be incorporated into the comprehensive system. But this was not to be the end of the matter, for in later speeches and media interviews, Blunkett let it be known that what he had really meant to say was 'no further selection under a Labour government'. This was much more than a slip of the tongue; it was actually the announcement of a change in traditional Labour Party policy. The phrase 'no selection' signified an end to the existing grammar schools; 'no *further* selection' was, in effect, a *guarantee of their retention*.

## A renewed commitment to choice and diversity

New Labour's first big education act, the 1998 School Standards and Framework Act, was largely concerned with systems and structures. While ending the Conservative policy of grant-maintained or opted-out schools receiving their funding direct from central government, the 1998 Act followed up the proposals in the previous year's White Paper by stipulating that, in future, there would be three main types of school: community, aided and foundation. Community schools would be similar to the existing county schools; aided and foundation schools would employ their own staff and own their own premises. There would be permitted levels of selection in the existing grammar schools and in some of the new specialist schools. By 1999, most former grant-maintained schools, enriched by many years of preferential funding, had opted for foundation status, while most faith schools – of which there were around 700 in 1998 – continued as voluntary-aided schools.

It was Clause 102 of the 1998 Act that gave legislative backing to a pledge in the 1997 White Paper that 'secondary schools with a specialism will continue to be able to give priority to those children who demonstrate the relevant aptitude, as long as that is not misused on the basis of general academic ability'. The Clause stated that a maintained secondary school may 'make provision for the selection of pupils for admission to the school by reference to their aptitude for one or more prescribed subjects', where:

- the admission authority for the school are satisfied that the school has a specialism in the subject or subjects in question;
- the proportion of selective admissions in any relevant age group does not exceed 10 per cent.

This Clause caused considerable disquiet among teachers and many Labour MPs, even as the 1997 Bill was in the process of becoming an Act. It was felt that specialist schools could easily create (or exacerbate) an unbalanced academic and social mix in many inner-city schools. And who could say how children could be tested for specific 'aptitudes', rather than for 'general ability'?

As we have already seen, New Labour had no wish to make it easy for campaigners for the comprehensive school to abolish the existing grammar schools. In an interview with the *Sunday Telegraph*, published on 12 March 2000, Education Secretary, David Blunkett, left readers in no doubt that he had no intention of concerning himself with the grammar-school question. It was time, he said, to 'bury the dated arguments of previous decades' and reverse 'the outright opposition to grammar schools' that had been 'a touchstone of Labour policy for at least 35 years'.

This interview was given just two days after the announcement of the voting figures in the only ballot on the future of a grammar school held as a result of the policy leaving the future of 11+ selection in the hands of local parents. The future of Ripon Grammar School in North Yorkshire, founded back in 1556 and one of the oldest in the country, was, in fact, assured as local parents decided by a clear majority of two to one to reject the proposition that the school be required in future to 'admit children of all abilities'. On a 75 per cent turnout, 1493 of the 3000 or so parents who were 'entitled to vote' because their children went to one or other of 14 'feeder' state primary or independent preparatory schools voted to reject the proposition, with 748 voting in favour.

While grammar schools were being allowed to prosper, with admissions having increased by around 20 per cent between 1992 and 2000, New Labour was also pursuing the Conservatives' Specialist Schools Programme with great vigour. By September 2004 there were as many as 1,955 Specialist Schools, by far the largest number specializing in technology, arts, sports, science or modern languages, with a smaller number offering maths and computing, business and enterprise, engineering, humanities or music. Those specializing in technology, arts, sports, modern foreign languages or music were allowed to select up to 10 per cent of their intake on the basis of pupils' 'aptitude' for the subject. Almost as soon as the Specialist Schools had been set up, claims were made that pupils did better in this type of school, but, as Professor Sally Tomlinson (2003) has pointed out, 'there was no way of separating factors relating to preferential funding and a socially skewed intake in order to make any valid comparisons'.

As a way of bringing private sponsors into the system, New Labour launched its own version of the Conservatives' City Technology Colleges Project in March 2000. This was the programme for City Academies (to be discussed more fully in a future section on the privatization of education); and at its launch, David Blunkett said that it must be seen as 'a radical approach' to 'breaking the cycle of underperformance and low expectations in inner-city schools'.

A White Paper published in October 2005 was enthusiastic about the whole idea of 'independent non-fee-paying state secondary schools', and was anxious to promote the new City Academies and the idea of Trust Schools where schools could either create their own trust or work to form links with an existing trust made up of the sort of bodies already sponsoring academies. By the time Francis Beckett published his book *The Great City Academy Fraud* in 2007, there were already 46 academies in existence, and Tony Blair had announced a new target of 400 such schools to be up and running by September 2010.

An important book that covers the Conservative administrations and the two early New Labour governments (1997–2005) is Professor Sally Tomlinson's *Education in a Post-welfare Society* (2005); it includes lists of all the main education acts and key policy documents.

**Key figure: Sally Tomlinson**

Sally Tomlinson is currently a professor in the Department of Educational Studies at the University of Oxford, having previously held professorships at several other universities. She has written numerous articles and books on a wide range of education areas including policy, race and education, special education, 14–19 education and much more. Her prize-winning book on *Education in a Post-Welfare Society* (2005) has been very much appreciated by education studies students. She has always been committed to fairness and greater equality in education and has long been a supporter of comprehensive schools. You can find out more about her and her recent articles and books by visiting: www.education.ox.ac.uk/people/academics

When Gordon Brown replaced Tony Blair at the end of June 2007, the education system was more divided and divisive than at any time since the end of the Second World War. Parents were faced with a bewildering array of secondary schools, and a place for their child at the school of first choice could not be guaranteed. Attempts to make the system fairer and more transparent by the publication of a succession of Admissions Codes were hampered by the existence of a number of schools that acted as their own admissions authority.

---

**Activity: New Labour's emphasis on standards**

There seems no doubt that New Labour's commitments to education and to raising standards were summed up in Tony Blair's 1995 statement of his three future priorities – that, if elected, his policies would promote 'education, education, education'. Unsurpassed high levels of spending on education were to follow. But, in your view, did the prime focus on 'targets, testing, tables (league tables) and tick lists' in order to drive up standards, undermine the quality of education? Make two lists, one justifying the emphasis on standards and how it was conducted and another listing the drawbacks and negative effects.

---

## Key theme 5: the privatization of education

The privatization of education has assumed many different forms over the past 30 years and has generally enjoyed the enthusiastic endorsement of both Conservative and New Labour ministers. Yet not all the privatizing initiatives have met with long-term success. For example, in 1998, Surrey County Council invited companies to bid for the contract to run a 'failing' comprehensive school, King's Manor, in Guildford. And, in February 1999, it was announced that the contract had been won by 3Es Enterprises Ltd, a private company set up as the commercial arm of Kingshurst City Technology College, which had opened in the West Midlands Borough of Solihull in the autumn of 1988. The Managing Director of 3Es Enterprises was, in fact, the husband of the Principal of Kingshurst CTC. At the time, it was confidently expected that handing over everything to a private company would revitalize the school and lead to lasting academic success. But, in March 2010, Ofsted announced that King's had failed its inspection and that the school would be placed in the 'special measures' category. Surrey County Council successfully applied to the Department for Children, Schools and Families to replace the Governing Body, which effectively ended all links with 3Es Enterprises Ltd.

### PFI and (city) academies

This section is largely devoted to two major projects that have transformed education in England: PFI (Private Finance Initiative) and academies (the word 'city' soon being dropped to allow for the establishment of new schools in rural areas).

The Private Finance Initiative is in many ways the most radical and far-reaching of the various privatization schemes of the past 20 years. It involves the use of private-sector funding and ownership to provide new buildings and carry out major refurbishments right across the public sector. Private capital is injected into a wide range of essential public services, particularly education, health and transport, in return for lucrative long-term service contracts and the pleasing prospect of a considerable period of financial stability and steady growth. PFI contracts normally last for between 25 and 35 years, during which time the private company can look forward to being handsomely reimbursed by the relevant public body, whether it be a health trust or a local authority. Where schools are concerned, the company or consortium responsible for providing the new buildings will normally enjoy the additional benefits of taking over the maintenance and management of the premises, and this will involve such things as repairs, grounds maintenance, catering, cleaning, and the provision of furniture and IT equipment.

The PFI had actually been launched by Conservative Prime Minister John Major in late 1992. It was not discussed during the 1997 general election campaign, but Tony Blair still felt he had a mandate to expand its scope in the period of his administrations. Its great attraction for ministers was that it reduced capital spending – or at least postponed it to future years. It was also very attractive to local authorities in that PFI projects provided much needed funding for building at a time when money might not be forthcoming from other sources. It was claimed that PFI schemes provided 'value for money' and delivered more efficient services, although there was considerable evidence that PFI schemes were often more costly than large publicly funded projects of a similar nature. It often cost local authorities more to borrow money from the private sector than from the government, taking into account such factors as the large fees for consultants and the profits to go to the companies themselves.

As we have already seen, New Labour launched its new Academies Project in March 2000. Education Secretary David Blunkett actually outlined his vision for these privately sponsored schools in a speech to the Social Market Foundation on 15 March. This is what he said:

> These academies, to replace seriously failing schools, will be built and managed by partnerships involving the government, voluntary, Church and business sponsors. They will offer a real challenge and improvements in pupil performance, for example through innovative approaches to management, governance, teaching and the curriculum, including a specialist focus in at least one curriculum area. (http:/www.gov.uk/speeches)

In resurrecting the Conservatives' CTC project, which had come to a sudden end in 1991 with the creation of just 15 schools, New Labour was determined not to repeat some of the Conservatives' more obvious mistakes. Whereas Kenneth Baker had believed that private sponsors would be prepared to pay 'all or most' of the estimated £10 million cost of setting up a new CTC, New Labour ministers opted for the more realistic sum of £2 million. As time went by, and in a bid to give the academies greater respectability, New Labour was even prepared to allow new academic sponsors, particularly independent schools and universities, to dispense with any contribution towards the starting costs.

By September 2006, there were 46 academies in existence, and in a speech to the Specialist Schools and Academies Trust in November 2006, Tony Blair announced a doubling of the original target figure, to 400. It was also made clear that some of the new academies would be aimed at catering for pupils aged from 3 to 19. A total of 67 new academies were opened at the beginning of the school term in September 2009, bringing the grand total of these new schools to 200.

The growth of academies and the increasing privatization of education are now slowly but surely beginning to be researched by education academics and others. Two important books to read in connection with these developments include Stephen Ball's *Education plc* (2007) and Francis Beckett's *The Great Academy Fraud* (2007).

---

### Activity: the impact of privatization

It is often said that privatization is a convenient way of bringing money and sponsorship into the education system. Can you think of reasons why many people are opposed to this development – and what do you think is lost or gained if decision-making power no longer resides with the LEA?

---

## Key theme 6: curriculum change since 1988

### The primary curriculum

It was obvious right from the outset that Tony Blair's government would try to transform the existing primary school curriculum. The 1997 education White Paper, *Excellence in Schools* (HMSO 1997), announced that literacy and numeracy would now be a clear priority for all primary school pupils. Each primary school would be expected to devote a structured hour a day to literacy from September 1998 and then introduce a daily numeracy hour the following year. This drive to improve pupils' literacy and numeracy skills would be accompanied by a rigorous programme of assessment and testing at the ages of seven and eleven.

There was to be much criticism of the primary curriculum for providing young children with experiences that were restricted and dull. The emphasis on literacy and numeracy taking up a large part of the morning sessions was seen by many commentators as having the undesirable effect of 'narrowing' and 'impoverishing' the curriculum, with little room left for creative/aesthetic experiences. It was conceded by Mike Tomlinson, a former Chief Inspector of Schools, in an interview with the BBC Radio Four Programme, *The World Tonight*, broadcast on 16 May 2002, that a once broad and rich primary curriculum had been steadily 'whittled away' to facilitate a harmful concentration on literacy and numeracy. In this interview, he said that the new emphasis on 'core skills' amounted to 'a silent revolution', whereby there was little time available for such important subjects as history, geography, art and music. And it was to be one of the main conclusions of the Final Report of the Cambridge University-led *Review into Primary Education*, published in 2010, that New Labour had introduced a primary-school diet even narrower than that of the Victorian elementary schools (Alexander et al. 2010).

## The curriculum for older students

Where the curriculum for 14 to 16 year olds in Years 10 and 11 is concerned (the years known as key stage 4), very little was left of Kenneth Baker's 1987 model by the time New Labour came to power in 1997. Maintained secondary schools in England were now required to teach the authorized programmes of study in: English, maths, science (as a 'single' or 'double' programme), design and technology (a short course being the 'minimum requirement'), information technology (either as a separate subject or co-ordinated across other subjects), a modern foreign language and physical education. Secondary schools also had a statutory obligation to provide a programme of 'clearly identified' religious education, in accordance with a locally agreed syllabus, and a programme of 'carefully structured' sex education – although in accordance with Section 241 of the 1993 Education Act, parents now had the right to withdraw their children from all or part of the programme. Careers education would become a statutory part of the key stage 4 curriculum from September 1998. And it had been decided that there would be 'greater scope' for vocational options by providing courses leading to GNVQs (General National Vocational Qualifications).

Further proposals for 'slimming down' the key stage 4 curriculum were announced in 2002. It would now comprise: English, maths, science and ICT, alongside citizenship, religious education, careers education, sex education, physical education and work-related learning. Modern foreign languages and design and technology would no longer be 'required study' for all students but they would now join the arts and the humanities as subjects where there would simply be 'a statutory entitlement of access'.

Throughout his period in office, Tony Blair was resolutely opposed to the idea of bringing together academic and vocational subjects for older students, by creating a sort of 'British Baccalaureate' and thereby breaking the stranglehold of A levels and GCSEs. It was not until the end of 2007 that Gordon Brown's Education Secretary, Ed Balls, began the process of reforming and broadening the 14 to 19 curriculum by the introduction of Vocational and Academic Diplomas suitable for all students, but these proposals were criticized by many for being both half-hearted and lacking in conviction. You should look at two important books on the curriculum and on the education of young people: these are *Rethinking the School Curriculum: Values, Aims and Purposes*, edited by John White (2004), and *Lost Generation? New Strategies for Youth and Education* by Martin Allen and Pat Ainley (2010).

---

**Activity: your experiences of the curriculum**

If you look back to your own schooling,

1. were there subjects on the curriculum that were unattractive to you?
2. were there subjects and topics you would have liked to have studied but they were not offered on the timetable?

---

## Key theme 7: New Labour and inclusion

Where education is concerned, it is not always clear what is meant by the term 'inclusion'. Certainly, New Labour believed in 'an inclusive society', where all groups can flourish in a non-threatening environment. Following a number of nail bomb atrocities carried out in April 1999 and designed to bring bloodshed and chaos to various 'marginalized' communities in London: in Brixton, Brick Lane and Soho, Prime Minister Tony Blair spoke eloquently of the need to build 'the tolerant, multiracial Britain the vast majority of us want to see'. In a speech delivered in Birmingham on 2 May 1999 and intended to mark the 300th anniversary of the founding of the Sikh religion, Mr Blair argued powerfully that an attack on any section of the community was an attack on Britain as a whole:

> When one section of our community is under attack, we defend it in the name of all the community. When bombs attack the Black and Asian community in Britain, they effectively attack the whole of Britain ... When the gay community is attacked and innocent people are murdered, all the good people of Britain, whatever their race, their lifestyle, their class, unite in revulsion and determination to bring the evil people to justice.

The Prime Minister went on to emphasize that education had an important role to play in defeating any form of vicious nationalism that tolerated attacks on minorities and then replacing it with 'a vision for the 21st century based on respect for human diversity'. Schools had to teach that patriotism and pride in one's national identity should never be defined 'by reference to those excluded from that identity'.

At the same time, a rhetoric of 'inclusion' and a declared commitment to social justice has not resulted in an education system that is fair and egalitarian. There have been policies designed to 'lift poor children out of poverty', but by 2004, the Institute of Fiscal Studies was able to demonstrate that Britain had become one of the most economically unequal countries in Europe, with poor children in the UK poorer than the worst off in other industrial societies. The point is that inclusion remains a contested concept. Research has shown that the schools with higher levels of inclusion tend to serve the more disadvantaged areas, while schools serving advantaged areas are more likely to reject 'undesirable' pupils. This is particularly true where young people with 'disabilities' and 'special educational needs' are concerned. Good intentions for reducing inequality and exclusion have to be balanced by the political reality that the New Labour government had no wish to pursue policies that may alienate the middle and aspirant classes, and thereby threaten its electoral base. Policies to promote inclusion and fairness will always be negated by an emphasis on choice and diversity and a blind faith in market forces.

The dual educational policies of New Labour – raising achievement and promoting inclusion – although apparently in unison, can also be viewed as essentially contradictory: the drive to constantly promote success, perhaps for the majority, further alienates and stigmatizes the minority. An interesting book on New Labour and inclusion is *A More Equal Society? New Labour, Poverty, Inequality and Exclusion,* edited by John Hills and Kitty Stewart (2005).

### Key figure: Susanne Wiborg

Dr Susanne Wiborg, who teaches at the Institute of Education in London, and is from Denmark, is one of this country's leading experts on comprehensive systems in Scandinavia and much of her work has sought to explain why the comprehensive reform has made great headway in large parts of Scandinavia while the same cannot be said with regard to the situation in England and Germany. In her book *Education and Social Integration: Comprehensive Schooling in Europe* (2009), she argues that the key to understanding this phenomenon is to be found in the strength of Social Democratic political parties in Scandinavian countries, which pursue progressive education policies, and in the genuine alliances they have been able to form with Liberal groups. Her most recent research study, which attracted a good deal of media publicity in July 2010, found that plans to create hundreds of Swedish-style 'free schools' in England will risk increasing racial and social segregation as middle-class parents are encouraged to pull their children out of local comprehensives.

### Activity: inclusion

New Labour had 'inclusion' as its other major educational policy to that of raising standards. This policy very much differentiated the New Labour governments from the previous 18 years of Conservative education policy.

Make a list of all the areas of education policy from 1997 to 2010 that you think might come under the heading of an attempt to foster inclusion.

### Key theme 8: education policy under the Liberal–Conservative coalition government (May 2010 onwards)

The general election of 6 May 2010 produced an unstable situation where the Conservatives gained 306 seats in the House of Commons, Labour 258, the Liberal

Democrats 57 and other parties 28. On 11 May, the Liberal Democrats under Nick Clegg decided to join the Conservatives rather than New Labour, in a new coalition government and, as a result, David Cameron became the Prime Minister, with Nick Clegg as his Deputy. Michael Gove replaced New Labour's Ed Balls as the new Education Secretary.

The Coalition Agreement drafted on 11 May said that the new government would set up a network of Swedish-style 'free schools', allowing parents, charities and business organizations to set up their own schools outside local authority control. At the same time, the new government would press ahead with greatly extending the number of privately sponsored academies at the secondary level and expand the programme to include primary schools as well. There were currently 203 academies in existence, and the government wanted this figure to reach over 2000 within a very short period of time. Whereas under New Labour, the original idea was that academies should be seen as a 'radical approach' to breaking 'the cycle of underperformance and low expectations' in inner-city schools, the Conservative idea was that 'outstanding' primary and secondary schools should automatically be awarded Academy status. Many critics argued that this would create a two-tier education system divided into 'the best and the rest'. There would be a financial incentive to become an academy; and the new schools would have special powers in connection with teachers' pay and conditions, length of school terms, curriculum content and, in some cases, admissions policy. A new Academies Bill was introduced into the House of Lords on 26 May 2010 and, on the same day, Michael Gove wrote to the headteachers of 20,000 primary and secondary schools inviting them to seek academy status.

On 24 November 2010, the coalition government published a White Paper called *The Importance of Teaching*. It included many proposals such as plans for a new National Curriculum. It was later announced, in January 2011, that a Review of the National Curriculum would start work guided by a group of advisers and open to public consultation. There was also a plan for a new kind of training for teachers based in proposed new Teaching Schools, and therefore implying an even more reduced role for educational theory and debate in Schools of Education, which rightly feel threatened by these proposals. The Education Bill to implement the main proposals in the White Paper moved through the stages in Parliament in 2011 and included these features but also the proposals for the right of groups to set up more academies or a 'free school', with no local authority consultation, and the transfer of land to the new schools – so taking away land from local authorities. These schools will be funded from central government coffers.

**Key figures: New Right policy analysts**

While it is safe to say that many of the eminent academic analysts of education policy are orientated towards the political Left, there are many who are considered to be more conservative – and who also offer provocative and insightful commentaries on education. These include:

- **James Tooley**, Professor of Education Policy at the University of Newcastle; he is a fervent believer in the privatization of education;
- **Alan Smithers**, Professor of Education at the University of Buckingham; he is a great believer in the value of vocational education;
- **Anthony Seldon**, the Headteacher of Wellington School; although many of his instincts are conservative, he does believe that private schools should share their facilities with state schools.

---

**Activity: Liberal–Conservative coalition – a radical departure?**

In relation to the Liberal–Conservative coalition from 2010 onwards, what aspects of developing education policy mark a radical departure from New Labour's policies from 1997 to 2010?

---

## Conclusion

There seems to be a real possibility that the new government's education policy will denote the end of a publicly accountable state education system in England. As I argued in an article in spring 2011 (Chitty 2011), these plans will further destabilize the schools system in the UK and deny local scrutiny from the LEAs in terms of their admission procedures and plans to meet local needs. Labour education spokespersons attack the education policies of the coalition government claiming that excessive privatization has its drawbacks, but they seem to forget that they were themselves part of a government that paved the way for the policies being pursued by David Cameron and Michael Gove.

---

**Further research**

Having read the chapter, think about and ask yourselves the following questions.

- Successive governments since 1979 have been committed to driving forward higher levels of achievement amongst pupils in our schools. This has been conducted by reliance on a culture of 'performativity', by emphasizing accountability, public scrutiny of results, quality assurance via Ofsted, and constant assessment and measurement of results. A more popular way of describing this would be the culture of targets, tick lists, tests and tables (league tables). Critically assess the successes and failures of this approach.
- Under all governments since 1979, there has been an increase in privatization or the use of the private sector in education – at the levels of central government, local government and at the school. To what extent is this inevitable/desirable?

## Key readings

### Books

Ball, S. (2008) *The Education Debate*. Bristol: Policy Press. A lively and accessible paperback book that contains an analysis of English education policy, especially in relation to issues of equality and equity, by one of the UK's foremost policy researchers.

Chitty, C. (2009) *Education Policy in the Britain* (2nd edn). Basingstoke: Palgrave Macmillan. An overview of policy development that brings the history fairly up to date.

Lingard, B. and Ozga, J. (eds) (2005) *The RoutledgeFalmer Reader in Education Policy and Politics*. Oxford: RoutledgeFalmer. A wide-ranging collection of some of the key writings.

Tomlinson, S. (2005) *Education in a Post-welfare Society* (2nd edn). Maidenhead: Open University Press, second edition. Very readable analysis of policy changes from 1945 but with an emphasis on the governments from 1979 to 2005, when this second edition was published.

### Websites

Since education policy is changing radically almost by the day since the Liberal–Conservative coalition government was formed in May 2010, it is vital to keep up with key developments by visiting the following websites:

Department for Education: www.education.gov.uk
The *Guardian*: www.guardian.co.uk
The *Independent*: www.independent.co.uk
The *Times Educational Supplement*: www.tes.co.uk (but especially the weekly supplement)
The *Daily Telegraph*: www.telegraph.co.uk
The National Union of Teachers: www.teachers.org.uk
The National Association of Schoolmasters and Union of Women Teachers: www.nasuwt.org.uk
BBC News: www.bbc.co.uk/news

### Journals

*Forum*, a journal for promoting 3–19 comprehensive education and founded in 1958 by Brian Simon, Robin Pedley and Jack Walton. It is published three times a year and contains a wide mix of critical refereed and non-refereed articles on education policy. Details are available online at www.wwwords.co.uk/FORUM

The *Journal of Education Policy*, published by Routledge six times a year. It has a wide and impressive editorial board and range of articles. It is available on subscription and in university libraries in electronic and paper form. The 25th-anniversary edition of 2010 includes selected key articles from the journal's back editions.

The *Journal for Critical Education Policy Studies* is a peer-reviewed, international journal published as an e-journal, twice a year, by the Institute for Education Policy Studies, based at the University of Northampton. It has an editorial board that is worldwide and adopts an openly Marxist and Left orientation. It contains impressive articles on the UK and other countries, largely mounting a critique of neo-liberal and market approaches to education.

## References

Alexander, R. et al. (2010) *Children, Their World, Their Education: Final Report and Recommendations of the Cambridge Primary Review*. Abingdon: Routledge.

Allen, M. and Ainley, P. (2010) *Lost Generation? New Strategies for Youth and Education*. London: Continuum.

Ball, S. (2007) *Education plc*. Abingdon: Routledge.

Beckett, F. (2007) *The Great City Academy Fraud*. London: Continuum.

Callaghan, D. (2006) *Conservative Party Education Policies 1976–1997: The Influence of Politics and Personality*. Brighton: Sussex Academic Press.

Chitty, C. (2011) A massive power grab from local communities: the real significance of the 2010 White Paper and the 2011 Education Bill. *Forum,* 53(1).

Chitty, C. and Dunford, J. (1999) *State Schools: New Labour and the Conservative Legacy*. London: Woburn Press.

Chitty, C. and Simon, B. (1993) *Education Answers Back: Critical Responses to Government Policy*. London: Lawrence and Wishart.

Edwards, T., Fitz, J. and Whitty, G. (1989) *The State and Private Education: An Evaluation of the Assisted Places Scheme*. Basingstoke: Falmer Press.

Hennessy, P. (1986) *Cabinet*. Oxford: Blackwell.

Hills, J. and Stewart, K. (2005) *A More Equal Society? New Labour, Poverty, Inequality and Exclusion*. Bristol: Policy Press.

HMSO (1992) White Paper, *Choice and Diversity*. London: HMSO.

HMSO (1996) *Self-government for Schools*. London: HMSO.

HMSO (1997) *Excellence in Schools*. London: HMSO.

HMSO (2010) White Paper, *The Importance of Teaching*. London: HMSO.

Jones, K. (1988) *Right Turn: The Conservative Revolution in Education*. London: Hutchinson Radius.

Knight, C. (1990) *The Making of Tory Education Policy in Post-war Britain, 1950–1986*. Lewes: Falmer Press.

Lawton, D. (1984) *The Tightening Grip: Growth of Central Control of the School Curriculum*. London: Institute of Education.

Letwin, O. (1988) *Privatising the World: A Study of International Privatisation in Theory and Practice*. London: Thomson Learning.

Marquand, D. (1988) *The Unprincipled Society: New Demands and Old Politics*. London: Jonathan Cape.

Perry, A., Amadeo, C., Fletcher, M. and Walker, E. (2010) *Instinct or Reason: How Education Policy is Made and How We Might Make it Better*. Reading: CfBT Education Trust.

Simon, B. (1991) *Education and the Social Order, 1940–1990*. London: Lawrence and Wishart.

Tomlinson, S. (2003) New Labour and education. *Children and Society,* 17.

Tomlinson, S. (2005) *Education in a Post-welfare Society* (2nd edn). Maidenhead: Open University Press.

White, J. (2004) *Rethinking the School Curriculum: Values, Aims and Purposes*. London: Routledge.

Wiborg, S. (2009) *Education and Social Integration: Comprehensive Schooling in Europe*. Basingstoke: Palgrave Macmillan.

# 3

## WILL CURTIS
## The Philosophy of Education

---

### Learning outcomes

By the end of this chapter you should be able to:

- identify the main areas of interest for philosophers of education;
- outline and critically evaluate philosophical perspectives on the nature and purpose of education;
- outline and reflect on philosophical concepts and their value to educational theory and practice;
- apply a philosophical approach to aspects of educational practice.

---

## Introduction

Perhaps more than any other discipline in this book, it is difficult to write an introduction to the philosophy of education without it becoming a 'potted history' – a selection of the author's favourite writers, quotes and ideas presented as a tidy, ordered and complete narrative. After all, the discipline of philosophy has been around for more than 3000 years, and philosophers have been engaging with questions of education, learning and teaching throughout this time and across the world. There is so much that could be talked about and so little space in which to do it.

With this in mind, the following chapter has as its main focus six key themes:

1. Thinking philosophically about education;
2. Philosophy of education – policy and practice;
3. The aims of education;
4. Meeting the needs of society or the individual;

5. Teaching, morality and the cultivation of virtue;
6. Philosophy of education in the 21st century.

In focusing on these themes, many of the key issues of interest to philosophers of education are introduced. These include:

- the extent that everyone has a 'right' to an education;
- what it means to be an 'educated' person;
- whether or not schooling should be compulsory;
- how far the aims and content of education should be universal or should differ between individuals and/or groups;
- the relationship between education and morality, and the extent that it is possible (or indeed desirable) to teach a child to be moral;
- conceptions of teacher and learner and the relationship between the two;
- similarities and differences between education, training and indoctrination;
- the relationship between education and the wider world, especially to working life, adulthood, culture and democracy;
- knowledge as objective reality or social construction;
- similarities and differences between formal schooling and informal learning;
- the role, purpose and content of curriculum and assessment.

## A brief history of philosophy

The tradition of 'western philosophy' began in Ancient Greece around 2500 years ago. You have probably heard of Plato, his mentor Socrates and his star pupil Aristotle. You may have heard of philosophers like Pyrrho, the sceptic who believed he could know nothing, or Diogenes, the cynic who became entirely disillusioned with the human way of life. Of course, this western tradition of philosophy is only one of a number of philosophies around the world. 'Eastern' philosophies pre-date the Ancient Greeks, with many arguing that the Greeks acquired their philosophical interest during their travels eastwards. There are many overlaps and similarities as well as many real divergences between different philosophies around the world. For example, it is worth looking at the writings of al Ghazali, a 5th-century Islamic scholar, to compare his educational philosophy with current western ideas and practices.

Traditional western philosophy tells a compelling yet oversimplistic story of the history of ideas – that the fall of the Roman Empire in AD 476 was followed by 1000 years of darkness, where religion and superstition dominated thought. Scholars at the time were priests who wielded tremendous power. These priestly scholars communicated in Latin, making them disconnected from 'ordinary' people. According to this story, in the 15th century the combined forces of the 'Renaissance' centring around Italy and humanist ideals from northern Europe led to a celebration of human capacity, individuality, creativity and genius, which freed Europe from these so-called 'dark ages'. This led swiftly to a scientific revolution (the 17th century), an intellectual revolution (the 18th-century Enlightenment) and then a social, industrial and political revolution (19th century). It is during these periods of great social, cultural and material upheaval that many of the other disciplines you encounter during this book had their origins. Interestingly, Islamic philosophy tells an almost entirely contrary story – where those 1000 years of darkness are seen as the period of great intellectual development and that these were lost around the time the West was apparently being emancipated.

As the world has seemingly got 'bigger' and more complex, the domain of the philosopher has narrowed. During antiquity, philosophers had ambitious, whole-system projects – to tell us the meaning of life, to redesign society, to elucidate an entire theory of knowledge or morality, to prove God's existence. Philosophers were the scientists, historians, mathematicians, astronomers, sociologists and psychologists – Aristotle is famously claimed to be the last person who knew everything that could be known at the time he lived. Today, knowledge is increasingly compartmentalized into specialist disciplines (and disciplines within disciplines). Generally, modern philosophers have projects that are far more modest than their predecessors. For much of the 20th century, philosophers were preoccupied with language and the meaning of words and other symbols. In the philosophy of education, these projects have meant exploring a particular concept or feature of schooling such as care, well-being, forgiveness, authority or discipline.

Nevertheless, the main branches of philosophical enquiry that existed in Ancient Greece remain today.

- *Moral philosophy* – what makes an action right or wrong?
- *Epistemology* or *philosophy of knowledge* – what can we know? How do we know it? How certain is knowledge?
- *Political philosophy* – how should we organize society? Who should rule? What is the relationship between the state and the people?
- *Philosophy of mind* – what makes me me!? How can I know your thoughts and how can I express mine to you?
- *Religious philosophy* – does God exist? How should religion be organized? How can different religions exist alongside one another?
- *Aesthetics* – what gives an object beauty? Is it intrinsic to the object or in the eye of the beholder?

As you shall see during this chapter, questions of interest to educational philosophers span each of these branches.

## Key theme 1: thinking philosophically about education

Unlike all of the other disciplines you encounter in this book, philosophy of education does not depend on empirical evidence. In fact, many philosophers would want to challenge the validity of empirical evidence, claiming that inductive reasoning (using the observation of events to make general rules or predictions) can, at best, tell you what *has* happened, but not what *will* happen.

Instead of gathering empirical evidence, educational philosophers ask questions – difficult questions! Thinking about education in a philosophical way is certainly thought-provoking, engaging and challenging. It can also be annoying and frustrating – there is a lack of final 'right' answers – because philosophers, as 'lovers of wisdom', tend to seek out complexity rather than straightforward answers. Socrates was famously referred to as the 'Gadfly', because he buzzed around asking infuriating questions and making people distrust things they previously knew with confidence. Socrates, and philosophers who have followed him, wanted to challenge the perceived truths that people hold to, claiming that when we think we know something we stop thinking about it. Think of all the knowledge humankind believed to be entirely true that has since been proven false – the world is flat and the centre of the universe, draining blood cures the sick, kings and queens are appointed by God, etc. We would be complacent to think that none of these falsehoods remains. So we should continually examine and question the assumptions that underpin our knowledge.

There are three types of question philosophers of education (and philosophers more generally) enjoy.

- Divergent questions about what *is* – though these are usually not surface but underlying: questions like – *what is education for? Why are assessments generally based around the unseen, timed exam?*
- Normative questions – these are 'should' questions that elicit judgements like – *what should education be for? How should we organize the curriculum/timetable/classroom?*
- Speculative questions – these are theoretical questions that ask 'what if . . .?' *What could schools be like if we started with a blank slate? How might education be organized in 50 years? What would happen if we replaced human teachers with robots?*

One device philosophers make use of to analyse reality is the 'thought experiment' – an imaginary episode designed to analyse current states, uncover assumptions, meanings or values. You may have heard of Bishop Berkeley's famed question of whether a tree that falls on an uninhabited island makes a sound or not. Or Descartes meditation where he imagines that he is being deceived by an all-powerful malignant demon, so that he can determine which knowledge he possesses is utterly irrefutable – this thought experiment gave rise to his celebrated utterance, 'I think therefore I am'. You might have seen the film *The Matrix*, which bears a striking resemblance to a thought experiment by the American philosopher Robert Nozick, who considers whether one would plug into a dream machine that could provide you with the whole life experience you would desire. The latter illustrates one of the more popular forms thought experiments might take – the design of utopian or dystopian visions. Perfect and/or terrible images of an entire society or a particular institution can prove highly revealing both as a tool for evaluating current practice and to orientate towards future goals.

An educational utopia might look something like this:

- children and young people designing their own education to suit their individual needs, interests and skills;

- happy teachers – with less contact time, more preparation time and smaller group sizes;
- engaging lessons characterized by deep relationships and 'profound learning', where pupils and teachers are 'learning together' to create knowledge and meaning;
- a 'learning society', where learning is inherent and valued throughout life;
- education as whole-community as well as individual enrichment;
- free curriculum – with minimal centralized assessment;
- technology harnessed to reduce inequalities, especially for children with special educational needs.

Whereas an educational dystopia might have the following features:

- bureaucracy – an 'iron cage' of paperwork, email and form-filling;
- separate 'interest' schools teaching children to distrust the 'other';
- massive content curriculum;
- successful schools for the rich, sinking schools for the poor;
- education owned by Sky, Google and Microsoft;
- class sizes topping 100;
- no teachers – all learning is done in front of a computer or with mega-powerful robot-teachers;
- drugs used to sedate the 'out of control' mass of youth.

---

**Activity: utopian and dystopian educational futures**

Looking at the qualities of utopian and dystopian education futures above, which one do you think we are closer to today? Are we moving in the direction of one more than the other?

Now think about your own educational ideal and nightmare – remember these do not need to be constrained by practicalities.

- What can you learn from your own depictions?
- Can the education system in its current form do anything to move towards your ideal and away from your nightmare?

---

## Key theme 2: philosophy of education – policy and practice

As a discipline, the philosophy of education is more grounded and pragmatic than philosophy itself. Like the sociology and psychology of education, it is an *applied* discipline, existing to inform, examine and critique existing educational contexts (Carr 2004). Two important modern philosophers of education, Paul Hirst and Wilfred Carr (2005), disagree about whether philosophy is primarily concerned with theoretical or practical philosophy, but both agree on a core purpose to interrogate and inform educational policy and practice.

Contributions to the philosophy of education derive from three distinct but interrelated sources.

1.  Philosophy and philosophers (in a wider sense) add to our understanding of education. While not primarily concerned with education, the ideas of influential philosophers have proved fruitful in the analysis of educational practices and structures. For instance, a great deal of educational philosophy has been provoked by:

    - Michel Foucault's exploration of power – in particular, that modern societies utilize surveillance to discipline and normalize behaviour;

    - Hannah Arendt's critique of modernity and her account of public action;

    - Friedrich Nietzsche's critique of moral and knowledge claims, and his analysis of human nature as the 'will to power' (the desire to dominate other objects and people);

    - Ludwig Wittgenstein's analysis of the meaning of words and their uses.

2.  Other philosophers have a specific interest in education, often stemming from their own practical experience as educators – for instance, Freire, Dewey and Plato were all teachers. Philosophers in this category might focus solely on education. Others might have broad philosophical interests, but engage in a detailed and systematic manner with education. Theorists in the 'Key figures' boxes that follow fit within this second group.

3.  Given the applied nature of the discipline, practising professionals make up a key constituent of philosophy of education. This informal source is made up of practitioners who reflect on their work in a philosophical way, asking questions and having conversations about their position in the classroom, the purpose of schooling and the nature of learning.

Of course, if philosophy of education is to be meaningful, these sources must be connected. Oancea and Bridges identify two ways that philosophy of education can impact on practice: the encouragement of 'democratic conversations' and 'practical deliberation' (2009: 557). 'Formal' philosophy of education supports practitioners to reflect on and critique their own practice. It also stimulates open public dialogue about the many aspects of schooling. They cite the *Nuffield Review of 14–19 Education and Training in England and Wales* (see Pring et al. 2009) as a contemporary example of this kind of philosophical policy analysis, based as it was around the question, 'What is an educated 19 year old in this day and age?'

**Activity: the relationship between philosophy of education and policy and practice**

It is easy to think that texts written hundreds or even thousands of years ago can have little relevance to educational practices today. After all, schools in the 21st century bear little resemblance to schools of the 1970s, let alone the 450 BCs! Yet, education-alists today frequently return to key historical works in the philosophy of education and find resonance with, and stimulus for, current thinking. As Oancea and Bridges put it, such writings have 'continuing power to illuminate and reinterpret contemporary experience' (2009: 553). The following rap considers the highly influential American educator and philosopher, John Dewey.

### Dewey rap

*Education is life itself, not just about the wife or the wealth, under stealth, to help societies health, this is what John Dewey felt, me and you is a result of what he dealt, so take his book of a shelf, need to read, heart will melt, if not starve yourself, need to read, heart will melt,*

*So what was his purpose, for students to be the 'Spirit Of Service', the whole education system needed a refurbish, otherwise kids will leave school feeling nervous, continue like a vicious circle or a circuit, so it was put into play and made to work it, education revolutionised so perfect,*

*The education system, moved and proved progressive education, in relation the system, encouraged and molded, critical thinking and problem solving, offloading passive thinking, upholding active thinking, the link comes from his pens ink, extinct is the old and boring, where you sit there and stare and start snoring, the boredom was unfolding, so Dewey told them, his ideal was golden, so he showed them and got the ball rolling,*

*For generations and generations, there's bin a rigid unchanged stipulation, where education was in the need of levitation, army based learning more like a interrogation, different size paddles, a teachers recreation, children would sit there hating, I don't blame them, what a shame for them education remained in the bin, active intelligence remained a sin, John Dewey changed to win, children engaged entertained as they grin, heads are put together, whatever the weather, much more pleasure, trust formed better, actuality treasured, ideas and character was built and bettered, total reliance on the teacher was severed, it was about adapting not who's the most clever*
By Arjun Sokhi – Education Studies student, De Montfort University (2010)

Create a piece of art (lyrics, short story, drawing, play, storyboard) that reflects how *educational* philosophy relates to policy and practice today.

## Key theme 3: the aims of education

Perhaps the most pressing question for the philosopher of education concerns what education exists for. The answer is dependent on issues that go well beyond the school gate, relating to wider political, religious, moral and epistemological considerations. Meanings and purposes of education are complex and multi-faceted, highly fluid and dependent on the contexts in which the question is asked, and the personal and political values of the respondent. This section briefly discusses the four most enduring philosophical positions. The first two are traditional teacher-centred ideas; the second two are progressive and learner-centred.

## Education as conservation

Arguably the most established and widespread educational aim is to pass on an existing body of knowledge from one generation to the next. Within philosophy of education, there are two schools of thought that adopt such a position. These perceive the aim of education as:

1.  transmitting culture (customs, conventions, norms, values, roles, language) from one generation to the next – *essentialism*;
2.  encouraging learners to grasp eternal and universal truths – *perennialism*.

The first and most traditional position, known as essentialism, holds that the aim of education is the socialization of young people into a shared culture. Education exists to transmit culture, values and knowledge from one generation to the next, thus ensuring the continuation of a common culture. This position is intrinsically conservative, based on a belief in stability, gradual progress and respect for established ideas. Children should leave formal education with a sound grasp of 'essential' knowledge and skills in order to contribute to the society they belong to. Popularized by the American philosopher William Bagley (1938), essentialism advocates a disciplined and rigorous approach to study, with the teacher as intellectual and moral role model. As a reaction against the fashionable learner-centred approaches that were popular at the time, Bagley argued that children should be taught respect for authority, tradition and scientific truth. Learning should be hard work, requiring persistence and the guidance of a subject-expert teacher. Building on basic skills, students should acquire a systematic and detailed knowledge of 'traditional' disciplines such as maths, science and literature.

The second position, perennialism, is premised on the idea that there is an objective reality and that knowledge of this is within our grasp. While there may be many differences within and between cultures, there are absolute and irrefutable truths. The role of the teacher is to enable learners to grasp everlasting principles that are common to all people, rather than specific and culturally bound skills or 'facts'. Perennialists seek to support learners in their personal development, through the discovery of truths present in great works of literature, art, philosophy and religion.

Universal and timeless truths might take a number of forms.

*   *Religious* – this earliest form of perennialism was articulated by the renowned scholastic philosopher of the 13th century, St Thomas Aquinas. Still important today, it claims that the aim of education is to support personal development through engagement with spiritual truths.

- *Idealistic* – Plato (2007) famously argued for an eternal world of ideas (the 'Forms') that existed beyond the physical world. While the world of experience is changeable and subjective, the world of ideas contains objective moral and epistemological truths.
- *Realist* – from this perspective, the aim of education is to teach young people empirical, scientific and 'human' truths. Among the philosophers to put forward this position are Robert Hutchins (1953) and Mortimer Adler (1982). Both argued in favour of a non-specialized liberal education, connecting each generation with the 'great books' and teaching what is common to all humanity.

### Key figure: Plato (428–348 BC)

Plato is often referred to as the 'father of western philosophy'. As you have already seen, the areas he wrote about have become the traditional branches of philosophy. Plato famously established the *Academy* – an institution for the study of philosophy that is generally viewed as the first university. Unlike many philosophical texts, Plato's writings are highly accessible and readable – he uses the dramatic device of dialogue to present and interrogate his ideas. He wrote these dialogues using Socrates as his central character, who debates with (and generally defeats) well-known Athenians of the time. Many argue that Plato's early dialogues represent the true teachings of Socrates, while his later ones use the character of Socrates to voice his own ideas. The two dialogues that are most concerned with the philosophy of education are:

1. *The Republic* – in which Plato articulates his version of the ideal state and develops the first western account of education;
2. *Meno* – here Plato explores the nature of learning and recollection; the 'Socratic method' of teaching is presented, in which the learner is directed to an answer by responding to a series of structured questions.

The education system that Plato outlines is one where the interests of society, and not the individual, are of prime concern. Plato argues that individuals are born with different moral and intellectual capacities, and education shapes us into what we become. So one key purpose of education is to sift out those with the potential to become Guardians – rulers ('philosopher-kings') or auxiliaries (who help the rulers). Potential rulers are to be educated differently from 'ordinary' people. Through dialogue and questioning, teachers lead students away from ignorance and to an understanding of objective reality – a realm of ideas that exists beyond the surface impressions of the material world.

There is much in Plato's account to be commended and much that resonates with education today. For Plato, education is universal and meritocratic. Every citizen is educated and educational success or failure is the determinant of one's position in society – the initial stage provides basic literacy and identifies those children with the potential to become Guardians. Plato argues that educational undertakings ought to tally with a person's strengths at different stages of life; put simply, learners should be active when young and engage in abstract reasoning when they are old.

There are other aspects of Plato's education that might seem somewhat sinister and at odds with our contemporary way of thinking – it is certainly a very conservative model of education aimed at upholding the status quo. For instance, since Plato views children as easily corrupted, and since the good of society is paramount, he argues for a curriculum that is to be strictly controlled and censored: children should not experience any form of artistic expression that might lead them astray. Perhaps most alarmingly, Plato advocates removing children from their parents to be educated by Guardians, as well as indoctrination in the form of a 'noble lie' (see below).

To read key extracts from *The Republic*, the whole of *Meno* and an excellent commentary on Plato's contribution to the philosophy of education by Robert Brumbaugh, see Cahn (2009).

## Progressive educations: education for change

So this first group of aims focuses on the transmission of a body of knowledge (whether universal or culturally specific). One might argue that the aim of education is to foster particular qualities in the learner – rather than teaching children *what* to think, education might primarily be concerned with teaching children *how* to think. John Dewey, who argued for an education with the aim of cultivating young people who are self-confident and engaged, most famously articulated this position. Dewey viewed education as central to a healthy and continually advancing society. By developing the skills and qualities of active citizens, schools should create young people able to participate fully in a democratic life.

**Key figure: John Dewey (1859–1952)**

The American philosopher, John Dewey, is arguably the most influential 20th-century educationalist. His most important educational works include:

- *The School and Society* (1899);
- *Democracy and Education* (1916/1997);
- *How We Think* (1933);
- *Experience and Education* (1938).

Dewey's view of education developed out of his philosophical pragmatism. According to pragmatism, 'truth' is defined by what is useful at a particular point of time – an instrument used by people to solve problems and to make sense of current situations. As contexts change, truth changes. Philosophers should not be interested in pretentious, abstract questions, but in practical and everyday living. Knowledge is uncertain, fluid, rooted in experience and meaningful only in as much as it has practical consequences.

In 1896, while Head of Department for Philosophy, Psychology and Pedagogy at the University of Chicago, Dewey established the legendary Laboratory School. The school had two main experimental aims – 'to exhibit, test, verify and criticize theoretical statements and principles' (Mayhew and Edwards 2007) and to allow learners to approach their studies in an active and investigational manner. In one of his most quoted passages, Dewey (2008: 29) defines the school as:

> … an embryonic community life, active with types of occupations that reflect the life of the larger society, and permeated throughout with the spirit of art, history, and science. When the school introduces and trains each child of society into membership within such a little community, saturating him with the spirit of service, and providing him with the instruments of effective self-direction, we shall have the deepest and best guarantee of a larger society which is worthy, lovely, and harmonious.

Dewey was especially concerned with the cultivation of democratic community, whereby citizens actively question and participate in a social life rich with communication and experimentation. He perceived schooling as central to this aim, as an environment in which appropriate skills and attitudes can be experienced and fostered. He viewed learning as social and interactive: requiring experience, interaction and reflection on the part of the student. Teachers are partners, rather than instructors, in the learning process so that students can take ownership of their own experiences.

While Dewey clearly disliked traditional, authoritarian approaches to education, he was also critical of much 'progressive' education for being too unstructured, free and child-centred. He viewed the experiences of learners as fundamental, but he argued that learning activities needed to be purposeful and guided rather than entirely free.

To find out more about Dewey's educational philosophy, you should read:

- *The Child and the Curriculum* – to view Dewey's criticisms of traditional and child-centred approaches;
- *My Pedagogic Creed* – in which Dewey outlines his own philosophy of education.

Dewey is the most prominent of a number of writers and practitioners who advocate 'progressive' education. While progressive educational philosophers differ from one another in many ways, they share a number of common characteristics. While knowledge-based aims tend to prioritize the content of curriculum and the teacher (who possesses expertise), progressive theories prioritize the learner. Learning is experiential, experimental and active – based on dialogue, questioning, problem solving and discovery. Knowledge is seen as tentative, open to exploration, contestation and critique. Based in real-life experiences and activities, learners can contribute to its development. There is an emphasis on the growth of personal qualities such as self-esteem, confidence and communication, all seen as encouraging learners to think and act for themselves.

In the later stages of the 20th century, a more radical form of progressivism emerged – sometimes referred to as 'reconstructionism'. Based on the work of Paulo Freire, and developing into the theory and practice of *critical pedagogy*, it pronounced the aim of education as to instil in young people the awareness of injustice in the world and the desire and capacity to transform it. Education must raise *critical consciousness* – an awareness of social issues and the development of skills to be able to transform the world. Critical of more Deweyian forms of progressivism for being apolitical, critical pedagogy argues that teachers are moral agents who simply cannot be neutral. In a fundamentally oppressive world, they either support the status quo (and therefore the oppressors who are gaining from current conditions) or fight for *change* (and side with the oppressed) (see Apple 2009). By encouraging learners to confront injustice, to challenge dominant ideas and to develop visions of a better future, education has the capacity to be transformational – on both individual and system-wide levels.

**Key figure: Paulo Freire (1921–97)**

Perhaps the most influential educationalist of the late 20th century is Paulo Freire, who grew up in poverty in Recife, Brazil. His experiences taught him to view education as simultaneously the source of, and solution to, social injustice and oppression. He spent his life as an educator, developing literacy programmes for adults in deprived communities, and developing truly democratic, empowering and grassroots educational theory and practice. He wrote a number of important texts, the most notable being *Pedagogy of the Oppressed* (1970/1996). Among his other major contributions were *Education for Critical Consciousness* (1973/2005), *Pedagogy of Hope: Reliving Pedagogy of the Oppressed (1994)* and *Pedagogy of Indignation (2004)*

In *Pedagogy of the Oppressed*, Freire critiques practices he terms 'banking education'. This traditional form of education is based on very unequal roles, with the teacher as active, powerful and knowledgeable and the learner as passive recipient of the teacher's knowledge. For Freire, classroom relations and communications are inauthentic and artificial – the teacher possesses all legitimate knowledge and the learner none. This 'jug and mug' version of education reduces learners to receptacles: effectively to memorize and store the information transmitted to them. 'Banking' pedagogy creates dependent, uncritical, ignorant and passive members of society: they are unable to conceive of alternatives to existing inequalities and oppressions. In doing so, Freire argued, it perpetuates a social system that is fundamentally unequal and unfair.

So Freire offers an alternative pedagogy – termed 'liberatory' or 'problem-posing' education. At the heart of this pedagogy is dialogue – open, authentic and trusting communication between learners and teachers. For Freire, thinking happens actively in conversations based around problem solving, not in listening and memorizing. He argues against a strict demarcation between teachers and students, in favour of 'teacher-students' and 'student-teachers': as 'critical co-investigators', teachers and students have joint responsibility for the construction of knowledge and meaning. In this pedagogy, knowledge is not an abstract entity possessed by the teacher; it develops from learners' experiences and is relevant to their lives. And, most importantly, it is the source of 'conscientization' – enabling people to think critically about the world and to develop the confidence and capacities to transform it. For Freire, then, education is not about the acquisition of decontextualized facts; it is a process of 'mutual humanization', in which people learn to care for one another and seek to make the world a better, more equal and less oppressive place.

To find out more about Freire and his influence on 'critical pedagogy' you should read:

- his seminal work – *Pedagogy of the Oppressed*;
- *The Critical Pedagogy Reader* (Darder et al. 2008).

## Activity: assessing competing aims of education

You have encountered four philosophical positions in this theme – that education aims to teach objective truths, to transmit culture, to create active citizens, or to transform the world.

- How do you think each position would criticize the others? Fill in the following table, considering how the position at the top would view the one on the side.

|  | Objective truths | Transmit culture | Active citizenship | Transform the world |
|---|---|---|---|---|
| Objective truths |  |  |  |  |
| Transmit culture |  |  |  |  |
| Active citizenship |  |  |  |  |
| Transform the world |  |  |  |  |

After completing the table, consider the following questions.

- How far does each position prioritize the needs of society or the individual?
- What are the main similarities and differences between each position?
- Which one do you favour most/least? Why?
- Which one(s) most closely resemble education in its current form?

## Key theme 4: meeting the needs of society or the individual

Related to the aims of education, philosophers question the extent that education should have as its prime intent the needs of society as a whole or those of the individuals that constitute it. There are broadly two schools of thought here.

There is a strong tradition within educational thought that elevates the needs of society above the interests of the individual. Plato suggested education should promote a 'noble lie' (2007: sections 414–17); that once education has sifted those with greater talents from those with lesser, it ought to propagate a myth. By claiming that educators can identify children who are born with golden, silver and bronze souls, Plato argues society as a whole benefits. Citizens feel happy with their place in society because they believe those above and below them in the social order are essentially unlike them. One might argue a reverse myth is perpetuated today: that the education system gives the impression of meritocracy when, in reality, we know that the class, gender and ethnicity one is born into is a marked indicator of educational success or failure.

The lie Plato outlines sounds a lot like indoctrination to the modern ear. Yet many would argue education retains societal priorities: to educate children and young people with the appropriate skills to enable them to contribute effectively in society (broadly) and for the world of work (narrowly). You have already seen that Dewey argued in favour of a more instrumental educational purpose, though he viewed the teaching of these skills and characteristics as equally advantageous to the individual. More narrowly, since the beginning of state education, theorists and politicians have argued for an education that produces effective and efficient workers. And this instrumentalism has become increasingly narrow in recent years – arguably the prime purpose of education today is the furthering of economic interests. Resembling Functionalist sociology, education's economic purposes are two-fold. First, to sift children, who possess different skills and abilities – or 'merits' – into appropriate employment. Second, to foster in them the kinds of qualities that make effective, efficient and profitable workers – these might be the kinds of qualities fostered in the formal curriculum, such as numeracy and literacy. It might be qualities instilled in children through the 'hidden curriculum' – dispositions like respect for authority, punctuality, obedience or the capacity to cope with a mundane and repetitive environment. Moreover, this has led to educational structures increasingly mirroring the characteristics of the world of work: an education 'production line' – prioritizing standards, more-for-less efficiency and an emphasis on measurable performance indicators.

The ascendancy of educational structures based on such philosophies has spawned a number of radical alternatives. One of the key figures is Ivan Illich (1973), who articulated a vision for a 'de-schooled' society: free from the constraints of formal schooling and professional authority, where children learn what they want, when and where they want. Other prominent figures include John Holt (1990) and later John Taylor Gatto (2002). Both agreed that formal schooling had harmful emotional, social and intellectual impacts on children – teaching them to fear failure and to turn against their natural and impulsive love of learning.

Theorists like Holt and Gatto found child-centred educational philosophies more attractive. Their thinking was influenced by Rousseau's novel *Emile*, which outlined an approach to education that placed the interests and well-being of the child at its heart.

From a child-centred perspective, children are not the miniature adults that schooling tends to depict them as. Each child is unique, fundamentally good but easily corrupted. Schooling should start from the interests and needs of the child, not those of society. It should equip children with the character to resist the excesses and difficulties of the adult word. Child-centred education was taken forward and put into practice during the 19th century by Pestalozzi and Froebel, among others, the latter originating the 'kindergarten' model (see Doddington and Hilton 2007 for a brief history).

**Key figure: Jean-Jacques Rousseau (1712–78)**

Rousseau was born in Geneva and lived in Paris, the centre of the so-called 18th-century 'Enlightenment' during which time intellectuals advocated the use of reason and scientific enquiry – to combat ignorance, as the source of authority, and as a tool for building a better world. Rousseau was acquainted with many of the key figures of this movement and contributed towards Diderot's *Encyclopedie* – a collection of writings that represented the thoughts of the Enlightenment. But Rousseau was not typical of Enlightenment thinkers. His work is regarded as straddling Enlightenment and Romantic movements, because of its interest in the capacities of both reason and emotion in human development. Rousseau's romantic inclinations are most forcefully illustrated in the opening line of his most famous work, *The Social Contract* of 1762: 'Man is born free, and everywhere he is in chains' (1968: 47). Individuals are trapped or imprisoned by the artificial institutions and conventions of society (wealth and poverty, family, etiquette, schools, etc.). In another of his influential treatises in political philosophy, *Discourse on the Origins of Inequality* from 1755, Rousseau examines how inequality is created by society, and how this inequality leads to envy and unnatural desires – an unhealthy shift in individual mindset from '*amour de soi*' (natural self-love) to '*amour propre*' (pride).

These concerns are at the heart of Rousseau's educational philosophy. In his novel *Emile* (1762), arguably the most important book on education since Plato's *Republic*, Rousseau tells of the one-on-one education of Emile. Like his earlier writing, he starts with the premise that children are naturally good – again he has a provocative opening line – 'God makes all things good; man meddles with them and they become evil' (2007: 11). This is very different from the dominant perspective of the time (and one that remains today) that children need to be socialized or 'civilized' into appropriate or 'good' behaviour through schooling. In the debate between the so-called *dionysian* (evil and dangerous – prominent in the Christian doctrine of original sin) and *apollonian* (natural innocence and goodness) conception of the child, Rousseau clearly sides with the *apollonian* (see Jenks 2005). Put simply, character flaws and poor behaviour are a result of society and not of nature.

For Rousseau, therefore, one of the prime functions of education is the protection of the child's natural state. Childhood is distinctive from adulthood, so the child should be educated away from the corrupting influences of society. Emile is educated in nature – he should be happy and free in this setting. His learning is directed by his own natural inclinations – he is not told what to do or how to behave. Rather, his own interests and developing capacities motivate him. He learns from experience, sensation and example – not from lecture or instruction, and especially not from moralizing, which Rousseau claims is likely to prove counterproductive. Most importantly, the central pedagogic approach is that of *discovery learning*.

Rousseau argues that educational activity is dependent on the *natural* physical, emotional and intellectual stage a child has reached. He asks the kinds of questions that have become typical of 20th-century psychologists – what are children like? How are they different from adults? How do they develop? His answers to these questions led him to propose separate and distinct stages of education:

- up to 12 – freedom, play, nature, developing senses;
- ages 12–15 – speedy physical development, learning to read, but only read one book (*Robinson Crusoe* – as a guide of self-sufficiency), developing reason;
- ages 15–20 – becoming an adult, gradually entering community life, exploring morality, religion and philosophy.

In *Emile*, Rousseau articulates child-centred educational philosophy – with the needs and interests of the child at the centre of learning activities. It is noteworthy, however, that Rousseau does not grant this child-centred education to Emile's life partner, Sophie – and this has proved a source of heavy and ongoing criticism of his educational writing.

To find out more about Rousseau's educational philosophy you should read:

- Rousseau's novel, *Emile*;
- a clear outline of Rousseau's contribution, in Flanagan (2006).

In the UK, A.S. Neill is the most celebrated child-centred educationalist. Neill, who was also influenced by Freudian psychoanalysis, believed social ills were the result of unhappy childhoods. Unhappiness is perpetuated as teachers impose their own neuroses and repression onto the children they are charged with. Neill disliked the strict disciplinary nature of schooling, favouring instead 'the discipline that interest draws' (1968: 16): that children learn when they want to, not when they are made to. Neill viewed the purpose of education as the fostering of happy and free individuals. He put this child-centred philosophy into practice, creating Summerhill school in 1921; the school successfully continues today in Leiston, Suffolk (Neill 1970).

**Activity: exploring alternative schooling**

There are a large number of schools worldwide that draw from progressive or child-centred educational philosophies like the ones you have encountered in the previous two sections. Among them are:

- Montessori schools;
- Steiner Waldorf schools;
- Summerhill school in Leiston, Suffolk;
- Sands School in Ashburton, Devon;
- Reggio Emilia schools;
- Sudbury schools.

Find out about one of the above. Try to identify school practices as well as the philosophies that underpin them. What are the similarities and differences with the education you had? Would you want to send your children to the school you researched – why?

## Key theme 5: teaching, morality and the cultivation of virtue

For much of the 20th century, formal education prioritized intellectual mastery over moral development. More recently, a focus on standards, efficiency, 'performativity' (the production of measurable and continually improving outcomes) and 'technicism' (the acquisition of specific skills) has largely removed moral language from educational discourses. On the whole, philosophers abhor such trends, believing that the role of philosophy of education should be 'to develop richer more humane and, in the end, more educational conceptions of education' (Smith 2005: 206). Nel Noddings, an important advocate for teaching children about care, is highly critical of a school system for the head that ignores the heart. She argues in favour of an education that 'encourage(s) the growth of competent, caring, loving and lovable people' (Noddings 2005: xxvi).

### Activity: moral dilemmas for the teacher

Teachers are continually faced with moral decisions. Consider the following situations. In each case, think about what you would do and how you would reach your decision.

- One of your pupils has poor personal hygiene. Do you tell her?
- A pupil asks for an extension for his homework. Do you give him one?
- Two students submit identical essays. It is clear that one of them has copied, but you cannot be sure which one. What do you do?
- You really fancy one of your students. They feel the same way. Do you have a relationship with him/her? Does your answer depend on factors such as age, sex, other contexts? Why?
- You have strong views on a particular issue. Should you express this view in class or should you always try to remain impartial? What if a pupil directly invites your perspective?
- A student makes a comment that is likely to offend other members of the class. How do you react?
- A student invites you to join their social networking group. How far do you engage with your students outside formal class settings?

So what might 'moral education' look like? There are at least three approaches:

1.  instructing children towards specific moral rules;
2.  teaching children to think morally in different situations;
3.  developing in children the qualities of a 'good' person.

The first approach posits that moral rules exist and are teachable. These might be abstract or concrete, universal truths or specific to a particular time and place. Most commonly, these derive from religious doctrine – for example, the Ten Commandments of Christianity or the Five Precepts (Pancasila) of Buddhism. But such rules might also be obtained through reason: whereby moral rules are constituted by the *motivation* or *effect* of action. The 18th-century Enlightenment philosopher Immanuel Kant's categorical imperative – that one should always act in a manner that could be universalized rationally – is an example of the former. The utilitarian rule – always act in a manner that will maximize happiness and minimize suffering – is an example of the latter. Moral education involves transmitting these rules to learners, so that they know, understand and enact them.

The second approach involves cultivating in learners the facility to think independently about moral situations. Rather than passive adherence to a conventional rule, learners acquire the capacity to reflect on and critically engage with established moral ideas. In the 1960s, the American psychologist and philosopher, Lawrence Kohlberg, developed a highly influential theory of moral development that illustrates the distinctiveness of this second approach. Kohlberg (1984) argued that children pass through different moral stages – from 'pre-conventional', through 'conventional', to 'post-conventional' morality. Until they reach the 'post-conventional' stage, children simply 'follow the rules'. But when they reach this third stage, children become able to engage critically with socially accepted rules. Kohlberg believed that children acquire the ability to evaluate conventional moral rules by using universal moral principles like 'justice', 'human rights' or Kant's 'categorical imperative' (see above) to develop their own self-chosen and reasoned principles. Encountering moral situations, recognizing the complexity of moral decision making, and conversing with one another, children learn to deliberate morally and develop 'moral reasoning' or 'intelligence'.

The third approach was originated by Aristotle and applied in modern society by Alasdair MacIntyre (see MacIntyre and Dunne 2002) and David Carr (1991). Rather than focusing on moral *beliefs* or *situations*, this approach stresses the importance of individual moral *character* – the living of a moral or 'virtuous' life. Education, both in its formal sense and as a lifelong pursuit, involves the cultivation of virtues – through engagement with positive role models (including teachers) and the practice that makes being virtuous habitual. Importantly, virtues might be intellectual as well as moral, and traditionally include generosity, forgiveness, tolerance, perseverance and integrity. Claxton (2008) suggests the 'big 8' virtues for the 21st century are:

1.  curiosity;
2.  courage;
3.  exploration;

4. experimentation;
5. imagination;
6. discipline;
7. sociability;
8. thoughtfulness.

There are strong arguments in favour of each approach. The key point is that educa-tion should have a strong moral component. Highly 'educated' individuals have been responsible for numerous atrocities. Teaching people to think about the impact of their action – on one another and on the social and natural worlds – should be at the heart of any education system.

## Key theme 6: philosophy of education in the 21st century

The final theme of the chapter considers some central concerns for the philosopher of education within contemporary culture. Recent changes in the way social life is organized – especially in terms of globalization, digitization, cultural fragmentation and uncertainty – impact considerably on educational meanings, purposes and prac-tices. As Oancea and Bridges argue, philosophy of education plays a key role in mapping and shaping this changing educational landscape:

> National and international debates about the aims of education and the principles which should govern educational practice, the scope of the curriculum, education for citizenship, faith schools, parents' and children's rights, education in a multi-racial/culturally diverse society, the role of the university in a mass higher educa-tion system – all rest on essentially philosophical considerations, as well as empirical data. (2009: 554)

While there are many areas of contention for the philosopher of education today, four important areas are discussed below.

### Learning and cultural pluralism

Numerous social commentators have argued that the last 30 years or so have witnessed a radical restructuring of culture and society – sometimes termed late or post-modernity. Previous systems of order and structure have been replaced by plurality, fragmentation and increasing senses of unpredictability and uncertainty. Claims we used to make with certainty are open to contestation today. As Usher points out, 'knowledge is multiple, based on multiple realities and the multiplicity of experience. It is neither canonical or hierarchical' (2009: 173). We live among individuals and groups who hold to a wide variety of truths, defined by an immense breadth of experience and beholden to the many competing sources of knowledge each has access to. Today, the western world might be characterized by concepts such as fast-paced, consumerist, multicultural, globalized, free and individualistic.

Such changes transform education. Recent years have seen the emergence of an educational marketplace, with parents 'shopping around' for the 'best' educational experience for their children. There has been a shift in power relations, with children and parents gaining and teachers losing out. Private companies have thrived by providing 'more for less' services, in such diverse fields as catering, building or supplying teachers. There has been a rapid growth in the number of schools intended for particular or sectional interest groups, for example faith or specialist schools. Perhaps most significantly, as Usher (2009: 171) puts it, the 'boundaries defining "acceptable" learning are breaking down' resulting in a 'multiplicity of sites of learning'. The scope of learning has widened to include:

- a huge increase in the numbers continuing into further and higher education onto a far wider range of courses;
- greater opportunities for less 'traditional' forms of learning, such as home schooling, distance, online and 'lifelong' learning;
- learning outside formal settings, through non-formal organizations offering training and experiences;
- opportunities for informal learning opened up by new media technologies.

While many embrace such changes – seeing truly 'democratic' opportunities arising out of the breakdown of unequal and divisive social orders – others are wary of them, fearing the potential for conflict caused by people entrenching into their interest groups and a collapse in authority resulting in relativism and the chaos of an 'anything goes' mentality. Either way, educational theorists and practitioners need to be engaged and responsive – either to make full use of new possibilities that open up, or as the best protection against the excesses and conflicts of this rapidly changing world. Indicative of the latter perspective, Vokey (2006: xix) starkly claims, 'only a radical change of heart and mind effected through transformative education will enable us to respond adequately to the social, political, economic, environmental, moral and/or spiritual crises'.

## The changing nature of curriculum

As society changes, so do requirements for the content and delivery of our children's learning. As a result, the last few years have seen a number of reviews of each stage of the curriculum – early years, primary, 14–19, higher education – asking philosophical questions about the changing nature and role of curriculum in and for the 21st century.

Changes in society result in an assortment of new philosophical questions regarding curriculum, including:

- What constitutes a 'good' citizen in the 21st century, and how might appropriate qualities be taught and learned?
- What might religious education look like in a society with a plurality of religions and increasing secularization?

- How far should schools representing particular sectional interests have the freedom to develop their own curricula?
- Can a National Curriculum encompass all the interests and needs of its citizens?

Among the most significant of social and cultural changes to impact on curriculum is the emergence and proliferation of new technologies. Technological advances bring with them numerous curriculum opportunities – to enable children to discover independently, to learn at a distance, to communicate and collaborate with other children around the world. But technological advances also bring new risks – access to inappropriate or dangerous material, increased potential for plagiarism, a more sedentary and solitary lifestyle. Futurelab undertook a philosophical exploration of educational futures in the contexts of this changing social and technological landscape (Facer 2009): *Beyond Current Horizons* suggested that the 21st century required curricula built around formal and informal learning networks.

## Power, classroom relations and voice

Since Dewey, considerable interest in the discipline has been paid to the relationship between democracy and education – both in the ways that education might produce citizens capable of participation and autonomous decision-making and in terms of democratic classroom relations. The work of the modern German philosopher and sociologist, Jurgen Habermas, on 'ideal speech' has proved particularly influential: Habermas (1991) argued for conditions whereby participants attempt to reach consensus through open dialogue. In such conditions, all participants should have equal opportunities to contribute, unconstrained by power, role, status or authority. Participation depends on 'communicative competence' – the capacity to talk and listen effectively.

Emphasis on dialogue, communication and democratic relations is central to constructivism, a theory of learning and teaching that has become very important today. Constructivism claims that real learning takes place in communication, where learners construct knowledge and meaning in conversations with one another. This makes the voice of the learner central to educational activity – highlighting the capacity to articulate one's viewpoints effectively, to discuss openly and effectively, to be heard and to have those views taken seriously and acted upon. In the UK, the most prominent advocates of pupil/student voice have been Jean Ruddock and Michael Fielding (2006), who suggest three 'big issues' that impact on effective voice strategies:

1. *power relations between teachers and pupils* – the extent that a perception of equity exists between all participants;
2. *commitment to authenticity* – how far strategies are engaged with genuinely, are meaningful and result in action;
3. *principle of inclusiveness* – the extent that less articulate and conspicuous voices are heard.

## Teaching philosophy in schools

Should philosophy be part of the curriculum? And if so, at what stage of education should children encounter it? What areas of philosophy are appropriate? And what should the curriculum look like – should it be a distinct and explicit subject area, or embedded within subjects that children already study? Such questions are of considerable interest to philosophers of education today. Recent curriculum changes have given philosophy a more prominent (but implicit) role, for instance through the study of Citizenship, and Personal, Social and Health Education (PSHE).

Some, drawing on a tradition beginning with Plato, argue that learning about philosophy at too young an age can turn children off it for life. Others argue that children should start philosophizing at an early age. For instance, Haynes (2008: 2) makes a compelling case for primary school teachers stimulating 'thinking that expresses both collaboration and independence of mind and spirit in situations where critical, democratic values are being actively promoted'. Accordingly, children do not necessarily need to encounter great philosophical works, but will benefit from learning to think philosophically – and this depends as much on classroom activities and relations as it does on the content that is taught. Hand and Winstanley's (2009) recent book brings together many influential contemporary philosophers of education to discuss such issues. It provides a detailed and engaging account, considering among other things how teachers promote critical thinking, and how controversial issues and children's literature can be ideal sources for philosophical thinking.

---

**Key figures: contemporary philosophy of education**

The most influential 20th-century British philosopher of education is **Richard Peters**, who established an analytical tradition in the UK at the Institute of Education, University of London, in the 1960s alongside another key figure, **Paul Hirst**. Analytical philosophy involves assessing language, concepts and arguments. It involves analysing the meaning of education and what distinguishes it from indoctrination, instruction, initiation and reform. Peters' liberal approach, which perceives education as leading to the achievement of rational autonomy, is being further developed today in the work of prominent figures like **John and Patricia White**. Routledge reprinted a 24-volume set of distinguished texts in 2009 – *International Library of the Philosophy of Education* – which contains key texts by each of these authors. **Paul Standish**, the current Head of the Philosophy section at the Institute of Education, works in the areas of democracy and citizenship, and considers the relationships and tensions between analytical and continental philosophies.

Evidence of the link between philosophy and policy can be found in the work of **Mary Warnock and Richard Pring**. Warnock's definitions of special educational needs, learning difficulties, 'mainstreaming' and 'statementing' have informed practice for more than 40 years. Richard Pring was Lead Director of the Nuffield Review of 14–19 education and training. He has written about the relationship between philosophy and education, and values and vocationalism in education, as well as leading discussions on the ethics of educational research (Pring 2005).

To find out more about current philosophy of education in the UK, you should read *The RoutledgeFalmer Reader in Philosophy of Education* (Carr 2005) and *An Introduction to the Philosophy of Education* (Barrow and Woods 2006).

And beyond the UK, *Leaders in Philosophy of Education: Intellectual Self Portraits* (Waks 2008), a collection of autobiographical essays by top scholars.

---

**Activity: an education for the 21st century**

Think about the following questions.

- What do you consider to be the main priorities for schools and teachers in the 21st century?
- What knowledge, skills and personal qualities should young people possess when they leave formal education?
- What changes would you make to the organization of schooling in the UK so as to maximize opportunities to develop these skills and qualities?
- What place should philosophy occupy in the curriculum of the 21st century?

---

## Conclusion

There is a contention among some today that philosophy of education has rather lost its way (see Standish 2006 for an outline and critique of this viewpoint). The 1980s' Thatcher government did much to diminish the place of educational disciplines within teacher training – as part of a broader move to denigrate and deprofessionalize the teacher – so that philosophy of education has little presence on training courses today. The discipline itself can appear somewhat imprecise and disorderly, lacking the points of focus and distinguishable perspectives of the others you encounter during this book. Instead, 'there remains a distinct sense that philosophy of education is what those who write it and teach it say it is' (Chambliss 2009: 251). But this 'messiness' gives the discipline its potency – there is an 'adventurousness in the form of openness to ideas and radical approaches' (Phillips 2008: 3) that makes it distinctive from the other disciplines. Philosophy of education is *what good teachers do* as part of their daily lives: informed by historical and contemporary ideas, they think critically and reflectively about their professional practices and the purpose and scope of educational activity.

> **Further research**
>
> - To what extent, if at all, should teachers confront social and political issues in the classroom?
> - To what extent can and should education teach young people to become moral?
> - Evaluate the claim that there is no such thing as absolute knowledge and therefore no need for education.

## Key readings

### Books

Bailey, R. (ed.) (2010) *Philosophy of Education: An introduction*. London: Continuum. The most accessible introduction to the discipline for Education Studies undergraduates, including chapters by current theorists on many of the important issues for philosophy of education today.

Cahn, S. (ed.) (2009) *Philosophy of Education: The Essential Texts*. Abingdon: Routledge. Extended extracts from significant educational philosophers, each followed by an 'interpretive essay' written by present-day specialists.

Curren, R. (ed.) (2003) *A Companion to the Philosophy of Education*. Oxford: Blackwell. A comprehensive reader, including a history of educational philosophy and contemporary educational issues approached from a philosophical perspective.

Titone, C. (2007) Pulling back the curtain: relearning the history of the philosophy of education. *Educational Studies*, 41(2): 128–47. An excellent article that reflects on the key contributions of women to the development of philosophy of education.

### Journals

*Educational Philosophy and Theory* – journal of the Philosophy of Education Society of Australasia.

*Journal of Philosophy of Education* – journal of the Philosophy of Education Society of Great Britain.

*Studies in Philosophy and Education* – offers an international perspective.

### Websites

www.philosophy-of-education.org/ – homepage to Philosophy of Education Society of Great Britain, with links to its journals, its booklet *IMPACT* and its magazine *Questa*, as well as links to other useful resources.

www.vusst.hr/ENCYCLOPAEDIA/doku.php – *Encyclopaedia of Philosophy of Education* – with lots of up-to-date essays in the field of educational philosophy.

## References

Adler, M. (1982) *The Paideia Program: An Educational Syllabus*. New York: Macmillan.

Apple, M. (2009) Is there a place for education in social transformation? In H. Svi Shapiro (ed.) *Education and Hope in Troubled Times: Sociocultural, Political and Historical Studies in Education Studies*. Abingdon: Routledge.

Bagley, W. (1938) An essentialist's platform for the advancement of American education. *Educational Administration and Supervision*, 24: 242–56.

Barrow, R. and Woods, R. (2006) *An Introduction to the Philosophy of Education*. Abingdon: Routledge.

Cahn, S. (ed.) (2009) *Philosophy of Education: The Essential Texts*. Abingdon: Routledge.

Carr, D. (1991) *Educating the Virtues: An Essay on the Philosophical Psychology of Moral Development and Education*. London: Routledge.

Carr, W. (2004) Philosophy and education. *Journal of Philosophy of Education*, 38(1): 55–73.

Carr, W. (2005) *The RoutledgeFalmer Reader in Philosophy of Education*. Abingdon: Routledge.

Chambliss, J. (2009) Philosophy of education today. *Educational Theory*, 59(2): 233–51.

Claxton, G. (2008) Character curriculum for a learning age. Available at: http://www.teaching expertise.com/articles/guy-claxtons-character-curriculum-for-the-learning-age-2793

Curren, R. (ed.) (2007) *Philosophy of Education: An Anthology*. Oxford: Blackwell.

Darder, A., Baltodano, M. and Torres, R. (eds) (2008) *The Critical Pedagogy Reader*. Abingdon: Routledge.

Dewey, J. (1916/1997) *Democracy and Education: An Introduction to the Philosophy of Education*. New York: The Free Press.

Dewey, J. (2008) *The Child and the Curriculum Including, the School and Society*. New York: Cosimo.

Doddington, C. and Hilton, M. (2007) *Child-centred Education: Reviving the Creative Tradition*. London: Sage.

Facer, K. (2009) *Beyond Current Horizons: Technology, Children, Schools and Families*. Bristol: Futurelab.

Fielding, M. (2007) Beyond 'voice': new roles, relations, and contexts in researching with young people. *Discourse: Studies in the Cultural Politics of Education*, 28(3): 301–10.

Flanagan, F. (2006) *The Greatest Educators . . . Ever!* London: Continuum.

Freire, P. (1970/1996) *Pedagogy of the Oppressed*. Harmondsworth: Penguin.

Freire, P. (1973/2005) *Education for Critical Consciousness*. London: Continuum.

Gatto, J.T. (2002) *Dumbing Us Down: The Hidden Curriculum of Compulsory Schooling*. Gabriola Island: New Society Publishers.

Habermas, J. (1991) *The Theory of Communicative Action: Reason and the Rationalization of Society*. Oxford: Polity Press.

Hand, M. and Winstanley, C. (eds) (2009) *Philosophy in Schools*. London: Continuum.

Haynes, J. (2008) *Children as Philosophers: Learning through Dialogue and Enquiry in the Primary Classroom*. Abingdon: Routledge.

Hirst, P. and Carr, W. (2005) Philosophy of education: a symposium. *Journal of Philosophy of Education*, 39(4): 615–32.

Holt, J. (1990) *How Children Fail*. Harmondsworth: Penguin.

Hutchins, R. (1953) *The University of Utopia*. Chicago, IL: University of Chicago Press.

Illich, I. (1973) *Deschooling Society*. Harmondsworth: Penguin.

Jenks, C. (2005) *Childhood*. Abingdon: Routledge.

Kohlberg, L. (1984) *The Psychology of Moral Development*. San Francisco, CA: Harper and Row.

MacIntyre, A. and Dunne, J. (2002) Alasdair MacIntyre on education. *Journal of Philosophy of Education*, 36(1): 1–19.

Mayhew, K. and Edwards, A. (2007) *The Dewey School: The Laboratory School of the University of Chicago, 1896–1903*. Upper Saddle River, NJ: Transaction.

Neill, A. (1968) *A Dominie's Log: The Story of a Scottish Teacher*. London: Hogarth Press.

Neill, A. (1970) *Summerhill: A Radical Approach to Education*. Harmondsworth: Penguin.

Noddings, N. (2005) *The Challenge to Care in Schools: An Alternative Approach to Education*. New York: Teachers College Press.

Oancea, A. and Bridges, D. (2009) Philosophy of education in the UK: the historical and contemporary tradition. *Oxford Review of Education*, 35(3): 553–68.

Phillips, D. (2008) Philosophy of education. *Stanford Encyclopaedia of Philosophy*. Available at: http://plato.stanford.edu/entries/education-philosophy/

Plato (2007) *The Republic*. Harmondsworth: Penguin.

Pring, R. (2005) *Philosophy of Education: Aims, Theory, Common Sense and Research*. London: Continuum.

Pring, R. et al. (2009) *14–19 Education and Training: Looking to the Future*. Oxford: Routledge.

Rousseau, J. (1968) *The Social Contract*. London: Penguin.

Rousseau, J. (2007) *Emile or On Education*. Sioux Falls: Nuvision Publications.

Ruddock, J. and Fielding, M. (2006) Student voice and the perils of popularity. *Educational Review*, 58(2): 219–31.

Smith, R. (2005) Paths of judgement: the revival of practical wisdom. In W. Carr (ed.) *The RoutledgeFalmer Reader in Philosophy of Education*. Abingdon: RoutledgeFalmer.

Standish, P. (2006) John Wilson's confused 'perspectives on the philosophy of education'. *Oxford Review of Education*, 32(2): 265–79.

Usher, R. (2009) Experience, pedagogy, and social practices. In K. Illeris (ed.) *Contemporary Theories of Learning*. Abingdon: Routledge.

Vokey, D. (2006) *Philosophy of Education 2006 Yearbook*.

Waks, L. (ed.) (2008) *Leaders in Philosophy of Education: Intellectual Self Portraits*. Rotterdam: Sense.

# 4

## REBECCA ALLEN
## The Economics of Education

---

### Learning outcomes

By the end of this chapter you should be able to:

- identify the types of policy questions in education that economists are equipped to answer;
- explain how education can lead to greater economic growth;
- understand how economists use criteria of equity and efficiency to judge the success of education policies;
- design policies to improve the functioning of the teacher labour market;
- construct arguments for and against encouraging greater parental choice.

---

### Overview of the discipline

### What is the economics of education?

Economists analyse the production of education in this world where resources such as the capital invested in buildings or technology and the labour of the teacher workforce are necessarily scarce. This scarcity of resources means that policy-makers must decide:

- how much to spend on each stage of education (i.e. what to produce);
- how to provide educational services in a way that maximizes its benefits to society (i.e. how to produce education);
- who should have access to each stage of education (i.e. for whom is education provided).

Economic theory is able to help policy-makers by providing both facts about the education system and values to inform decision-making. The part of economics that is concerned with establishing facts about the world is called *positive economics*. It asks questions such as 'Can we improve the quality of teachers by increasing pay?' or 'Will smaller class sizes raise pupil attainment?' *Normative economics* asks questions that require value judgements such as 'Is it fair to charge higher education students tuition fees?'

A social welfare framework underpins the dominant approach in the economics of education. According to this framework, society should strive to arrange educational services to be produced and distributed in a manner that is both *efficient* and *equitable*. Efficiency means that educational outputs are maximized, given a set of constrained resources. Equity means that services are distributed according to some principle of social justice or fairness.

Individuals and governments often face hard choices because of the scarce resources they possess. For example, expanding higher education and increasing provision of early years care might both appear to be policies that have the potential to improve the well-being of society overall, but which should a government prioritize? Economists describe the costs of taking a particular action as *opportunity costs*, because the greatest cost of expanding higher education might be the lost benefits of not undertaking the next best alternative policy, such as increased provision of early years care.

## Short history of the economics of education

Economists are normally associated with ensuring that profit-making companies and the overall economy functions well, but they have slowly expanded their interests to new spheres of society. The origin of the economics of education as a significant field within economics dates back to the theoretical and empirical developments made by American economists such as Gary Becker, Jacob Mincer and Theodore Schultz in the 1960s (Machin 2008). Their work introduced the idea of education as human capital and they attempted to calculate the economic returns to acquiring education. These ideas are discussed in the first key theme below.

Over the past decade there has been an enormous growth of interest by economists in education policy, both in the UK and across the world. This has been accompanied by a growing political interest in market-based reforms across the public sector that is briefly covered in key theme five. These types of reform include devolvement of financial planning to front-line institutions such as hospitals and schools, and giving consumers of public services choice about which provider to use. Economists from other fields such as labour economics have been attracted by the growing availability of large-scale datasets that facilitate complex statistical analysis to analyse the impact of particular policy initiatives. Examples of these data include the National Pupil Database in England, which has collected annual information on the background characteristics and key stage attainment data of all pupils in state-maintained schools since 2002, and the PISA, an international survey of the skills of 15 year olds across many industrialized countries.

## What is the economic paradigm?

Economic theory makes certain assumptions about human behaviour in order to make predictions about the effects of policy changes. The starting point of economic analysis is that individuals and institutions are rational agents (often given the name *'homo-economicus'*), operating with self-interested intent as they make decisions about providing or participating in education (Le Grand 2003). Individuals are assumed to set themselves a goal of maximizing their own well-being (or utility), given fixed preferences or tastes for education and a well-defined money constraint. Many economic theories assume that human brains possess perfect computational powers to process all the information needed to make optimal choices at all times!

These economic models of individuals and institutions present a simplified version of reality and for this reason they have been criticized by many sociologists and psychologists who claim they bear little resemblance to the real world. However, economists would argue that these simplifying assumptions are necessary to make precise predictions about the likely impact of policies in this complex world we live in. To put it another way, economists do not really believe that humans are so selfish and simple in their motivations; they just believe that this simplification is a useful analytical tool to help us understand the world better.

---

**Key figure: Gary Becker**

Gary Becker (born 1930) is a US economist who has spent most of his career at the University of Chicago, one of the foremost institutions in the world. He was one of the first economists to branch into the analysis of new areas such as education, racial discrimination, family organization and crime. He is known for arguing that many different types of human behaviour can be seen as rational and utility maximizing, even apparently altruistic behaviour. He is seen as the modern founder of the field of economics of education for his work on human capital theory in 1964. This is the idea that individuals make the choice to invest in their own knowledge and skills based on rational calculations of the benefits and costs to them in both time and money. He won a Nobel Prize in Economics for his work in 1992.

---

## Key theme 1: education as human capital and economic growth

Why does any individual choose to get themselves an education? Although we might choose to take educational courses for pure enjoyment (and this is particularly true of certain types of courses such as adult evening classes), the starting perspective of the economics of education is that individuals usually invest in their own education in order to raise their future earnings. The knowledge, skills, competencies and attitudes that an individual acquires from education are said to increase the amount of human capital the individual has. The use of the word human *capital* emphasizes that the skills we have as individuals are as useful to us financially as other capital we might possess, such as bank savings and houses.

According to human capital theory, education is worth investing in if the value of the future returns it brings to individuals exceeds the costs of the resources used to provide education. The largest cost of an educational course is not usually the tuition fees; it is the opportunity cost of losing wages because you are not working while being educated. Economists add up all the costs of acquiring an education and compare them to the future increased wages that the individual is likely to get as a result of their extra human capital. This comparison of costs and benefits is called a *rate of return* to education.

The relationship between education and human capital is not a straightforward one. Some courses, such as an introductory photography evening class, will not lead to knowledge and skills that are ever likely (or indeed intended) to raise an individual's wage potential. So, although an individual might learn new skills, they do not increase human capital because the skills they learn will never have a value in the labour market. Also, much of the human capital that we have and that is valued by our employers does not come from formal education because we acquire useful experiences in our everyday life. For example, our capacities to persuade, negotiate and compromise are invaluable to employers but are as likely to have been learned in the home as they are in school.

Governments calculate the rates of return to education to help make policy decisions about what types of educational provision they should expand and subsidize. This decision that is taken from the perspective of society as a whole is slightly different to that taken by individuals because society takes into account the benefits of having an educated society beyond the narrow economic potential. For example, we know that educated individuals are more likely to vote and participate in the democratic process, are more likely to do charitable work, are more likely to maintain a better state of health and are less likely to commit crime (McMahon 2004).

## Does education cause economic growth?

Given that human capital theory predicts that education will lead to more productive workers who are able to make valuable goods and services, we should expect that countries that expand their education system will experience higher economic growth as a result. For example, educating young people in India in the English language and IT skills has led them to be able to work in IT and in call centres. These are more productive jobs than working in agriculture. However, it has been surprisingly difficult to prove that education facilitates growth. Hanushek and Woessman (2009) use 40 years of data from across the world to show that there is actually little relationship between a country's improvement in average years of schooling received and economic growth. There are many examples of countries in Africa and South America that have expanded education and have failed to see corresponding economic growth and prosperity. There are many reasons why this might happen. For example, graduates with significant human capital may fail to find jobs that allow them to use their skills and competencies for institutional or political reasons. Education also has the perverse effect of damaging an economy in the short term as children are taken out of jobs in agriculture and placed in schools where they are not productive for many years. Most importantly, though, teaching quality is often insufficient in developing countries for children to be able to learn useful skills. Hanushek and Woessman show that this last explanation is likely to be the most important since the relationship between a country's growth in academic test scores and economic growth is very strong (see Figure 4.1).

Governments are responsible for deciding both the overall level of education spending and the mix of levels of education. Rates of return to education analysis can be useful in informing the latter by helping society direct resources to the areas that

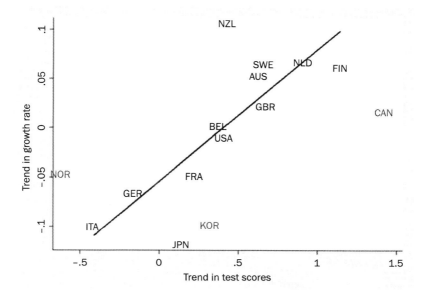

**Figure 4.1** Trends in growth rates versus trends in test scores
*Source:* Hanushek and Woessman (2009).

have the potential to generate the greatest return. For example, suppose a government in a developing country has a choice between making primary education universal and free for all children or expanding provision for secondary schooling to reach one-third of the population. Economists could explore which policy would be most likely to generate economic growth for a country. Psacharopoulas (1994) and other economists at the World Bank have analysed data across almost every country in the world and claim that investments in primary education, rather than higher levels of education, have almost always generated the greatest rate of return in terms of high wages for individuals. It is for this reason that the World Bank and UNESCO have supported and funded *Education for All*, a programme of universal primary education across the world that aims to reach its goals by 2015.

---

### Activity: the costs and benefits of your education

Economists carry out a cost–benefit analysis of education to decide whether a course is a worthwhile investment. Your task is to think about the costs and likely future benefits of the course that you are currently taking.

1.  Write down the amount of tuition fees that you are paying each year. This might seem like a lot of money, but the government is probably also subsidizing your course. Try to use the internet to find out approximately how much the government is contributing to the costs of your course.

2.   Your largest cost is actually your forgone earnings. This is the amount of money you would be earning in a job that you could have done if you hadn't taken your course. Write down a few examples of jobs that you could be doing now if you weren't on a university course. Use the internet to find out approximately how much you could earn in total from this work.

3.   We now need to make a list of the benefits of taking the course. First, write down all the knowledge, skills, competencies and attitudes that you think you are acquiring on your course.

4.   Write down the job that you hope to do when you complete your course. Find out what salary it pays. How much more money is this than the job you would be doing if you hadn't taken the course?

5.   What other non-money benefits might you and society receive as a result of your education?

**Key figure: Jacob Mincer**

Jacob Mincer (1922–2006) was a Polish-born labour market economist who spent most of his career at Columbia University in New York, having survived prison camps in Czechoslovakia and Germany. Alongside Gary Becker he made a great contribution to the development of human capital theory and understanding income inequality. His greatest contribution was a book called *Schooling, Experience and Earnings*, published in 1974. In this book he showed the empirical relationship between education, on-the-job training and the income of workers. The field of economics of education continues to use a statistical approach called Mincerian earnings equations to measure the rate of return to education.

## Key theme 2: efficient resource usage in the production of education

In this world where resources are scarce, economists use ideas of efficiency to judge whether education is being effectively produced in the interests of society as a whole. In their analysis of educational institutions they compare the amount of outputs such as educational qualifications that are produced from a given amount of inputs such as teachers, books, infrastructure and technology. A school is judged as being productively efficient if it maximizes its output for a given level of inputs. This type of analysis treats educational institutions as 'black boxes' where only inputs and outputs are measured, and the processes that take place within the institution are largely ignored.

There are multiple ways in which we can judge the outputs of school or university. For example, does the student accumulate new skills or knowledge? Did students enjoy the course? Have students successfully found relevant jobs? Researchers usually take student test scores in national exams, such as GCSEs in England, as the main indicator of the output of a school. This is clearly not a comprehensive indicator of school quality since it ignores other educational and social benefits, but we know that academic success is valued by both parents and students in surveys of schooling. We might think that the wages that former students eventually manage to earn in the job market are a better indicator of the true economic value of their educational experiences, but these cannot be measured until many years after the pupil has left the school.

This analysis of productive efficiency, in other words maximizing outputs for a given level of inputs, is critical to judgements of whether resources are being sensibly used to improve social welfare. However, it doesn't take full account of the extent to which the outputs are actually valued by society. For example, a nursery school could be productively efficient at using its resources to produce a set of children with important social skills, such as getting on with other children, sitting still when an adult is talking, getting dressed and undressed, and so on. Another nursery school could be exceptional at ensuring four year olds can count, write their names and read some words. The concept of productive efficiency cannot help us decide which of these two nurseries is the more efficient because the outputs are incomparable. Instead, economists use the criteria of *allocative efficiency* to decide which type of output society values the most.

Suppose we decide to give a school some additional money to spend on resources. We should expect the school to spend the money on teachers or other resources that improve the academic achievement of the pupils. However, evidence for a causal relationship between school funding and pupil achievement is surprisingly weak (see Dewey et al. 2000 for a review). This statistically significant, yet notably small, association has been found in many developed countries across the world so does not appear to be an artifact of the institutional structure of schooling in the UK. It is a problem as allocation of larger government budgets is the usual means by which governments attempt to improve the public services they value most. For example, the first decade (1997–2007) of the last Labour government in the UK produced a massive 56 per cent real increase in school budgets, with very large rises for the most deprived schools, yet the empirical evidence suggests that this admirable attempt to improve schools and to close the social class gap in attainment may not reach its policy goals. Indeed, the increased expenditure has not seen outputs rise at the same rate and so school productivity has fallen (Wild et al. 2009).

All this evidence suggests that schools do not appear to spend money on the resources that are the most efficient route to improving test scores, but we know little about why this is. One possible reason is that headteachers lack the knowledge to make the best resource deployment decisions, so there is a greater role for government in helping them learn about best practice in this area. Another suggestion is that governments place great constraints on how money can be spent. Money is often tied to specific government initiatives spent in a piecemeal fashion with no opportunity for long-term planning on the part of schools. In England the initiative to install interactive whiteboards in classrooms had no associated funding for training teachers to use them. The Excellence in Cities programme earmarked money specifically for learning mentors, learning support units and programmes for 'gifted and talented' pupils. These restrictions to school spending are marginal, however, compared to the very large restrictions that the trades unions and government impose on the teacher labour market in most countries across the world. These are discussed in key theme 4.

In England, national pay bargaining and precisely mandated working conditions and hours make it impossible for school leaders to use their *human* resources efficiently. Teacher pay generally accounts for over 60 per cent of school expenditure (and total staff costs up to 80 per cent). If schools are unable to make efficient spending decisions with this part of their budget it is not surprising that the overall relationship between spending and test scores appears to be weak.

Even free of constraints on spending decisions, we should not expect schools to make resource decisions efficiently if doing so has little impact on the well-being of the school community. Teachers, school leaders and governors all have their own goals, of which the overall test scores of pupils may be only one. Without effective incentives, education systems can be dysfunctional and individual teachers may pursue their own interests. For example, in the UK, a large proportion of the increased schools budget has been spent on a three-fold increase in the numbers of teaching assistants to support teachers in the classroom. They are generally popular with teachers, not least because they reduce their administrative workload, but evidence suggests this increase in resources has almost certainly had no impact on pupil test scores and may have damaged learning experiences in many cases (Blatchford et al. forthcoming).

## Productive efficiency and class sizes

One of the most important questions in judging the productive efficiency of schools is, should we reduce class sizes? This would clearly increase education costs because teachers are a very expensive resource, but it might be a good use of money if the smaller class sizes improved children's achievement. Many economists have tried to answer this question in different countries and with different ages of children. However, it isn't a straightforward question to answer because we often observe that children in smaller classes do worse! How could this happen? One reason is that popular schools tend to have larger class sizes, yet they could be popular because they are strong academically. The other reason is that schools that use ability grouping for teaching usually ensure that class sizes for the less able students are slightly smaller, leading us to wrongly infer that the larger class sizes are improving attainment.

Despite these difficulties of using real-world examples for analysis there are two types of study that economists have used to look at the causal impact of class size on educational attainment. The first is a randomized experiment called Project STAR than ran in Tennessee in the 1980s (cited in Krueger 1999). Teachers and pupils were randomly assigned to small classes, regular-sized classes or regular classes with a teaching assistant. They found that children who attended the small classes did a little better in academic tests and that these advantages of smaller class sizes were larger for ethnic minority students and those from low-income families. Teaching assistants had little effect on pupil achievement so did not appear to represent a good use of school financial resources. Overall the gains in performance were relatively small compared with the magnitude of the reduction in class sizes.

The second type of study uses an institutional rule in Israel which means that class sizes must never rise above 40 (see Angrist and Lavy 1999). This means that if a school year group has 39 pupils in it and one extra pupil joins the school, the school is forced to split the class into two groups of 20 pupils each. This is known as a *natural experiment* because a chance event – the arrival of one extra pupil – has a very large impact on class size. This study shows that reducing class size produces a significant and substantial increase in test scores for fourth and fifth graders in Israel, although not for third graders. The findings suggest that the idea that school resources have no causal effect on learning may be premature because studies are often confounded by a failure to isolate a credible source of variation in school inputs.

---

**Activity: improving the efficiency of university teaching**

In undergraduate studies, students are usually taught using a variety of teaching methods, including large lectures, smaller seminar groups and self-study activities. Your university would like to improve the efficiency of the delivery of your course by reorganizing teaching. It can do this by changing the mix of teaching methods, by changing the class sizes or by changing the type of lecturers that it uses.

1. Suppose it would like to improve the quality of the course while maintaining the existing course budget. Would it be possible to do this?
2. Suppose it needs to halve the cost of delivering the course. How would you suggest it does this in order to minimize the impact on quality?

---

**Key figure in the economics of education: Stephen Machin**

Stephen Machin (born 1962) is Professor of Economics at University College London and is Director of the Centre for the Economics of Education. Like many other economists in the field of economics of education, most of his early research analysed labour markets. His recent papers explore whether UK education policy has made schools operate more effectively. For example, he has evaluated the impact of the Literacy Hour, new technological investments and the Excellence in Cities initiative. He has also investigated whether large-scale institutional reform such as the academies programme can improve schooling. His other strand of research has tried to establish the extent to which parents really value pupil attainment, by measuring how much they are willing to pay for a house that guarantees them access to a popular school.

---

## Key theme 3: equity in the distribution of education

In *normative economics* – the study of questions concerning what society *should* do – principles of social justice sit alongside efficiency as a goal of resource allocation. Economists working in education are able to analyse whether the distribution of educational access, take-up of these opportunities and educational outcomes are equitable. However, deciding whether policies meet equity criteria is exceptionally contentious because equity means many different things to different people.

Economists and political philosophers have worked alongside one another to produce a set of theories concerning social justice.

We can use a real policy question to illustrate how different the policy conclusions are that result from competing theories of social justice. Suppose a government is trying to decide how to organize its secondary education system. It could introduce a system where everyone can attend their nearest school (a comprehensive system) or it could retain a selective system where the most academically able quarter of children will attend academic grammar schools and the rest will attend less academic schools (a grammar system). This was the choice facing local authorities in England in the 1960s and 1970s. Our question is which system is the most equitable?

## Equity as concern for the least advantaged

The first set of theorists would argue that social justice means concern for the least advantaged in society, so faced with the choice described above, governments should choose the policy that makes this group the best off. There are several different theoretical perspectives that are taken, but each has a similar policy conclusion. For example, egalitarians believe that society's equity goal should be equality of outcomes, whereas Rawls (1971) would argue that policy should maximize the well-being of the person who is worst off in society.

If we class the least advantaged as those children from low-income households, any system of academic selection is unlikely to benefit this group. This is because there is a correlation between a child's ability and household income at the age of 11, so the children who are able to progress to academic grammar schools will always be disproportionately from wealthier families. Furthermore, performance in an academic entrance test can be purchased by wealthier families in one of two ways. A higher-income family can simply send their child to a private primary school or purchase private coaching in the years leading up to the test. Even without this purchased help, a family from a higher social background is much more likely to be able to help their children through the test than a lower social background family.

So clearly, those who are most concerned with the least advantaged in society would not favour a grammar school system, even though some children from low-income families would do very well out of it. However, they would also be concerned that wealthier families are able to purchase a house close to a good-quality school in the comprehensive system and that this might also be unfair.

## Equity as concern for fairness of processes based on protecting the rights of individuals

Another set of theorists would argue that a system is equitable, provided the process of allocating pupils to schools is implemented fairly. There are many who would argue that any system of academic selection at age 11 will be procedurally unfair and therefore is necessarily inequitable. One reason is that selection by ability involves splitting a population of children into two groups, one of which gets to attend grammar schools, and that this will violate the principle of the equal treatment of equals in the system. This is because if we allow only the top 25 per cent of pupils into grammar schools, the system treats the child who just gets into a grammar school and the child who scored almost the same mark in the test but who just misses out very differently. Another equity argument contends that the test itself will rank pupils inconsistently and so is unfair. Suppose we asked a set of pupils to take five entrance tests over the course of a week and select the top 25 per cent of pupils on each of the five occasions. Some pupils will appear in the top 25 per cent in every test, but others will 'pass' or 'fail' depending on the vagaries of the test. This variation in performance for the individual pupil is impossible to avoid, thus we cannot devise a consistent measure of who should, and should not, attend a grammar school. Another inconsistency results from the timing of the test. It was well documented in the 1960s that if we selected at 11, we would chose a completely different set of pupils than if we selected at age 14, 16 or indeed 7. The choice of age 11 is arbitrary and favours relatively early developers. A final procedural equity argument claims it is impossible to directly test 'intelligence' so instead we test a child's academic capabilities. However, it is arbitrary how we devise this test, for example a test with a greater weight on maths and science skills relative to literacy skills would benefit children from lower-income households.

Nozick (1974) has the most radical views on what constitutes a fair process, arguing that individuals should be free to act as they please without state interference, so the only role for governments is to ensure that property right laws are upheld. He would therefore argue for an education system run entirely by the private sector. Buchanan (1986) has a more moderate view on this, arguing that differences in educational opportunities and outcomes result from four factors: choice, luck, birth and effort. If we observed that some children get greater educational opportunities from passing an entrance exam, then Buchanan wouldn't have a problem with this so long as their differences in performance were the result of the child's choice, their luck or their effort. For him, only differences that result from inequalities in 'birth' or family circumstances justify government interventions. He would therefore have some problems with a selective schooling system because wealthier families are able to purchase advantages for their children. He would not worry that any test is arbitrary or gives advantages to those who are lucky enough to be of a higher ability.

---

### Activity: equity in access to higher education in England

Figure 4.2 shows recent statistics for the proportion of young people attending higher education in England. Overall, about 29 per cent of this cohort of pupils attended higher education, but there is a steep social gradient. Almost 50 per cent of students who come from high-income families continue into higher education, but this figure is around 15 per cent from low-income families.

1.   Does this chart tell you that higher education policy in England is equitable? Why, or why not?
2.   What additional information would you like to know about these groups of children to help you decide whether England's current higher education policies are fair?

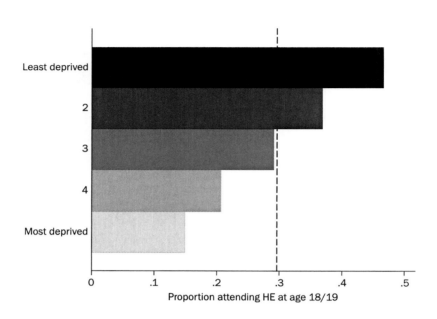

**Figure 4.2** The proportion of 18–19 year olds who attend higher education in England, by socio-economic group
*Source:* Chowdry et al. (2008).

3. Why do you think that students from low-income families are unlikely to go to university?
4. How do you expect the Conservative–Liberal Democrat coalition higher education policy reforms of 2011 to affect equity?
5. What types of policy might succeed in making access to higher education more equitable?

**Key figure: Simon Burgess**

Simon Burgess (born 1960) is a Professor of Economics at the University of Bristol and is Director of the Centre for Market and Public Organization, currently one of the largest research centres in the field of economics of education. He has a particular interest in the experiences of ethnic minority pupils in the English schooling system, analysing why schools are ethnically segregated and how this impacts on pupil achievement. He has written extensively about parental choice of school and school competition, covered in key theme 5 in this chapter. He has also researched teacher labour markets, including measuring how much variation in teacher effectiveness exists within schools and whether threshold payments for teachers have had any impact.

## Key theme 4: the labour market for teachers

Teacher labour market reforms, such as changes to the way we recruit and pay teachers, hold the promise of the greatest gains in the overall success of education policy. Spending on teacher pay accounts for around three-quarters of total spending on schools in most developed countries, and so small pay reforms can have potentially large impacts on the costs of education. More importantly, we know that variation in teacher quality accounts for the greatest proportion of the differences that schools have on pupil outcomes: having a good versus an average teacher can make a substantive difference to your educational success. As an example of the magnitude of the importance of teachers, being taught for a GCSE course by a high-quality teacher rather than a lower-quality teacher adds almost half a GCSE grade for each student in the class (Slater et al. 2009).

The labour market for teachers is unusual because in most countries it is dominated by a state employer that controls pay and conditions of service, with little discretion for teachers and schools to bargain over individual pay rates. Where there is a single buyer of labour, such as a government, economists call it a *monopsony* market and predict that the monopsonist will choose to maintain teacher shortages in order to keep wages low. This is rational because if it wants to attract, say, 100 extra teachers to work in English state schools, it would have to offer a slightly higher wage than the existing pay scale to attract these people into teaching from other jobs. However, it can only do this by raising the national pay scale for all the teachers it employs, thus making the overall costs very high indeed.

There are three features of the UK teacher labour market that support the view that the government is acting as a monopsonist by depressing wages and leaving a shortage of teachers who are willing to work at the going rate. First, there are persistent teacher vacancies in many parts of the labour market, particularly for schools in London and those trying to recruit maths and science teachers. Second, the government makes widespread use of 'perks' to attract additional teachers without having to raise the pay of existing teachers. These include the use of 'golden hellos' for shortage subjects, writing off student loans and offering housing schemes for younger workers who are not yet on the housing ladder. Third, shortages in the supply of well-qualified teachers are 'plugged' through the use of staff who are not subject to the normal pay scale. These include overseas teachers from countries such as Australia, New Zealand and South Africa who do not have qualified teacher status and new graduates on schemes such as TeachFirst.

## Should we pay teachers more?

Headteachers in England have long claimed that learning at their school is hindered by a shortage of teachers or by inadequacies in the teachers that they employ. International surveys of education such as PISA suggest that this problem is greater in England than it is in most other countries. However, the argument that England could solve this problem by raising teacher pay is a contentious one. There are all kinds of moral arguments that can be made about what an appropriate level of pay should be for such a critically important job. However, from an efficiency perspective we should raise the wages of teachers only if we can demonstrate it would improve pupil outcomes sufficiently, given the additional costs. This can only be true if higher pay is successful in recruiting and retaining high-quality teachers or if high pay can somehow induce the existing pool of teachers to work more effectively.

It is clear that there has been a problem in England with recruiting new graduates to become teachers, not least because of greater opportunities elsewhere in the labour market. Vacancy rates suggest an overall shortage, but of more concern is the decline in the academic credentials of new teachers entering the profession now, compared to the 1960s. Academics from the UK and the USA have shown that the relative pay of teachers compared to other graduate occupations does have a significant effect on graduates' choice of teaching, but this relationship is not particularly strong. The reason for this is that people are attracted into teaching, in part, because of a vocational attraction and the perceived non-money benefits, such as the pleasure of working with children or disseminating subject knowledge. The prestige of the profession may also be an important factor in attracting teachers, and this is not necessarily very closely related to pay (Finland has average teacher salaries, but it is a high-prestige profession and the Finnish schooling system is very successful as a result).

The retention of teachers is an equally serious problem, and the exit rates from the teaching profession are staggeringly high. After about four years, only half of a cohort of new entrants is still teaching in state schools in England. It has been shown that higher relative earnings would increase the retention of teachers, and in particular the retention of teachers who themselves were more academically successful (Chevalier et al. 2007).

These recruitment and retention problems suggest a need to improve the pay of teachers to make the profession more attractive overall. However, the evidence does suggest that this will have only a small impact on the numbers that are willing to teach overall, and it may do little to improve the average quality of teachers because salaries will rise for all teachers, regardless of the quality of the learning experience they provide for pupils in their classroom.

## Paying teachers for the performance of their pupils

Most countries across the world give school teachers almost guaranteed jobs for life with salaries that automatically increase each year regardless of teacher effort or quality. There is little formal performance assessment or sanction of dismissal for poor teaching standards. These types of pay system provide no financial incentives to reward the most talented teachers for their efforts and encourage them to remain in the profession.

One reason that teacher pay systems work in this way is that it is hard to identify the individuals that have the greatest potential to be high-quality teachers and pay them more to join and then remain in the profession. This is because teacher quality is not really related to the individual's own characteristics (Eide et al. 2004). For example, teachers who themselves were academically very successful do not seem to be much more successful teachers. Even the subject they studied for their degree does not appear to be as important as many people assume it is.

Performance-related pay schemes have been proposed by economists as a possible financial incentive to reward teachers if their pupils are academically successful. They have the potential to encourage all teachers to improve the quality of their teaching and may also cause poorer-quality teachers to leave the profession altogether since they will not qualify for extra pay.

The theoretical rationale for performance-related pay is that teachers, like all workers, act to maximize their own well-being. Le Grand (2003) suggests that some teachers are 'knights' who are altruistic, motivated by intrinsic job satisfaction and the desire to promote the welfare of pupils. However, many teachers occasionally display 'knavish' behaviour, making them more self-interested or even opportunistic. For example, they may not give the highest quality of feedback on pupils' homework assignments if they believe that parents or inspectors will never monitor the exercise books. Where this knavish behaviour is present it can be modified by rewarding teachers directly for actions that are also in the interests of the pupil.

There are many different ways to introduce performance-related pay. All schemes retain a fixed salary part that is paid to everyone and the performance-related part is intended to reward teachers for their contribution to educational progress made by children. Where these schemes have been introduced around the world they have generally been found to improve the quality of teaching overall. For example, Mexico introduced a successful voluntary scheme that rewarded teachers for student learning achievement and evidence of professional development. The UK 'threshold' on the existing national pay scale is a type of performance-related pay since it allows teachers who have reached the top of the main pay scale to apply for additional pay if they meet criteria including demonstrating student progress and achievement. However, most teachers do successfully pass through the threshold so the criterion of high performance is not particularly onerous.

One problem with these schemes is that when pupils do well in exams we do not know whether this is due to their teacher's effort and talents or whether the pupil has social characteristics that mean they were likely to do well regardless of the teacher they were assigned. It is very costly for headteachers to monitor the true quality of teaching that is taking place in their school. Furthermore, performance-related pay can lead to tensions within a school teaching body if some teachers feel the distribution of rewards is not reflective of true quality or effort. In light of this problem, Israel and several states in the USA have experimented with school-based performance pay where all teachers in the school are awarded additional pay if the school's results have improved (Ladd 1999; Lavy 2002). These school-wide pay schemes have been successful in raising pupil test scores while maintaining a sense of collegiality within a school and removing individual incentives for teachers to choose less disruptive classes to teach.

---

### Activity: introducing performance-related pay for teachers

The government has announced that it intends to link teacher pay to the performance of the pupils that they teach in order to incentivize teachers to work hard to raise educational standards. You have been asked to recommend a new performance-related pay scheme.

1.  In your scheme the amount that teachers are paid should be related to how good a job they do. Your first task is to decide how you will judge teacher quality. For example, will you rely on classroom observations, pupil surveys or pupil test score results?
2.  In your scheme, high-quality teachers should be paid a bonus. How much extra money would you give your best teachers?
3.  Do you think your scheme will work, or might it have unintended consequences?

**Key figure: Eric Hanushek**

Eric Hanushek is a Senior Fellow at the Hoover Institution at Stanford University in California. He has worked in the economics of education field throughout his academic career and has a made a great contribution to further understanding of schooling systems, particularly in the USA. His research spans the impact on achievement of teacher quality, high-stakes accountability and class-size reduction. He pioneered measuring teacher quality on the basis of student achievement, the foundation for current research into the value-added evaluations of teachers and schools. His work on school efficiency is central to debates about school finance adequacy and equity, and his analyses of the economic impact of school outcomes motivate both national and international educational policy design.

## Key theme 5: market reforms in education

A market is any place where buyers and sellers come together to exchange goods, whether physically or virtually via the internet. Very competitive markets are desirable for consumers because they are able to choose between many producers who are selling similar goods, with good information about prices and quality, and with the constant threat of new suppliers forcing existing suppliers to keep prices and profits low. Examples of very competitive markets are the curry houses on 'curry mile' near the universities in Manchester or the market for foreign exchange that you might use before going on holiday.

In most countries there exists a well-functioning market for private school places where wealthier parents can choose a school based on price and quality, and schools are incentivized to make themselves as desirable as possible to parents so that they can survive and often make a profit. Economists argue that competition for pupils can incentivize these schools to use their resources such as buildings, materials and teachers to maximize pupils' achievement because this is the school output that parents value the most. This is known as productive efficiency. Economists also suggest that competition forces schools to produce the type of education, such as the mix of subjects and extra-curricular activities, that is most desired by parents. This is known as allocative efficiency. If they fail to do this in a competitive market, other schools might be able to attract away their potential pupils by producing an environment that is more desirable to parents, with better teaching and learning experiences for the same fee.

By contrast, government-funded schools often operate on a very different basis, with administrators deciding the rules for who gets to go to school where, and little incentive for schools to use money efficiently since they cannot keep surplus money at the end of the year. This has led some economists, such as the American Milton Friedman, to suggest that government-run schools could be made more efficient if they were required to compete for pupils with one another and with private schools. His idea was that parents would each receive a school voucher that would be redeemable against tuition fees at the public or private school of their choice. Thus, schools would receive money only if they successfully attracted students to their school. The English state schooling system has been a 'sort of' (economists call this 'quasi') voucher scheme for over two decades, with parents able to express a preference for any state-funded secondary school and school funding that is partly based on pupil numbers. This means that if English state schools become unpopular they will lose funding. Schools are, in theory, incentivized to improve academic standards through the publication of league tables because parents use these to decide which schools to apply to. Local authorities have traditionally overseen English schools, but there are now hundreds of academies that are independently operated, receiving all their funding from central government. Furthermore, not-for-profit 'free' schools are currently in the process of being opened. The new groups who are planning to open free schools include teachers and parents who want to run schools relatively free of government restrictions on curriculum and organization.

Voucher schemes for schooling have been introduced all over the world to attempt to improve the functioning of schooling systems. In 1981, Chile introduced radical reforms to education that allowed teachers, parents, religious groups or companies to set up private schools, with government vouchers paying the tuition fees for children who decide to attend them. In Chile today about half of all pupils attend a private school and the government voucher means that companies have found it profitable to set up schools in both very deprived and very affluent neighbourhoods. Private schools are able to 'top up' their income from the government by charging very limited additional fees to students, though many choose not to do this, and schools are able to choose which students they wish to educate at their school. The result is that schools in Chile have become rather stratified, with children from poor families concentrated in certain schools and other schools attracting the social elite by charging fees or requiring children to sit entrance exams. So, overall, the scheme does not appear to meet the equity criteria of equality of educational opportunity. Many economists have analysed the impact of the Chilean reforms on pupil achievement at the end of compulsory schooling and have reported mixed findings on the impact of this greater school competition on efficiency (Hsieh and Urquiola 2006).

Sweden has been operating a similar voucher scheme since 1992. Private schools can be set up by anyone and are given funding via a voucher for each of their pupils on exactly the same terms as government schools. However, unlike in Chile, private schools are not able to charge extra tuition fees and they must admit pupils on a 'first-come, first-served' basis. A wide variety of types of private school now educate around 10 per cent of pupils, with specialist language schools, special pedagogy schools and religious schools, alongside general education private schools. Private schools are a little more likely to be used by families with highly educated parents and also by second-generation immigrants, leading to concerns that the system is starting to become socially stratified. Economists have analysed the impact of this reform by comparing areas of Sweden that have seen a growth in private schools with other areas that are still entirely state run. They have shown that children who are educated in areas with many private schools are performing better in subject exams at the end of compulsory schooling. However, the advantages that these children appear to have gained by age 16 do not persist so that they are no more likely do well academically at the age of 19 or participate in higher education than those who were educated in areas with no private schools (Böhlmark and Lindahl 2008).

Overall, most market-based reforms that have tried to improve school standards by encouraging schools to compete for pupils have not achieved the educational improvements that proponents of the reforms hoped for. This may be because education is a very strange product and schools tend to be unusual institutions. For competition to improve school standards we need schools to actually be motivated to attract more pupils and grow; yet headteachers are usually not financially rewarded for doing this. We also need parents to be most attracted to the schools that offer the best-quality learning experiences, but it is difficult for them to know which these are. Parents often use exam results in league tables to indicate school quality, yet the social background of the pupils rather than the quality of teaching primarily determines the league table position of a school. This leads to the unfortunate side-effect of school choice, which is that in order to make themselves as desirable as possible, schools are actually incentivized to admit pupils from high-income backgrounds who are likely to do well academically.

---

### Activity: voucher reforms for schools

The government announces a radical reform to schooling in an area that you know well (perhaps the place where you went to school yourself). Private companies will be free to set up voucher schools, charge some limited additional fees, make profits from this activity and admit whichever pupils they choose. Answer the following questions.

1. Who do you think might set up new schools? For example, can you think of charities, firms, religious organizations, teachers or others who might want to?
2. What will these schools be like? How large will they be? Will they offer general or specialist education?
3. Will they all choose to charge additional fees? If not, why not?
4. Are there already private schools in the area? Will they choose to take part in the new voucher scheme? Why, or why not?
5. What will the impact on existing state schools in the area be? Which state schools are likely to close as a result?
6. Who will benefit from these new private schools? Who is likely to choose to attend them?

**Key figure: Caroline Hoxby**

Caroline Hoxby is an economist at Stanford University in California who has written extensively about education and local public economics in the USA. She is one of the leading US economists in the field of education and plays an important role in influential economic think-tanks, including the National Bureau of Economic Research and the Hoover Institution. She has won numerous awards for her work. She is best known for her work on school choice, and has written several articles that use empirical data to argue that US government schools perform best in situations where they are forced to compete with one another and with the private sector. She has also conducted research into university choice by students and the effects of tuition fees. In schools she has analysed the impact of teacher quality, classroom peers, class sizes and school financing on pupil achievement.

## Conclusion

Although the initial involvement of economists in education policy was limited to understanding the economic value of education in the labour market, their influence now spans large parts of education policy. The research they carry out continues to be appealing to governments because economists appear to provide concrete answers to specific policy questions through large-scale evaluations that often use administrative data. Economists also understand the tensions that are inherent in education policy-making: government budgets are constrained, so policy-makers can never implement every policy that they would like to. Economists provide a clear framework for choosing between education policies, even where policies are intended to affect completely different groups of individuals.

---

**Further research**

Choose an education reform that is proposed by a political party that you think is relevant to the economics of education. You should be able to find one in the manifesto of a political party, or alternatively as an announcement in a broadsheet newspaper.

Summarize the likely impact of the proposed policy on the efficiency and equity of the education system.

---

## Key reading

### Books

Checchi, D. (2008) *The Economics of Education: Human Capital, Family Background and Inequality*. Cambridge: Cambridge University Press. This book provides a comprehensive overview of all the work currently being carried out in the field.

Le Grand, J., Propper, C. and Smith, S. (2008) *The Economics of Social Problems*. London: Palgrave Macmillan. An introduction to economic theory applied to a wide variety of social problems, including education.

Machin, S. and Vignoles, A. (2005) *What's the Good of Education?* Princeton, NJ: Princeton University Press. A non-technical UK perspective on economics of education.

## Journals

Articles by economists about education policy are published in specialist journals such as *Economics of Education Review* and *Education Economics*. They also publish in other economic journals such as *Journal of Public Economics*, *Journal of Labor Economics* and *Journal of Human Resources*.

## Websites

IDEAS at RePEc. Almost all economics of education journal articles are first made available as working papers on the following website: http://ideas.repec.org/j/I2.html

Centre for Market and Public Organization. CMPO at the University of Bristol is one of the largest centres for research in economics of education in the UK: www.bristol.ac.uk/cmpo

Institute for the Study of Labor. The German think-tank IZA publishes many papers in the field of economics of education: www.iza.org

## References

Angrist, J.D. and Lavy, V. (1999) Using Maimonides' rule to estimate the effect of class size on scholastic achievement. *Quarterly Journal of Economics*, 114(2): 533–75.

Blatchford, P. et al. (forthcoming) The impact of support staff on pupils' 'positive approaches to learning' and their academic progress. *British Educational Research Journal*.

Böhlmark, A. and Lindahl, M. (2008) *Does School Privatization Improve Educational Achievement? Evidence from Sweden's Voucher Reform*. IZA discussion paper 3691.

Buchanan, J. (1986) *Liberty, Market and State: Political Economy in the 1980s*. New York: New York University Press

Chevalier, A., Dolton, P. and McIntosh, S. (2007) Recruiting and retaining teachers in the UK: an analysis of graduate occupation choice from the 1960s to the 1990s. *Economica*, 74: 69–96.

Chowdry, H., Crawford, C., Dearden, L., Goodman, A. and Vignoles, A. (2008) *Widening Participation in Higher Education: Analysis Using Linked Administrative Data*. IFS research report 2008/69.

Dewey, J., Husted, T.A. and Kenny, L.W. (2000) The ineffectiveness of school inputs: a product of misspecification? *Economics of Education Review*, 19(1): 27–45.

Eide, E., Goldhaber, D. and Brewer, D. (2004) The teacher labour market and teacher quality. *Oxford Review of Economic Policy*, 20(2): 230–44.

Hanushek, E. and Woessman, L. (2009) *Do Better Schools Lead to More Growth? Cognitive Skills, Economic Outcomes, and Causation*. IZA discussion paper 4575.

Hsieh, C. and Urquiola, M. (2006) The effects of generalized school choice on achievement and stratification: evidence from Chile's voucher program. *Journal of Public Economics*, 90(8–9): 1477–503.

Krueger, A.B. (1999) Experimental estimates of education production functions. *Quarterly Journal of Economics*, 114(2): 497–532.

Ladd, H.F. (1999) The Dallas school accountability and incentive program: an evaluation of its impacts on student outcomes. *Economics of Education Review*, 18(1): 1–16.

Lavy, V. (2002) Evaluating the effect of teachers' group performance incentives on pupil achievement. *Journal of Political Economy*, 110(6): 1286–317.

Le Grand, J. (2003) *Motivation, Agency and Public Policy: Of Knights and Knaves, Pawns and Queens*. Oxford: Oxford University Press.

Machin, S. (2008) The new economics of education: methods, evidence and policy. *Journal of Population Economics*, 21: 1–19.

McMahon, W. (2004) The social and external benefits of education. In G. Johnes and J. Johnes (eds) *International Handbook on the Economics of Education*. Cheltenham: Edward Elgar.

Nozick, R. (1974) *Anarchy, State and Society*. New York: Basic Books.

Psacharopoulas, G. (1994) Returns to investment in education: a global update. *World Development*, 22(9): 1325–43.

Rawls, J. (1971) *A Theory of Justice*. Cambridge, MA: Harvard University Press.

Slater, H., Burgess, S. and Davies, N. (2009) *Do Teachers Matter? Measuring the Variation in Teacher Effectiveness in England*. CMPO discussion paper 09/212.

Wild, R., Munro, F. and Ayoubkhani, D. (2009) *Public Service Output, Input and Productivity: Education*. London: Office for National Statistics.

# 5

# RICHARD WALLER
## The Sociology of Education

### Learning outcomes

By the end of this chapter you should be able to:

- explain how sociology aids our understanding of educational processes and systems;
- demonstrate an understanding of key concepts and theoretical approaches in the sociology of education, and how they have changed over time;
- show an awareness of social context, of social diversity and inequality, and their impact on educational processes and outcomes;
- explain sociologically why different social groups achieve differential outcomes from engaging with education;
- outline an understanding of the appropriate use of research strategies and methods in gaining sociological knowledge.

## Introduction

When studying the sociology of education an inevitable overlap with most if not all of the disciplinary foci of this book's other chapters soon becomes apparent. We cannot examine the sociology of education without understanding its history, and the politics, economics, philosophy and psychology underpinning it. The notion of comparing education systems and people's experiences of engaging with them across different societies and over time in a given society is central to this process as well. This overlap is illustrated by reference to some key researchers and theorists cited in this chapter. American writers Samuel Bowles and Herbert Gintis are primarily considered economists, while Stephen Ball writes largely upon policy and its implications for people. As he himself notes: 'it is sometimes difficult to say who is a sociologist of education and who is not' (2004: 1), although Ball undoubtedly is.

Any account of something the size and complexity of the sociology of education is inevitably a partial one. There are many potential topics for inclusion in this chapter, and any student of the subject is strongly advised to read around it widely. Some pointers for further reading appear in this chapter, and I hope the subjects covered inspire you to explore this fascinating topic further.

---

**Activity: what is the sociology of education?**

Sociology is essentially the study of society and social life. With this broad definition in mind, suggest a list of key concerns and interests a sociologist of education might have. Compare your list to the one below; how closely aligned were you?

---

Lauder et al. (2009) recently outlined six key questions they suggest have structured the sociological study of education since the 1950s. I have developed their ideas to come up with a list of ten.

1. What is the purpose of schooling?
2. How does education affect the life chances of different groups in society?
3. Why do some social groups generally 'win' in terms of educational outcomes and others 'lose'?
4. What causes individual members of such groups to vary from these norms?
5. How can educational processes be understood?
6. What do pupils learn at school along with the official curriculum?
7. Does education liberate people or control them?
8. How are educational outcomes and economic success related for individuals and the wider society?
9. How do people's educational experiences affect their sense of identity?
10. What role does post-compulsory education play in society?

You will notice the overlap referred to in the chapter's introduction above with other academic disciplines. Question 1 for instance is central to the philosophy of education (Chapter 3), while question 9 is equally applicable to the psychology of education (Chapter 6), and question 8 to the economics of it (Chapter 4).

## A brief history of the sociology of education

### The 1950s: early days and political arithmetic

As suggested earlier, in the UK the sociological study of education began in earnest in the 1950s. Much early work was centred on the London School of Economics (LSE), which many credit with developing the popularity of sociology itself (Dale 2001; Halsey 2004; Lauder et al. 2009). The LSE's early work focused upon social mobility – that is, people changing social class (how we categorize people's jobs into a broad system of social stratification or hierarchy) during their working life from that they were ascribed (allocated) at birth. Studying educational opportunity and social mobility within an industrial democracy is known as the 'political arithmetic' tradition within the UK, and 'educational sociology' in the USA. It generally used large statistical datasets to examine social inequality over time, and was set within a particular paradigm (i.e. a way of seeing and understanding the world) dominating the sociology of education. This is often referred to as the Increased Meritocratic Selection (IMS). See Key theme 2 below for a fuller discussion of these issues.

Education policy changes followed the recognition that, despite the expansion of secondary schooling for all after the Second World War with the 1944 Butler Education Act, massive social inequality persisted, which the education system enjoyed limited success tackling. Comprehensive schooling was widely introduced in the mid-1960s, although it never fully replaced selection through the 11+ examination across the UK (see Key theme 3 below for further discussion of this). A new graduate-level teacher education qualification, the Bachelor of Education (BEd), was introduced around the same time, both longer and at a higher level than its predecessor. The sociology of education was central to the BEd, along with other disciplines featuring in this volume. This approach of 'educating' rather than merely 'training' new teachers, developing a deeper understanding of the role and purpose of education within society, held sway until Margaret Thatcher's Conservative government changed such programmes' content in the mid-1980s.

---

**Key text No. 1**

Ball (2004) provides a lively, accessible and informative collection, and at about 300 pages, far more portable than that by Halsey et al. (1997) The editor is probably the leading contemporary writer on the sociology of education, particularly on educational policy. This collection draws largely upon people still writing today, and is structured to demonstrate the concerns of contemporary sociologists of education. It contains seven sections each containing two readings: 'Social Class', 'Globalisation and the Economy', 'Gender', 'Regulation', 'Curriculum', 'Teacher', 'Students' and 'Classroom'. While there are obvious omissions here (ethnicity for instance), these are often covered in the selected articles – the reading on 'youthful masculinities' by O'Donnell and Sharpe for instance covers how the masculinity of young men is nuanced by class, ethnicity and rural/urban localities.

---

## The 1960s: the interactionists

Interactionist or ethnographic sociologists (studying smaller-scale, personal actions rather than the bigger population-wide outcomes of those from the political arithmetic tradition) grew in influence throughout the 1960s. Writers including Hargreaves, Lacey and later Ball demonstrated how, far from being a neutral 'black box' that pupils just passed through exempt from any effects, the structure of schools and expectations of those working in them impacted enormously upon children's education and wider social outcomes. This tendency to study the structures and processes of secondary schooling is explored in Key theme 2 below.

## The 1970s: the new sociology of education

In the early 1970s, an alternative, altogether more controversial approach to the discipline developed, the so-called 'new sociology of education' (NSOE), perhaps best exemplified by the early work of Michael F.D. Young (e.g. 1971). Young's edited collection, which included contributions from Basil Bernstein and Pierre Bourdieu, marked a change in direction for the sociology of education, exploring for the first time teachers' roles in reproducing social inequalities. The political arithmetic approach had positioned teachers and schools as neutral agents in this process, but work by Young and his collaborators demonstrated another side to education. It was no longer considered a primarily progressive force for greater equality and increased personal autonomy as intended by those introducing the raft of educational policies as part of the expanding post-war welfare state. Instead it was 'deeply implicated in the reproduction of (social) inequality' (Lauder et al. 2009: 573).

---

### Activity: education systems and the reproduction of inequality

Consider *how* the education system may reproduce social inequality. What factors may hinder some people succeeding at school or assist others? Write a list. Which of these are largely within an individual's control (i.e. their 'agency'), or a consequence of their place in society (i.e. 'structural')? To some extent all are a combination of the two, but consider which exerts the biggest influence. This notion of 'structure versus agency' runs through the study of sociology generally, just as 'nature versus nurture' is central to the study of psychology, or whether we are fundamentally competitive or cooperative beings underpins the study of politics.

---

As Dale (2001) suggests, the NSOE offered several new aspects to substantiate its claim to be a fundamentally differing approach to the political arithmetic tradition. The most important of these were its focus upon the curriculum as an appropriate topic for sociologists of education to study, and its emphasis on the potentially liberating activities of teachers and teacher educators – they were agents of potential social change. NSOE's primary focus remained persistent social class inequalities within the education system, similar to the political arithmetic tradition, but their proscribed remedies differed significantly. It moved away from tackling educational structures and towards the key role of individuals working within the system.

## The 1980s: an external ideological attack

Nearly two decades of Conservative government (1979–97), including the most ideologically antagonistic period under Margaret Thatcher's leadership (1979–90) led to major changes within UK educational policy and the sociology of education's response. This period is characterized by a significant legislative programme including the introduction of the National Curriculum, and of grant maintained schools and other market-led reforms, particularly to secondary schools. These reforms led to the neo-liberal (i.e. where individual wishes are promoted above strategic planning by the state) ideology of parental choice determining school provision, rather than Local Education Authorities; these changes have since continued under both Conservative and Labour governments, and, since May 2010, under the Conservative/Liberal-Democrat coalition.

In terms of its institutional location and wider status and significance, the 1980s witnessed a distinct downturn in the sociology of education's fortunes. This resulted from a clear ideological attack by the government of the day; sociology graduates were denied entry to teacher training courses; and the subject was effectively removed from the curriculum of teacher education courses (along with philosophy and psychology). Lauder et al. (2009) also point to what they consider attacks on the Open University, by then established as a leading centre of the discipline through its publications and study programmes.

---

**Key figures: Samuel Bowles (1939–) and Herbert Gintis (1940–)**

Contemporary American thinkers who generally work together, both of whom are more properly described as economists rather than sociologists, though Gintis is sometimes considered a 'behavioural scientist'. In their book, *Schooling in Capitalist America*, Bowles and Gintis (1975) developed an important idea in the sociology of education, the 'Correspondence Principle'. This explains how in its structures, norms and values, the internal organization of schools corresponds to that of the capitalist workplace. For instance, hierarchy systems in school reflect inequalities in the labour market's structure, with the head teacher as the managing director and pupils as factory workers. Formal education offers insights into interactions in the workplace, with young people preparing for entry into the labour market.

---

## The 1980s onwards: challenges from within

Simultaneously, within the discipline, during the 1980s onwards, some criticized the traditional emphasis placed upon white working-class boys and their education – Willis's study being a good example (see Key text No. 2 on p. 120), and this remains an ongoing concern. Feminists including Miriam David and Gaby Weiner helped the issue of gender adopt an increasingly central position within the discipline, while others including Heidi Mirza and David Gilborn kept ethnicity to the fore. Authors including Mairtin Mac an Ghaill and Debbie Epstein focused upon sexuality, while Len Barton and Harry Daniels among others explored students with disabilities. Stephen Ball (2004) termed this the period of 'minority epistemologies' or 'standpoint theories'; the attribution of a particularly focused analysis of the experiences of those traditionally marginalized by the sociology of education, and indeed other academic disciplines.

**Activity: researching key authors**

In your library or on the internet look up some of the names in the section above and read some of their work to get a flavour of their interests. Consider the criticism they might level at those primarily focusing upon the educational attainment of white working-class boys.

## The 1990s to the present day

Some writers identify a 'policy turn' in the sociology of education throughout the 1990s. Lauder et al. (2009) for instance outline how throughout the decade both major UK political parties sought to standardize or, pejoratively, 'teacher-proof' key areas of pedagogy (i.e. teaching), curriculum and assessment. Their primary area of interest concerned improving schools' performance through changing key personnel – or at least their approach – through managing them differently. More recently much government policy and the sociology of education has concerned the school effectiveness and school improvement (SESI) movement. This links with attempts from the 1970s onwards approaching issues of inequality in education through exploring factors present in 'good schools' and 'bad schools', and to improve schools by changing them accordingly. Much media coverage and local authority energies have gone into recruiting supposed 'super heads' to bring dramatic changes to schools, often based upon stricter discipline and uniform codes, in an attempt to raise standards.

Stephen Ball is often associated with studying such social policy, or perhaps more specifically, its impact upon people. Like Bernstein, who was writing on the topic in the 1960s, Ball is concerned with how the middle classes utilize policy for their benefit, effectively to the detriment of less privileged others. As I write this, a debate is taking place regarding the merits of 'free schools' (as championed by coalition government Education Minister, Michael Gove), set up by parents and other interested parties, the impact on the education of the children who might attend free schools, and, an area often of little concern to such parents, those excluded from such arrangements. This topic will be another key future area of work for sociologists of education. Stephen Ball explored the creeping privatization of state education in his book, *Education plc* (2007), an issue coming increasingly to the fore under the coalition government.

**Activity: Stephen Ball's work**

Using internet facilities see what areas of policy Stephen Ball has researched. You can use a library electronic journal search engine, look at his homepage at the Institute of Education (www.ioe.ac.uk) or just google his name.

The six key themes below cover various issues concerning sociologists of education, from the mid-20th century to today. The topics chosen are all key areas of interest and scholarship, but are just a selection from many possibilities, as any chapter this length could only ever be. The idea is to provide an overview of each topic, with references to related issues and recommendations for further study.

## Key theme 1: the role and function of education in society

If you have studied sociology before, for instance at A level or on a BTEC course, you will be familiar with the notion of functionalism; it approaches the study of society by considering an aspect of it – the education system in this instance – and examining what role it performs. Functionalism was the dominant theoretical perspective while the sociology of education was becoming established in Britain in the 1950s, as explained earlier. It underpins the political arithmetic tradition outlined below, which dominated the sociology of education until the early 1970s. The work of the French functionalist, Emile Durkheim (1858–1917), one of the founders of sociology, influenced Basil Bernstein. While functionalism has not always found favour among academic writers and theorists, it is generally popular with the media and policy-makers.

---

### Activity: the role and function of sociology

Having read the summary of the historical development of the sociology of education and the ideas of a few key theorists, make a list of alternative roles different sociologists think the education system plays within wider society. Remember, as with any group of 'experts', be they art critics, football commentators or economists, different people have different beliefs and values, and you should draw that out here. Consider what it does for individuals and organizations as well as wider society. Revisit this exercise when you have finished this chapter.

---

Durkheim's major concern was how modern industrial society held itself together following the breakdown of traditional religious-based forms of social solidarity or cohesion in agrarian society. He decided the answer was the social role played by the education system, whose central function was to make children 'social beings'. For Durkheim, education is the primary means for society perpetuating itself through recreating the conditions of its very existence; that is, preparing children for collective life. This involves encouraging both homogeneity (similarity) and diversification (difference). Societies are constructed by the values and practices of groups within them, and the education system imparts these to 'asocial beings', a process known as 'socialization'. School functions like an abridged form of society, with similar structures and rules, and the classroom is where a child learns to be disciplined within a social setting, and to strive for collective goals (see the following key figure box on Ivan Illich and the 'hidden curriculum').

**Key figure: Ivan Illich (1926–2002)**

Ivan Illich was a controversial figure in educational thinking, and another addressing disciplinary issues and concerns ranging across other chapters in this book. He was born in Austria, studying there and in Italy before becoming a Catholic priest, a role that led him to New York initially, then to Latin and South America. There he became outspoken against the impact of economic development upon traditional ways of life, blaming it for destroying knowledge and skills, and ultimately the self-sufficiency of non-industrial societies. Illich is best known for two key ideas, the first of which is from his book, *Deschooling Society* (1971). In this radical and influential text he proposed abolishing formal education, suggesting it did nothing positive for the poorest, and turned all of us into passive consumers. Long ahead of his time in terms of adopting technology to benefit educational processes, Illich called for its harnessing to develop mutually beneficial 'learning webs'.

Illich's second key contribution to the study of education was his role in developing notions of the *hidden curriculum*. In some quarters Illich is attributed with coining the phrase, while others suggest that a variety of other writers did so, including John Dewey and Phillip Jackson. However, even if Illich did not invent the expression, he did, along with other radical educators including the Brazilian Paulo Freire (1921–97) and John Holt (1923–85), develop it further. The idea strikingly expresses the notion that schools do not simply teach the official, formal curriculum, but also transmit values, processes, rules and, most importantly, social relationships. Schools thus help maintain the existing (unequal) social order, a function of schooling having far greater impact on students than learning the formal curriculum itself.

As well as socialization, functionalists see other key roles that education plays, including social selection – that is, determining how given social roles in society are allocated to particular individuals. For functionalists this is decided by ability, suitability and effort, and involves a degree of inter-generational mobility, with the children of, say, lawyers or road-sweepers not necessarily following their parents into similar-status occupations. Education has a central role in ensuring ascriptive (inherited) social status is not simply reinforced, but that the most capable and hardest-working pupils get the best-rewarded positions.

Through school, pupils internalize the value of achievement, meaning they accept inequality in outcomes of status and wealth later in life. This is an integrating function for schools, counteracting strains imposed by social differentiation. It is crucial here that whilst they see people's academic abilities as correlated with family status (academically high-achieving parents are more likely to have high-achieving children for instance) there must still be space in the system for a genuine selective process.

So functionalists including Durkheim and eminent American sociologist Talcott Parsons (1902–79) suggest the education system is meritocratic. However, problems arise from the existence of meritocracy, for example lower-class students may find the personal costs of achievement too great (see Key theme 6 on HE choice, *habitus* and risk). Personal stakes for bright, low-status pupils are high. They may reject school for fear of 'burning bridges' with peers and members of their family. But for functionalists this demonstrates the system's success rather than its failures, despite 'costs' to the individuals involved. As suggested throughout this chapter, much subsequent work in the sociology of education sought to demonstrate the continuance of ascriptive factors in education (see for instance the following section on the IMS thesis or political arithmetic approach, and the topics on strategies middle-class parents employ to ensure their children do not fall down the social ladder).

Unlike contemporary functionalists, Durkheim is not socially conservative (i.e. against large-scale social change). When writing in the late 19th and early 20th centuries he argued that society had not reached a point where people's place was determined by talent and effort, resulting in it being a source of 'anomie' (social disaffection or isolation) as a consequence. Durkheim's solution was to abolish inheritance to improve the class structure's fluidity, ensuring a fairer distribution of 'social goods'.

## Key theme 2: reducing inequality – social mobility and the political arithmetic approach

This section considers a view of education that dominated educational policy and in turn research within the sociology of education after 1944. Education is linked to the economy in providing employment skills, to the class structure in providing social fluidity and movement, and to democracy by offering individual fulfilment and opportunity. As society develops industrially, technological progress imposes growing demands for talent developed by the education system, which coincides with western societies' democratic ideology based on individual freedom and opportunity. Behind this lies a Durkheimian vision of a society where differences in outcome are accepted because *all* have the opportunity to succeed.

This notion is of a 'meritocratic' society where the rewards someone gets in terms of status and money are determined by their efforts and abilities rather than what they have inherited. The process of a society moving towards a meritocracy is in three stages, as Michael Young outlines (Young 1958). (Please note that, rather confusingly, this is not the Michael F.D. Young featured in the key figure section below). Remember, this is a 'macro' theory which considers society as a whole rather than just a given individual.

1. During industrialization, the link between people's social origins and their educational attainment weakens over time, as all human resources are developed to maximize economic productivity.

2. Meanwhile, the link between educational attainment and class destination strengthens over time as ability and motivation become dominant criteria for selection to the best-paid and most prestigious positions, and achievement prevails over 'ascription' – that is, social status at birth.

3. The link between class origins and destinations thus weakens over time, so society becomes more meritocratic.

As noted above, this *Increasing Meritocratic Society* (IMS) view dominated social policy in the second half of the 20th century, for example underpinning the New

Labour government's view of education during its time in office (1997–2010). As suggested earlier it also dominated the sociology of education; Dale (2001) for instance called it the discipline's 'dominant project'. Work including Halsey's *Origins and Destinations* (1980) study was highly influential to thinkers and policy-makers alike, and remains so today. This approach is also known as political arithmetic. The model is so powerful because education itself is; the whole of the rational, enlightened, industrial society requires an educated population, and for society to perform to its full potential requires everyone to have an equal opportunity to benefit from it fully. So, has it worked? Is Britain a more meritocratic society now than it was before the major post-war educational reforms?

The short answer is yes, but not by much or to the extent most people would hope. Returning to Young's three-point approach above, British research has failed to reveal any consistent movement to greater fluidity. As Halsey (1980: 205) suggested, 'the hereditary curse upon English education is its organisation upon lines of social class'. And this phenomenon continues today; just look at league tables for school performance or the social background of those accessing the most prestigious universities today. In both cases a clear link exists between economic advantage and higher performance, so education has not significantly removed the effect of class origins on destinations.

That is not to say no one was affected by this widening of opportunity, just that its effects were not as wide ranging as anticipated or hoped for. Research showed that in the middle period of the 20th century education *did* become more important in terms of destinations. Generally those people moving up the social order did so through gaining educational qualifications, my own father for instance. My dad was born in 1940 to a working-class family in London's East End. His father worked on a factory production line in a dirty, unpleasant and dangerous job using poisonous chemicals. My dad was the eldest of three sons, doing well enough in his end-of-primary school 11+ exam to go not to a grammar school but a technical school rather than the secondary modern his younger brothers later attended. My father left secondary school with sufficient qualifications to get an engineering apprenticeship, eventually becoming a senior engineer, a solidly middle-class job. My two uncles both left school with little by way of qualifications and worked in manual jobs until they retired – one was a docker, the other a lorry driver.

---

### Activity: family educational biographies

Using the example of my father and his brothers, or people from your own family if you prefer, think about what life chances and opportunities education offers (or denies!) people. Think too about the impact on the opportunities and life chances on later generations of the families concerned.

---

But stories such as my father's, of greater education leading to class mobility, are not the norm. Research shows presumptions of greater correlation between educational attainment and class destination not holding for recent decades – that is, 'by the later twentieth century the part played by education in mediating class mobility was no longer growing but, rather, in decline' (Jackson et al. 2005: 6). Work contrasting two cohorts, born in 1958 and 1970, found the association between origins and destinations is stable across this period, suggesting society had not become *more* meritocratic (as expected by the IMS thesis). For men and women the effects of education on the type of job they actually had are weaker in the latter period. Jackson et al. (2005: 6) argued the effect of class is largely explained by the difficulties associated with mobility strategies 'from below'; people trying to be upwardly mobile face greater barriers than those trying not to move downwards. The 'glass floor', an invisible barrier stopping people falling down the social hierarchy, is as impenetrable as the more familiar 'glass ceiling' preventing others rising higher. The 2009 government report (chaired by MP Alan Milburn, the ex-Minister for Health) on 'fair access to the professions' (Milburn 2009) proves interesting reading in this context; it can easily be obtained via the internet.

---

**Key figure: Michael F.D. Young**

Michael F.D. Young, a key figure in NSOE (see above), is based at the Institute of Education. Writing in the early 1970s, he led the move from sociologists of education being primarily concerned with the uneven distribution of educational outcomes, to one where the interplay of knowledge, the curriculum and power are to the fore – e.g. see his 1971 work *Knowledge and Control*.

However, Young's more recent work, brought together in a collection entitled, *Bringing Knowledge Back In: From Social Constructivism to Social Realism in the Sociology of Education* (2008), signals a change of emphasis with him now asserting the importance of 'knowledge' and subject-specific teaching in formal educational settings.

---

## Key theme 3: from meritocracy to the marketplace – the social impact of post-war changes in educational policy

Building on earlier work by Phillip Brown (1997), Taylor et al. (2005) subsequently identified four post-war phases of secondary school provision in the UK, especially England, each with particular characteristics, priorities and problems.

1.  *The rise of mass secondary education* (1944–60s)
    *   compulsory secondary education introduced;
    *   plurality of provision;
    *   tripartite system;
    *   state funding of faith schools;

- parents expressed preferences between schools, e.g. single sex or co-educational, religious or secular;
- sought to give opportunities to academically capable working-class children.

However, although schools were meant to cross social boundaries, the middle classes were massively over-represented in grammar schools.

2. *Introduction and expansion of comprehensive education* (late 1960s–early 1980s)
   - shift from plurality towards homogeneous provision;
   - part of wider welfare reforms, e.g. social housing;
   - greater *equality of opportunity*;
   - provision varied nationally – mixed Local Education Authority (LEA) enthusiasm;
   - geographical admission policies – i.e. school catchment areas.

Theoretically, there was considerable choice between types of school, especially in urban areas where higher population densities allowed greater provision. However, middle-class children were more likely to live near ex-grammar schools, generally in wealthier areas, or were more willing to travel to 'better' schools, reducing the actual social mix sought by policy-makers.

3. *Diversity through quasi-markets in education* (early 1980s–late 1990s)
   - neo-conservative attempts to confront comprehensive system's 'problems';
   - some state schools moved outside LEA control;
   - state/private partnership of some schools;
   - City Technology Colleges programme (1986);
   - grant maintained (GM) schools established in 1988 Education Reform Act;
   - some selectivity possible in GM schools.

Again, there were problems in some areas, with many LEAs unable to meet demand at high-performing GM schools. As previously, middle-class children again enjoyed the greatest opportunities.

4. *New Labour and school diversity* (1997–2005)
   - education *the* priority of New Labour government, which suggested 'standards, not structures are the key to success';
   - mixture of choice and competition with new public accountability practices;
   - attempts to end selectivity largely rhetorical, for example ballots on the abolition of the 160-odd remaining grammar schools involved only the parents of children studying there, but not the lesser status secondary modern schools adversely affected by policies of selection;
   - some policy shift from diversity to homogeneity of provision, for example through the abolition of the Assisted Places Scheme offering poorer working-class children funding towards private education fees;

- intervention to pursue higher standards, for example National Literacy and Numeracy Strategies, expansion of specialist schools, support for city academies;
- some 'privatization', for example the transfer of 'failing' schools in an era of increased surveillance to commercial organizations and out of LEA control;
- greater resourcing of disadvantaged communities, such as Education Action Zones, Excellence in Cities initiatives.

Again, despite progress in tackling social exclusion, the middle classes tended to benefit under these policies.

While writing this chapter, the precise educational policy direction of the new coalition government elected in May 2010 is unclear, though moves are afoot to increase the number of academies (self-governing but publicly funded schools), and to make it easier to establish 'free schools', independently established and funded by government but not regulated in the same manner. In my opinion neither of these policy directives will help equalize opportunities between working- and middle-class children; rather they will have the opposite effect. The UK's Equality and Human Rights Commission's October 2010 report *How Fair is Britain?* (EHRC 2010) is a good place to start when looking at inequality and educational outcomes in terms of class, gender, sexuality, disability or ethnicity – again this can easily be obtained online.

Other major coalition government changes include the abolition of the Education Maintenance Allowance, paid to 16–18 year olds from low-income households to stay in education, and the funding of HE, with universities being allowed to charge up to £9000 annually for undergraduate course fees. The impact of these policies is likely to be reduced rates of participation by students from poorer backgrounds in post-compulsory education, and a further polarization between elite and other universities in terms of their student intake.

It is not possible to include all of these elements in this chapter – a choice has to be made – and I have chosen to focus on class and gender issues. The issue of race and ethnicity in education has been touched on in Chapter 1 of this book, and some key books (Banks, Panayi, Gilborn) are cited there.

---

### Activity: the policy decision-making process

List the arguments for and against introducing a policy such as that of abolishing the Assisted Places Scheme referred to earlier, the money from which was used to reduce class sizes in all state primary schools. How should a government balance policies that greatly benefit a small number of individuals against those benefiting a larger number to a lesser extent? This dilemma has lain at the heart of educational policy making decisions for the last century or more, and such issues are discussed in this book's other chapters.

## Key theme 4: schools and gendered identity

Since the late 1990s the improved performance of girls in both exam results and progression to university has been allied to the view that the problem in education now revolves around boys' underachievement. Some now argue that problems associated with girls' education have now been dealt with, but this is interpreted by others as part of a backlash against feminism. This section looks at work questioning these assumptions. I highlight recent studies of femininity and masculinity in schools, to consider the gendered identities now readily available to children at school.

Three general themes emerge from the studies, namely that:

1.  certain forms of masculinity remain hegemonic – that is, dominant over other forms of masculinity and over femininity;
2.  some forms of femininity are still difficult to achieve, especially those associated with being clever;
3.  even girls choosing transgressive forms of femininity (i.e. those deviating from 'the norm') generally reinforce masculinity's dominance.

The work cited later generally sees gender as 'performance', in other words something needing to be 'achieved' and competently performed (Butler 1988). It is based on distinguishing between sex and gender. Sex is determined by biology – we are born male or female – while gender is socially constructed; this is another good example of the nature/nurture discussion referred to earlier. Boys and girls are actively engaged in constructing their own gender identities, and appropriate masculine or feminine behaviour in one context may be wholly inappropriate in another. In school, children are part of a gender 'regime', with a number of competing definitions of masculinity and femininity at play. These revolve around behaviour inside and outside the classroom, subjects discussed in formal and informal settings, and their presentation of themselves in terms of dress, speech and body language, etc.

The last decade or so has witnessed a large number of studies on this topic, and the most frequent conclusion is often one of hegemonic masculinity: it is better being a boy, an opinion shared by boys and girls alike. As Reay (2001:164) suggests, 'the contemporary orthodoxy that girls are doing better than boys masks the complex messiness of gender relations in which, despite girls' better educational attainment, within this peer group, the prevalent view is that it's better being a boy'. Many studies found that white middle-class masculinity is idealized, with academic boys being the most popular in class, especially if the boys concerned are thought to achieve academically without working hard, what Renold (2001: 586) referred to as boys positioning themselves as 'knowers'. In her study, high achievement for both boys and girls was problematic, often involving 'crossing traditional gender boundaries and/or being positioned outside conventional modes of "masculinity" and "femininity"'.

> **Key figure: Diane Reay**
>
> Possibly the most prolific current British sociologist of education, Diane Reay, an ex-primary school teacher, is now at the University of Cambridge. She has worked with a number of other key writers, notably Stephen Ball among those discussed here. A leading thinker and writer on Bourdieu, Reay's research usually revolves around issues of social justice, and she has written about class, ethnicity and gender inequalities across all sectors of education (see Reay 1998; Reay et al. 2005). She is on the editorial board of *BJSE* among several other publications. You can see a summary of her interests and access many of her recent publications via this link to her university homepage: http://www.educ.cam.ac.uk/people/staff/reay/

## Forms of femininity

Reay (2001: 158) wrote of 'Nice Girls' – middle class, hard-working and well-behaved, who 'exemplified the constraints of a gendered and classed discourse which afforded them the benefits of culture, taste and cleverness but little freedom'. Nice girls were seen as a 'contaminating presence', excluded from social activities by boys and considered boring by other girls. This is a recurring theme; Renold (2001) wrote of 'Square Girls' for instance, while the anti-academic working-class girls identified have been variously labelled 'Spice Girls' (Reay 2001) and 'Girlies' (Hey 1997).

## Forms of masculinity

As with studies of femininity in primary schools, there have been recent studies of boys and masculinity, though the classic ones tend to be of secondary schooling. The key one is Paul Willis's (1977) study of 'The Lads' – see key text box below.

> **Key text No. 2**
>
> In *Learning to Labour: How Working Class Kids Get Working Class Jobs*, Willis (1977) demonstrates how education reproduces social inequality. It is interesting methodologically. Willis, broadly speaking a Marxist sociologist, rather than simply doing one-off interviews with his participants, followed a group of boys intensively for an extended period. The book details how a group of anti-school white working-class boys – 'The Lads' – subverted school rules to increase their enjoyment of time spent there. While they disliked school's authoritarian structures intensely, they enjoyed the social activities it offered. Their whole approach involved 'having a laff', and they enjoyed challenging teachers and other authority figures. They treated pupils outside their group with disdain, particularly the more academic group, 'the ear 'oles', working-class boys studying hard, in an attempt to achieve social mobility and a better life than their parents enjoyed. Notions of 'manual' work being masculine and 'mental'

work feminine were clearly embedded in The Lads' world-view; the boys wanted to leave school and join their fathers, uncles and other male relatives in local factories. They considered work something to be endured rather than enjoyed, and a central tenet of masculinity. While they recognized similarities between work and school (see box on Bowles and Gintis and the Correspondence Principle, page 110) they were desperate to earn money, and approached school as a training ground for subverting and challenging the authority structures they would face at work.

Mairtin Mac an Ghail (1994) undertook a later study of masculine forms in a socially mixed comprehensive school, contrasting Willis's study of schooling in a predominantly working-class area. He found four clear forms of masculinity amongst the boys.

1. 'Real Englishmen'. Upper middle-class boys who considered themselves more intelligent than the teachers, and high in what Bourdieu would consider valuable cultural capital. They sought to achieve academically, but without being seen to work hard, and often studied subjects like drama and English which do not equate with traditional working-class forms of masculinity.

2. 'Academic achievers'. Hard-working boys from upper working- or lower middle-class backgrounds. Like Willis's 'ear 'oles', they saw education as a means to achieving social mobility and better-paid, higher-status work than their parents had.

3. 'New enterprisers'. These were also hard working, but generally studying topics like computing and business studies, neither of which were available when Willis was writing. They generally came from white or Asian lower middle or upper working-class families.

4. 'Macho lads'. Working-class boys with an anti-academic attitude, similar to Willis's 'Lads'. They too expressed their masculinity primarily through physical prowess.

A general conclusion from this range of studies is of the different forms of masculinity and femininity available to boys and girls in school, and that while they are usually associated with particular class (structural) groupings and ethnicities, each is difficult to achieve, requiring sometimes considerable personal effort to 'perform' (agency) convincingly. The subject of sexuality and gendered identities at school has also been explored by others – see Mellor and Epstein (2006) for instance.

### Activity: constructing gendered identities through education

Think back to your schooling, both primary and secondary. How familiar are the characterizations identified by the various writers mentioned above – Willis, Reay and Mac an Ghail? Consider your current college or university – are there different forms of gendered identity among students there too? This is an under-researched area of study, perhaps one you could consider exploring in an independent study or project on your course.

## Key theme 5: education and the middle classes

This section considers work examining social reproduction (i.e. how people come to fill the roles they do in society) by focusing on how reproduction is 'enacted' by the daily activities of middle-class parents and children. The importance of this has led writers including Bernstein to argue the need for 'a sociology of the middle classes'.

### The middle classes and social closure

Early work on social closure (the ability to restrict access to desirable resources including high-status, well-paid jobs) drew on the work of Weber who, like Marx and Durkheim, was another 'founder of sociology'. Weber wrote of how rationalization and bureaucracy were key features of modern society, and the rational pursuit of profit a key feature of capitalism. Bureaucracy's impact was to make formal qualifications necessary to take up positions in businesses or government offices. As Giddens (1971: 158) suggests, 'recruitment is based upon demonstration of specialised competence via competitive examinations or the possession of diplomas or degrees giving evidence of appropriate qualifications'.

For Weber an individual's class situation equated to their 'market situation', as defined by property and skills. This approach permits a clearer understanding of the situation of middle-class groups, whose position may be defined solely in terms of their skills or educational qualifications – doctors or university lecturers, for instance. This fraction of the middle classes has no significant property or wealth to pass to its children, so transmitting their privileged position is done through ensuring they gain the necessary qualifications to stay ahead in the race for social privileges.

As outlined earlier and throughout this chapter, the major response from sociology to class reproduction issues in education focused on either working-class failure, or on social and cultural reproduction. The former can be criticized for 'blaming' working-class children for their failure as a 'deficit' model, while the latter, with its focus on social structure, leaves little place for an individual's actions, in other words structure is overly prioritized above agency.

---

**Key figure: Basil Bernstein (1924–2000)**

Probably the most influential British sociologist of education, not least through the vast numbers of his ex-students working within the area. Bernstein's early thinking shaped the discipline of socio-linguistics through his work on speech codes, while his later writing on the structuring of knowledge and pedagogy is central to the sociology of education. He was, with Michael F.D. Young, a leader of the New Sociology of Education movement (see above), and was also perhaps the first sociologist to call for the sociological study of the middle classes, work that many others, including notably Stephen Ball, continue today. Bernstein's book *Class, Codes and Control* (1971) is his most important work, while a good recent account of his work comes in the Ivinson et al. (2010) book.

### Bernstein's language codes

For ex-A level Sociology students, Bernstein's work on speech codes is likely to be familiar. Bernstein developed a notion that middle-class children spoke in a more readily understood 'elaborate code' with a wider vocabulary than their 'restricted code'-speaking working-class counterparts, whose language may lack comprehensibility to 'an outsider' unfamiliar with the slang or specific vocabulary. The code spoken (which is learned from parents through socialization) acts as a marker of social identity, but more importantly affects how people assign meaning and significance to the things they speak of. However, Bernstein later distanced himself from this aspect of his early work, though that fact is not as well known.

### Bernstein's coding of knowledge

Bernstein also wrote of how knowledge itself is 'classified' and 'framed', with classification referring to how power regulates relations between contexts or categories of knowledge, and framing referring to relations of control within the contexts or categories of knowledge. The school curriculum for instance offers clearly defined subjects including maths or English with a strong classification or framing, and others like humanities where different disciplines (e.g. history, geography) are integrated, a weaker classification or framing. Education Studies is also an example of this weaker classification and integration at HE level.

More recently the question has been posed differently. Social mobility statistics show some middle-class children, who in terms of tests do not seem especially bright, still managing to gain qualifications and middle-class positions. Ability alone is insufficient in explaining their success; they draw on other, social, assets in achieving privilege. Similarly, 'gifted' working-class children will often remain in that class. So the question now asked is 'how the middle classes pass on their advantaged position to their children' rather than 'how working class families breed failure'. Recent work gives us a much clearer view of the strategies employed by the middle classes to maintain social closure. Stephen Ball also highlights strategies adopted to this end (e.g. Ball 2002), while writers including Power et al. (2003) demonstrate how the process of transmitting social advantage is not always straightforward in practice.

As witnessed above, in the post-war educational system, middle-class social advantages were exploited in a number of ways: by ensuring their children gained entry to grammar schools (or buying private education if not), or by getting to the best comprehensive schools where there were no grammar schools. Until the late 1970s this period was one of economic expansion, where developments in occupational structures meant there were plenty of middle-class jobs for middle-class children and for bright working-class students (e.g. Willis's 'ear 'oles').

Since the 1980s the context has altered in a manner threatening middle-class advantage. Changes to the occupational structure have increased the insecurity of some middle-class jobs, and a decade into the new millennium as I write this, the situation is worsening still, with the notion of 'the squeezed middle' (classes) becoming popular in the media. Comprehensive schools have increased the participation of children in education for longer, and higher education has expanded significantly over the last 25 years, meaning greater competition for both education and graduate-level jobs. When I went to university in 1984, only about 15 per cent of young people did so, but now about three times that number do. Middle-class parents needed to respond to this new context by devising strategies preserving their children's advantages. We will now focus upon HE to explore how they do so.

---

**Activity: university choices**

List the reasons why people choose the university and course they do. You can use your own experience or that of your friends if you wish. Once you have finished this, see how your list fits with the ideas in the next section.

---

## Key theme 6: HE choice – *habitus*, risk and the self

In recent decades in the UK and beyond, the issue of widening participation in HE has come to the fore. For instance, soon after coming to power in 1997, the New Labour government set a target of 50 per cent of young people experiencing HE by 2010, with several policy initiatives directed towards achieving this, including additional monies for universities, and the Education Maintenance Allowance paid to young people from poorer families staying in education beyond 16 (now abolished by the coalition government, as mentioned earlier). This target was met successfully in Scotland and Northern Ireland, but missed in both England and Wales. Interestingly, it was also met by young women across the UK as a whole, but not by young men. However, universities were opened up to people whose families had never experienced it before. I was one of those benefiting from an earlier phase of this expansion in the mid-1980s; perhaps you have too? A consequence of this move towards a system of mass higher education is a closer examination of the effects of social class in shaping HE participation, since the expansion has largely occurred in the working and lower middle classes, who traditionally did not continue in school beyond the earliest leaving age.

One area generating a lot of sociologically inspired research is the process of university choice. This has been based not on the quantitative data government tends to deal with, but on qualitative work, often longitudinal in nature. It tackles sociological concerns and develops concepts and theories to understand data generated through interviews, and forms the basis of this section. Whilst writing this chapter, I am just starting a large three-year project with colleagues following undergraduate students studying the same subjects at the University of Bristol and the University of the West of England (from the same city). Check the website, www.pairedpeers.com, to see what our methods and latest findings are.

**Key text No. 3**

*Education, Culture, Economy and Society* (Halsey et al. 1997) is a heavyweight (over 800 pages) compendium containing more than 50 contributions from key thinkers and writers in the sociology of education. It contains an extensive editorial outlining the major theoretical approaches within the discipline, and an assessment of their contribution to understanding its changing social, cultural, economic and political context. The book is divided into six parts: 'Education, Culture and Society'; 'Education, the Global Economy and the Labour Market'; 'The State and the Restructuring of Teachers' Work'; 'Politics, Markets, and School Effectiveness'; 'Knowledge, Curriculum, and Cultural Politics'; and 'Meritocracy and Social Exclusion'. Lauder, Brown and Halsey collaborated with another editor, Jo-Anne Dillabough, to produce a later edited collection with the same publisher in 2006, *Education, Globalization and Social Change* (nearly 1200 pages this time!), although while it is of a similar excellent standard, this later collection has yet to achieve the status of the earlier book. As with the earlier version, the individual chapters are rarely an easy read, but they are well worth persisting with!

## Theorizing choice

On the face of it, like much sociological study, the issue of whether to go to university, and, if so, what and where to study, is a simple issue facing young people in particular. 'Common sense' suggests it is a rational process of considering all available information; however, evidence suggests HE choice involves more than this rational appraisal of abilities, matching attainment at school to available opportunities. Look back at the list of reasons for your HE choices above and think again about why you made the decisions you did, or why others might.

Ball et al. (2002) suggested decisions regarding HE choice were pragmatic and based on partial information located in the 'familiar' and the 'known'. They claim that the family background, culture and life histories of the young people exerted enormous influence within the process, and decisions were at best only partly rational, being further influenced by feelings and emotions.

One aspect of 'non-rationality' is that students may not have the information needed to make rational decisions, e.g. about universities' ranking. Most students know there is a hierarchy of institutions, with Oxford and Cambridge at the top and some of the so-called 'new' universities (especially the ex-colleges of HE) at the bottom. For potential students who are more HE 'savvy', the choice of *which* university to go to is an important one. 'Lindsay', a mature student I interviewed for a research project, had applied to study Law at both the local 'new' university and the nearby 'elite', highly selective one. A single mum living very close to the new university, 'Lindsay', whose children went to school just half a mile or so away, felt it would be really convenient to go there. The new university was also reputed to be excellent for mature students, and its law school was considered one of the country's best, with a higher quality of teaching than the older university. However, the new university itself was lower status than its 'elite' neighbour, and although she felt it would have caused difficulties doing so, had the elite university offered her a place she would have taken it:

> If they had offered I would have probably gone there, but I don't think I would have enjoyed it, I think I would have struggled, and . . . I probably would have had more chance of being a failure there than I would at [new university] . . . (however) any lawyer would say 'if you have the chance to go to [old university], go . . . you'll just do so much better with it on your CV'.

However, unlike 'Lindsay', not all students know about the perceived hierarchies within universities, particularly if they come from families, schools and communities where people generally do not attend HE; for them the choice is often *whether* to go to university, rather than which one to attend. 'James', a working-class student from another study exemplifies this:

> I don't really know anybody who has completed university . . . so I suppose that's maybe why I don't know about . . . (their) reputations . . . or things like that, apart from what I was told by the prospectuses, the brochures, computers, what my teacher told me. I sort of worked it out as I went along really, played it by ear.

James's decision was a more conscious one. Like many working-class people he exhibits doubts, ambivalences and deliberate decision-making. These are 'choice biographies'. For Ball et al. (2002: 53), working-class students in HE are 'lucky survivors', and 'in terms of educational trajectories and aspirations, they are already exceptions'.

## Risk

For many working-class and other 'non-traditional' students, HE choice involves considering the potential risks of participation. Various studies of non-traditional learners identified a perception of significant risk as common amongst their working-class, mature and/or ethnic minority student participants. HE was seen as boring, involving hard work, high stress and periods of poverty (Archer and Hutchings 2000). The most commonly identified risk was the possibility of failure, with interviewees in Archer and Hutchings' study for instance assuming failure rates much higher than they actually were. The graduate job market was also commonly perceived as overcrowded; that is certainly the case as I am writing this in 2011, but it was not when their research was undertaken. Other risks include financial ones (i.e. will the outlay on tuition fees and loss of potential earnings for the period of study be recouped in a higher salary) and risks to relationships ('will my friends, family, partners or community still accept me if I become a student?'). And, equally importantly, 'I want to change my life by going to university, will I still want the same people?' See a co-written article of mine for a further discussion of this area (Brine and Waller 2004).

## Family and institutional *habitus*

Bourdieu's (see key figure, below) concepts of *habitus* and cultural capital have been employed to understand the choice processes described above. *Habitus* refers not merely to the external markers of social position, such as occupation, education and material wealth, but also to embodied dispositions (i.e. the beliefs and values that are an essential part of our make-up) generating thought and action. It is acquired through a gradual process of 'inculcation' – that is, 'absorbed' from the family, community, school and other influences around an individual, mainly during childhood. *Habitus* gives a sense of how to respond, orientates actions without strictly determining them, gives a 'feel for the game'. Diane Reay called family *habitus* 'the deeply ingrained system of perspectives, experiences and predispositions family members share' (1998: 527). Actions (including HE choice) cannot therefore be seen as a simple outcome of conscious calculation, but something far more nuanced and subtle.

**Key figure: Pierre Bourdieu (1930–2002)**

French sociologist Bourdieu (e.g. 1974, 1977, 1984) is an important thinker in a range of sociological areas, and quite possibly the most important ever sociologist of education. He proposed a number of key theories and ways of understanding and analysing the world that still influence the thinking of many sociologists of education. His idea of *habitus* is a powerful one, referring not merely to our defining external markers of social position, such as occupation, education and material wealth, but to the factors influencing our internal thought processes. *Habitus* is acquired through socialization by our family, community and other influences, including schools and peer groups around an individual. *Habitus* gives us a sense of how to 'naturally' respond to situations, and directs our actions which can no longer simply be seen as the result of rational calculation. Bourdieu's work on forms of 'capital' is equally influential. Of particular importance is his idea of cultural capital – what you know. Everyone has extensive cultural capital, but some forms of it are of greater benefit than others in a given setting. Middle-class children like my sons may well be taken to places like museums by their parents, an activity offering a form of cultural capital of direct benefit to learning in the classroom, and offering them an advantage in terms of formal learning. However, an encyclopaedic knowledge of popular music, computer games or football offers another form of cultural capital that may help the same middle-class children integrate with others in the playground. Both forms of cultural capital are valid, and both are valuable in different settings, though there has been less research on the latter form.

Schools and universities have an institutional *habitus*, independent of the student's family; 'perceptions and expectations of choices are constructed over time in relation to school friends and teachers' views and advice and learning experiences' (Ball et al. 2002: 58). The effects of *habitus* and cultural capital are seen within choice processes.

When looking at universities, students 'get a feel' for how they would enjoy being there. Students may reject universities that do not feel 'right', or where they do not feel 'at home'. Ball and Reay talk of 'class aversion' to high-status institutions by working-class students, institutions seen as not 'for people like us'. This self-exclusion derives from feelings about what is 'right for me' rather than a rational calculation of what is best.

## Conclusion

The purpose of this chapter is to offer an overview of some key issues in the sociology of education. As suggested previously, no such account can be definitive, and readers may feel some important areas have been neglected unnecessarily given the inclusion of others. Little is included here on ethnicity and education, for instance, or the specifics of differential attainment rates across various demographic cohorts – that is, different groups within the wider population. The purpose here is to offer pointers as to where such information could be obtained and I hope that is what this chapter has achieved.

---

**Further research**

Think of some of the issues raised in this chapter and how they may form the basis for your own research project. You could for instance consider the issue of gender identities amongst HE students, or how different forms of cultural capital have value in a variety of educational settings. Or research the educational biography of your own family members, including how it may have been affected by issues like social class, or how the twin notions of 'social structure' and 'agency' have impacted on the educational opportunities of someone you know. Enjoy it!

---

## Key readings

### Books

Giddens, A. (2009) *Sociology* (6th edn). Cambridge: Polity Press. A useful 'cross-over' book for A level sociology and first-year undergraduate studies. The education section, Chapter 19, contains details of useful websites for further study.

Haralambos, M. and Holborn, M. (2008) *Sociology: Themes and Perspectives* (7th edn). London: Collins. Another useful 'cross-over' introductory-level book. The education section is Chapter 10.

Lauder, H., Brown, P. and Halsey, A.H. (2009) Sociology of education: a critical history and prospects for the future. *Oxford Review of Education*, 35(5): 569–85. A useful summary of the history of the sociology of education in the UK. A far more accessible read than the Halsey et al. (1997) book (Key theme 3), though that volume is a useful reference book and well worth persevering with.

## Websites

http://www.guardian.co.uk/education
The education site of the *Guardian* newspaper, probably the best media coverage of key issues in education home and abroad. You can sign up for the useful daily summary, *The Cribsheet*, from this site.

http://socofed.com/
The new (November 2010) sociology of education website edited by David Mellor and me, the British Sociological Association's Education Study Group's co-convenors. The site is unofficial since it is not endorsed by the BSA. It includes links to lots of other useful sites and opportunities to contribute to current discussion topics via the message board.

en.wikipedia.org/wiki/Sociology_of_education
The Wikipedia site, with links to various writers and ideas. Be wary of the quality of the site's content though – the very nature of Wikipedia means it is open to anyone to put something there!

## Journals

*British Journal of Sociology of Education (BJSE)*
Although not always easily accessible in terms of its content as it tends to be rather theoretical, this is the key journal for the sub-discipline of sociology of education (see box below for a more detailed outline).

---

**Key journal: The British Journal of Sociology of Education (BJSE).**

This leading journal is published six times annually and has been going for some considerable time – it started in 1980 under the editorship of Len Barton, who is still editing it at the time of writing this chapter in 2011. Unlike other journals, *BJSE* has a dual focus on both theory and empirical studies. It has always maintained a board of executive editors reading a little like a 'who's who' of the discipline in the UK. It also draws upon research from elsewhere in the anglo-phonic world, notably Canada, Australia, New Zealand and the USA. The journal is available online (www.tandf.co.uk/journals/bjse), and a free sample copy can be obtained. A quick trawl through recent volumes (which can be done online) reveals what the key current issues in the sociology of education are. As well as the six or so main articles, each issue normally contains a list of recent doctoral theses awarded in the discipline, a review essay, an extended review and a review symposium on a major book or collection of books. Like other journals it also publishes responses to articles from other academics, encouraging a debate on key topics.

*British Educational Research Journal (BERJ)*
Not strictly sociological as such, but the journal of the **British Educational Research Association (BERA)**, and as such a useful indicator of key themes and issues for academics and educational practitioners alike.

*Gender and Education*
The journal of the Gender and Education Association. This has a more 'international' flavour than *BERJ*, and features articles covering issues including social class, sexuality, mature students and identity, as well as those indicated by the title.

## Acknowledgements

This chapter is based upon components of my sociology of education teaching at the University of the West of England, some of which was previously taught by Arthur Baxter, to whom a debt is owed for various materials and ideas expressed here. However, I take full responsibility for any errors or omissions.

## References

Archer, L. and Hutchings, M. (2000) 'Bettering yourself'? Discourses of risk, cost and benefit in ethnically diverse, young working class non-participants' constructions of higher education. *British Journal of Sociology of Education*, 21: 555–74.

Ball, S. (2002) *Class Strategies and the Education Market: The Middle Classes and Social Advantage*. London: Routledge.

Ball, S. (ed.) (2004) *The RoutledgeFalmer Reader in Sociology of Education*. London: RoutledgeFalmer.

Ball, S. (2007) *Education plc*. Abingdon: Routledge.

Ball, S., Davies, J., David, M. and Reay, D. (2002) Classification and judgement: social class and the cognitive structures of choice of higher education. *British Journal of Sociology of Education*, 23(1).

Bernstein, B. (1971) *Class, Codes and Control*. London: Paladin.

Bourdieu, P. (1974) The school as a conservative force: scholastic and cultural inequalities. In J. Egglestone (ed.) *Contemporary Research in the Sociology of Education*. London: Methuen.

Bourdieu, P. (1977) Cultural reproduction and social reproduction. In J. Karabel and A. Halsey (eds) *Power and Ideology in Education*. Oxford: Oxford University Press.

Bourdieu, P. (1984) *Distinction: A Social Critique of the Judgement of Taste*. London: Routledge and Kegan Paul.

Bowles, S. and Gintis, H. (1975) *Schooling in Capitalist America*. London: Routledge.

Brine, J. and Waller, R. (2004) Working class women on an access course: risk, opportunity and (re)constructing identities. *Gender and Education*, 16: 97–113.

Brown, P. (1997) The third wave: education and the ideology of parentocracy. In A.H. Halsey, H. Lauder, P. Brown and A. Stuart Wells (eds) *Education, Culture, Economy and Society*. Oxford: Oxford University Press.

Butler, J. (1988) Performative acts and gender constitution: an essay in phenomenology and feminist theory. *Theatre Journal*, 40(4): 519–31.

Dale, R. (2001) Shaping the sociology of education over half a century. In J. Demaine (ed.) *Sociology of Education Today*. Basingstoke: Palgrave.

Equality and Human Rights Commission (EHRC) (2010) *How Fair is Britain? Equality, Human Rights and Good Relations in 2010*. London: EHRC.

Giddens, A. (1971) *Capitalism and Modern Social Theory*. Cambridge: Cambridge University Press.

Halsey, A.H. (1980) *Origins and Destinations: Family, Class, and Education in Modern Britain*. Oxford: Clarendon.

Halsey, A.H. (2004) *A History of Sociology in Britain: Science, Literature and Society*. Oxford: Oxford University Press.

Halsey, A.H., Lauder, H., Brown, P. and Stuart Wells, A. (eds) (1997) *Education, Culture, Economy and Society*. Oxford: Oxford University Press.

Hey, V. (1997) *The Company She Keeps*. Buckingham: Open University Press.

Illich, I. (1971) *Deschooling Society*. [help][??263]? Calder + Boyars.[/help]

Ivinson, G., Davies, B. and Fitz, J. (eds) (2010) *Knowledge and Identity: Concepts and Applications in Bernstein's Sociology*. London: Routledge.

Jackson, M., Goldthorpe, J. and Mills, C. (2005) Education, employers and class mobility. *Research in Social Stratification and Mobility*, 23: 3–33.

Lauder, H., Brown, P. and Halsey, A.H. (2009) Sociology of education: a critical history and prospects for the future. *Oxford Review of Education*, 35(5): 569–85.

Lauder, H., Brown, P., Dillabough, J., Halsey, A.H. (2006) *Education, Globalization and Social Change*. Oxford: Oxford University Press.

Mac an Ghail, M. (1994) *The Making of Men: Masculinities, Sexualities and Schooling*. Milton Keynes: Open University Press.

Mellor, D. and Epstein, D. (2006) Appropriate behaviour? Sexualities, schooling and hetero-gender. In C. Skelton, B. Francis and L. Smulyan (eds) *Handbook of Gender and Education*. London: Sage.

Milburn, A. (2009) *Unleashing Aspiration: The Final Report of the Panel on Fair Access to the Professions*. London: The Cabinet Office.

Power, S., Edwards, T., Wigfall, V. and Whitty, G. (2003) *Education and the Middle Classes*. Milton Keynes: Open University Press.

Reay, D. (1998) Always knowing and never being sure: familial and institutional *habituses* and higher educational choice. *Education Policy*, 13(4): 519–29.

Reay, D. (1998) *Class Work: Mother's Involvement in Their Children's Primary Schooling*. London: Routledge.

Reay, D. (2001) 'Spice girls', 'nice girls', and 'tomboys': gender discourses, girls cultures and femininities in the primary classroom. *Gender and Education*, 13(2): 153–66.

Reay, D., Crozier, G. and James, D. (2011) *White Middle Class Identities and Urban Schooling*. London: Palgrave Macmillan.

Reay, D., David, M. and Ball, S. (2005) *Degrees of Choice: Social Class, Race and Gender in Higher Education*. Stoke-on-Trent: Trentham.

Renold, E. (2001) Square girls. *British Educational Research Journal*, 27(1).

Taylor, C., Fitz, J. and Gorard, S. (2005) Diversity, specialisation and equity in education. *Oxford Review of Education*, 31(1): 47–69.

Willis, P. (1977) *Learning to Labour: How Working Class Kids Get Working Class Jobs*. Farnborough: Saxon House.

Young, M. (1958) *The Rise of the Meritocracy*. London: Thames and Hudson.

Young, M.F.D. (ed.) (1971) *Knowledge and Control*. London: Collier-Macmillan.

Young, M.F.D. (2008) *Bringing Knowledge Back In: From Social Constructivism to Social Realism in the Sociology of Education*. Abingdon: Routledge.

# 6

## DIAHANN GALLARD AND ANGIE GARDEN
## The Psychology of Education

---

**Learning outcomes**

By the end of this chapter, you should be able to:

- identify some of the major areas of study in the psychology of education;
- understand the most influential theories of learning;
- outline and evaluate explanations for poor classroom behaviour, and strategies for improving behaviour;
- critically assess differing ways of understanding and measuring intelligence.

---

## Introduction to the psychology of education

---

**Activity: thinking about psychology in education**

Ask yourself the following questions.

1. Why do we need psychology?

2. Why might psychology be important in understanding education?

3. How might psychology be used to inform and evaluate educational practice?

---

Psychology is a subject area that deals with the human mind and behaviour, and the discipline has a key role to play in education. Psychology involves viewing situations from a number of different perspectives and so it is a particularly useful tool for understanding educational themes and processes. Primarily, psychology can help us understand how people learn; it can help us measure the ability and educational progress of a learner, and make comparisons with other learners. It can also make us aware of how each learner is (and must be viewed as) different and unique. Psychology enables us to understand human behaviour and how our motivation and engagement impacts on our educational attainment (think in terms of how your interest and ability in different subjects at school used to vary depending on how engaged you were in the lessons and also, now, in your various lectures!). Most importantly, psychology can help us place learner behaviour *within the context in which the learning is taking place* (recognizing the barriers and cultural bias that comes with diversity and individuality). It helps us to explain how both genetic inheritance and life context can influence how we learn within the educational provision available to children and young people. This chapter introduces you to some of these central issues. The purpose is to consider a number of core psychological concepts and theories that are applied to education. We have grouped these ideas into three key themes:

1.  behaviour;
2.  learning;
3.  intelligence.

However, before considering these three key themes, we should first focus on introducing you to the domain of the 'psychology of education'. Psychology is more than just common sense. It is an evidence-based study of how people think and what they do. Psychologists approach their work in more quantitative/positivistic/experimental ways than in many of the other disciplines covered in this book. Psychology searches for evidence using logical investigations based on the use of direct experiments, observations and interpretations of laboratory-based explorations and naturally occurring processes. However, whereas psychology has a scientific approach, education is not a science, and so there can be tension and conflict between the psychologist and educationalist positions within educational psychology.

It is also important to note that education has a tendency to be governed by the socio-political context of its time, and influenced by social processes and the social climate – and the (frequently harmful) agendas of individuals and groups. One example to illustrate this is 11+ testing (which began in the 1940s), which was implemented to stream children into different types of secondary school. There was a socio-political agenda attached to this educational policy, and less emphasis on substantiating the validity of the ideas underpinning it. Once psychological research established that there was no evidence for quantifying a set point for individual potential and life course for children at age 11 years, this education system was overturned in most local authorities.

## Key theme 1: behaviour

### Activity: behaviour in the classroom

Consider the following statements: do you agree or disagree? Why?

- Problem behaviour in the classroom should be dealt with through firm discipline and punishment.
- Teachers are the most important factor in the education of children.
- Children should be corrected by teachers so that they learn from their mistakes.

As you can probably appreciate from your responses to the statements, there are no clear right or wrong answers. However, we can apply psychological knowledge to such statements in order to clarify our perceptions and ideas, and to allow our viewpoints to be *informed* rather than based entirely on unfounded opinion.

There are various psychological terms used to make sense of behaviour within education. For example, the terms emotional and behavioural difficulties (EBD) and attention deficit and hyperactivity disorder (AD/HD) are commonly used today. As well as disruptive behaviours, children may be affected by emotional difficulties such as anxiety or depression.

### Activity: emotional and behavioural difficulties

Consider the various suggested definitions of EBD.

- A child's behaviour may endanger themselves, other people or property.
- A child's behaviour interferes with the education of other children or with their own educational progress.
- A child's behaviour means that they have difficulty forming social relationships or interferes with the relationships of other children.

For each of these points, think about how these difficulties may be observed in an educational context and suggest any reasons for such behavioural difficulties

A medical model may view problems such as disruptive behaviour and AD/HD as being primarily located within the individual child, although this view is not as common as it used to be. Problem behaviour would traditionally imply a 'problem child' – resulting in the child being removed from the classroom and educated in specialist off-site provision. More recently, a more widely held view is that problem behaviour is dealt with and viewed as an interaction between children, their past and present environments, home life and school life.

A large number of children referred to educational psychologists present with behavioural problems and these are often the source of conflict between home and school life. The school may have directed the child's problems back to the parents, who then feel threatened and defensive. The role of an educational psychologist in this scenario is to mediate between the two points of contact and try to gain the cooperation of both the school and home in order to progress work forward.

## AD/HD

AD/HD is a clinical diagnostic category in the American Psychological Association's *Diagnostic and Statistical Manual* (*DSM-IV*) and estimates of its prevalence indicate that it is a significant problem. Problems include behaviours such as:

- often has difficulty in sustaining attention in tasks or play activities;
- is often forgetful in daily activities;
- often does not seem to listen when spoken to directly;
- often fidgets with hands or feet or squirms in seat;
- often talks excessively;
- often has difficulty awaiting turn;
- often interrupts or intrudes on others, for example when playing games.

(APA 1994)

Children with problem behaviours such as those listed above will often be particularly demanding and challenging for teachers to manage in school. In order to meet a diagnosis, two out of three of the substantive list of *DSM-IV* symptoms must be present for at least six months, and they must have been present from an early age (before seven years). Educational psychologists ensure that these symptoms are present in at least two settings (e.g. school and home) and are not the result of another mental problem.

## Explanations, interventions and treatments

Whether or not it is useful to label children in this way is a matter for debate. The use of ability testing such as IQ testing in order to place children into a special needs category tends to suggest a 'within-child' belief. This belief suggests that the difficulties lie within the child, have a biological basis and little can be done to overcome them. Certainly for those children with IQs below 50, there is much evidence to suggest intrinsic biological limitations. A behavioural view may consider low educational achievement as being a result in part of limited general knowledge and understanding, poor understanding or comprehension of ideas, ineffective learning styles and poor general motivation.

There are a variety of treatments and interventions utilized to tackle poor behaviour. Treatments may include counselling given to parents after the trauma of giving birth to a baby with a disability, medication given for AD/HD, or an autistic child receiving training in functional communication skills in order to reduce self-injurious behaviour. Maintenance interventions aim to ensure that positive change in the child's or family's functioning continues into the future and that treated problems do not re-occur.

In general, interventions will follow a combined approach based on:

- a clear description of the nature of the problem;
- a thorough assessment of the problem at the individual and contextual level;
- a rationale for assisting the child who is experiencing difficulty in the current context;
- determination of how best to minimize such difficulty;
- a plan for the evaluation of attempts to minimize difficulty.

Other issues we can consider within this behaviour section include motivation, peer pressure and self-esteem.

## Motivation, self-esteem and classroom relations

Children need to be motivated to learn, to be able to concentrate and to pay attention in order to achieve. Bruner's (1996) theoretical framework contends that learning is an active process in which learners construct new ideas or concepts based upon their current or past knowledge. The learner selects and transforms information, constructs hypotheses and makes decisions, whilst relying on a cognitive structure to do so. Cognitive structure (i.e. schema, mental models) provides meaning and organization to experiences and allows the individual to go beyond any information given.

### Key figure: Jerome Bruner (1915–)

Jerome Bruner is the eminent American cognitive psychologist who has been heavily involved in education and theories of curriculum and teaching, proposing that knowledge is best gained by personal discovery, by active methods, with young or old developing concepts that lead to a better understanding. In schools, the teacher is the guide helping pupils to construct knowledge rather than just teaching it. This was perhaps best illustrated by Bruner's involvement in the famous social science/anthropology school curriculum project in the USA (and in the UK to some extent) in the 1960s and 1970s called MACOS (Man: A Course of Study). He is well known for many ideas such as the spiral curriculum, scaffolding, and the notion that anything can be taught to anyone at some level of sophistication as long as the instruction is appropriately organized.

Unlike Piaget, his early influence, he does not believe there are age-specific developmental stages, rather he believes that all forms of learning from the practical (action-based) and iconic (image-based) through to symbolic (language-based) can be taught or acquired at the same time given suitable teaching. He is the author of many books and is currently a senior research fellow at New York University. For more information you can go to his own website: www.psych.nyu.edu/bruner

Bruner felt that school experiences are different to other experiences because they are *de-contextualized* – that is, they exist separately from the actual process or thing being studied. Think about children learning about the pyramids. They will learn about the pyramids in the classroom, from pictures and text, but the likelihood is that they will not actually visit the pyramids.

Bruner argues that learning happens much more easily when it is contextualized and learning is much less formal. Early developments such as walking, talking and social interaction are not taught in a formal way and as such have more meaning for children. Decontextualized learning is partly as a result of a prescriptive curriculum and increased class sizes, which necessarily limit teachers' ability to respond on a more individual level. Bruner argues that it is still possible to develop learning through some direct experiences and in this way maintain a child's natural curiosity and motivation, while also encouraging positive behaviour.

In addition, Bruner states that a form of self-esteem known as *self-efficacy* influences children's *perceptions* of their own academic abilities. Past academic experiences can cloud these judgements, for example failure would reduce self-esteem whereas success would increase self-esteem and confidence in future learning. Bruner felt that children's judgements come not only from past academic performance but also the performance of their peers (peer pressure), general motivation and arousal, and from others such as teachers. Low self-esteem often triggers misbehaviour.

In school there exist *role expectations*, a set of norms and scripts for both pupils and teachers, and these influence to a large extent the view of 'normal' behaviour.

---

### Activity: thinking about what happens in the classroom

Consider the following questions.

1.  What are the normal/expected roles of a teacher?

2.  What are the normal/expected roles of a pupil?

3.  How many different learning experiences can you think of where children could be enabled to explore first hand the actual thing being studied?

4.  Can you think of any ways in which aggression may be directly or indirectly triggered in children?

---

A teacher's role is usually to control, organize, teach and exert authority. A pupil's role is usually to show obedience to the teacher's authority, conformity to the rules of the classroom and to learn. Normal behaviour involves to a large extent following these norms of behaviour and conformity to the majority influence. Problem behaviours in school may be seen as a general social process where pupils may act against the expectations or rules of the school in order to fit in with their own peer groups, for example contravening the school's dress code.

Another way of looking at problem behaviours in children is as a result of *operant conditioning*. The idea is that if children receive some kind of *reinforcement* (encouragement) when they are aggressive, they are then more likely to continue acting in an aggressive way on other occasions.

Direct acts of approval for negative acts may include attention, laughter or verbal comments. More indirect encouragement or reinforcement may be through television viewing, computer games or witnessing aggression in the home. Children can learn such processes from a very early age and rewarding consequences from a victim such as crying or passivity can reinforce the aggression in some circumstances. Children may copy the aggressive behaviour of others and if given positive consequences are then more encouraged to behave in this way again. It would seem that children develop their behaviours from observing the behaviour of those around them as well as from the consequences of their actions.

Indeed *observational learning* is a key concept in understanding how children develop their knowledge of social roles and their sense of identity in school. Social learning theory proposes that much behaviour develops due to us observing what other people do. Behaviour is traditionally studied by considering Bandura's social learning theory.

## Social learning theory

**Key figure: Albert Bandura (1925–)**

Albert Bandura was born in Mundare, Alberta. A Canadian psychologist, Bandura attempted in the 1960s and 1970s to make Freud's concept of identification more objective and scientific through developing a social learning theory. Social learning theory holds that we learn social behaviour through observing others and imitating them. Its origins are in the behaviourist perspective of classical and operant conditioning. Bandura emphasized the importance of observing and modelling the behaviours, attitudes and emotional reactions of others. Bandura's ideas were to dramatically change psychological theoretical perspectives in the 1980s.

Bandura (1977), in developing his social learning theory, attempted to account for personality and other aspects of social development in terms of learning mechanisms. Unlike most learning theorists, Bandura emphasized the active role that children play in their own development. He called this 'reciprocal determinism' (the world and a person's behaviour cause each other). Behaviourism essentially explains how one's environment causes one's behaviour. Bandura, who was studying adolescent aggression, found this too simplistic, and so he suggested that behaviour causes subtle shifts in the environment as well. Bandura went on to explain personality as an interaction between three components: the environment, behaviour and psychological processes – that is, the ability to entertain images in the mind and in language.

Bandura saw observation as the key way that children learn. This type of *observational learning*, or *modelling*, is involved in a wide range of behaviours. It depends on some basic cognitive processes such as having the child's attention, the child being able to encode the information (relate it to their own understanding), store the information and, lastly, being able to retrieve the information when it is needed. Learning does not always require direct reinforcement; it may be enough just to watch someone else perform.

According to Bandura (1974), the learning process for the child involved a number of observational learning steps.

- Paying attention: the child needs to be able to focus on the stimulus, that is the task to be achieved, and ignore anything that is incidental.

- Recording a visual image or semantic code: the child needs to have an adequate coding system in order to store information such as a sequence of numbers.

- Memory permanence: the child would be given the opportunity to rehearse and multiply the codes, such as a times table.

- Reproducing the observed motor activities: the child would have the opportunity to try out the observed task for her/himself and to repeat as often as necessary in order to reproduce the task, such as in a science experiment.

- Motivation: the child would be encouraged to keep motivated with the task through the nature of reinforcement and mere exposure.

---

**Activity: Bandura's observational learning steps**

Try this observational learning task for yourself. Imagine you have a group of pupils; how could you encourage them to learn the alphabet?

Using the Bandura's observational learning steps, consider the following.

- How could you encourage the child to pay attention and be interested in the task?

- What sort of coding system could you use to enable the child to learn the alphabet? What visual codes you could use for each letter of the alphabet?

- How could you encourage memory permanence? In what ways could the child rehearse the alphabet?

- How could you further keep the child motivated on the task?

---

As part of the learning process for children, *intrinsic reinforcements* or intrinsic rewards such as pride, feelings of satisfaction for a job well done or discovery are also centrally important. Bandura identified that such feelings help to keep a child motivated with the task and such reinforcements are internal to the individual.

In addition, as well as *observational learning* and *intrinsic reinforcements*, the third and perhaps most important way of learning, according to Bandura, is through *cognitive* elements in observational learning. This *Social Cognitive Theory* (Bandura 1986) emphasizes the mental elements in observational learning, for example modelling can encourage learning abstract as well as concrete skills or information. 'Rules' may be learned as well as 'specific behaviour', meaning that the child can acquire a whole range of values, attitudes and ways of solving problems or difficulties through the modelling process. The values and attitudes can be negative as well as positive, thus impacting on behaviour.

Social learning theory is sometimes described as a bridge between behaviourist and cognitive learning theories because it encompasses attention, memory and motivation. The theory is related to Vygotsky's social development theory (1978) and Lave and Wenger's situated learning (1990) as both also emphasize the importance of the social for learning.

## Key theme 2: learning

Traditionally the child has been seen as a passive agent in his or her own learning, simply absorbing knowledge that has been recited to them by the teacher. However, this mechanistic view of learning has been overtaken by a more cognitive paradigm. According to this, the child is an active participant in his or her own learning, in constructing knowledge, skills and ways of understanding. This perspective is mainly derived from the original ideas of Piaget, which emphasized the teacher as a facilitator of learning who gives opportunities for new experiences, and whose practice should include the observation of the child's changing needs and accomplishments.

### Cognitive development and learning – Piagetian theory

**Key figure: Jean Piaget (1896–1980)**

Jean Piaget, Swiss developmental psychologist and philosopher, placed great importance on the education of children. At age 11, while he was a pupil at Neuchâtel Latin high school, he wrote a short paper that is generally considered as the start of a brilliant scientific career made up of over 60 books and several hundred articles. His research in developmental psychology and genetic epistemology had one key question: how does knowledge grow? Piaget is one of the most influential developmental psychologists, influencing the work of Lev Vygotsky and of Lawrence Kohlberg as well as whole generations of eminent academics.

Jean Piaget (1972) developed the major theory in the area of cognitive development and learning (see also Piaget and Inhelder 1966). Mental structures called *schemas* were proposed. For young children this could involve the actions of 'reaching out' and 'grasping an object'. As a child matures, these schemas become more and more complex, ultimately representing abstract features. Overall, Piaget was concerned with the cognitive and logical nature of children's development.

Piaget described how information is only *assimilated* or fitted into other schemas. For example, the colour lilac may be understood as purple without recognizing the subtle differences in shade. A state of balance (of recognizing the new shade) is known as a state of *equilibrium*. However, there is a point at which the difference in understanding cannot continue, as a state of *disequilibrium* occurs. This new information must be fitted within existing concepts, in a process of restructuring known as *accommodation*. Following this process, a new state of equilibrium is reached. The child's understanding of colour will now consist of different shades of purple including lilac plus others.

Piaget believed that a child's mental abilities go through a series of developmental stages. Briefly these stages consist of the following.

- The *sensori-motor stage* covers 0 to 2 years of age. The focus is on sensory and motor reactions and responses. An infant's thinking is very much about doing and very young children find it difficult to believe that things still exist when they are not immediately present.
- The *pre-operational stage* covers 2 to 7 years of age. Children are now able to think about things in terms of consistent physical features. However, children at this stage are limited by their own perspective and have difficulty in separating appearance from fact such as number or quantity. The ability to do this is called conservation and Piaget highlighted this limitation through simple experiments such as the same quantity of liquid represented in a tall, thin glass and a short, fat glass.
- The *concrete operational stage* covers broadly 7 to 12 years of age. Children at this stage are now able to think about different features of things, but this is still limited to physical objects. Children are now more able to take on different perspectives.
- The *formal operational stage* from 12 years onwards involves much more abstract thought processes. Scientific thought is now much more likely with the ability to hypothesize and carry out experiments.

Piaget was more accurate in his description of the school-age child than anyone before him. The school-age child uses strategies to remember things such as rules for adding and multiplying, games, songs and so on, and these strategies develop with age.

---

**Activity: memory strategies**

Do you use the following memory strategies when you are attempting to memorize and recall?

- Chunking numbers together (for example, parts of phone numbers).
- Making a list and then rehearsing the items on it.

Do these methods increase the amount you can remember?

Certainly, having specific knowledge makes a big difference and the strategies that a child uses become more elaborate as they mature. There are, however, many criticisms of Piaget; for example, Piaget's observations were based on his own three children and the other children in his small research sample were all from well-educated professionals of high socio-economic status. Therefore, this unrepresentative sample makes it hard to generalize his findings to a larger population. Piaget's contention that children move automatically to the next stage of development has been disputed as environmental factors can also be seen to play a significant role in children's development. Additionally, most researchers agree that Piaget wrongly estimated the various ages at which children go through the various stages; for example, children are often able to take on another person's perspective at a much younger age than originally thought. Nevertheless, there is still general support for his theory of children as active participants in the construction of their mental structures. Piaget's work sparked a real interest in child development and had a huge influence on the future of education and developmental psychology.

## Social development theory

**Key figure: Lev Vygotsky**

Lev Vygotsky was born in Orsha, a city in the western region of the Russian Empire, in 1886. A Russian psychologist and educator, he extended and improved the work of Piaget, the Swiss educator who described what children are able to learn at different ages. Vygotsky's ideas are more flexible and less focused on the particular age of the child. He died of tuberculosis at the young age of 38. Although he was a contemporary of Skinner, Pavlov, Freud and Piaget, his work never attained their level of eminence during his lifetime. Nevertheless, his work has continued to grow in influence since his death, particularly in the fields of educational and developmental psychology.

Vygotsky's (1978, 1986) social development theory challenges traditional teaching methods. Historically, schools have been organized around *recitation teaching*. The teacher disseminates knowledge to be memorized by the students, who in turn recite the information back to the teacher. Children in the same teaching group will often be at around the same level of development. *Reciprocal teaching* would allow groups of children to work together in order to solve problems. The teacher's role would be to set up this group and facilitate it (rather like in a seminar group at university) as opposed to giving direct teaching input. You may find it surprising that children might be able to learn without being directly taught, but this is a strategy that has been found to be highly effective in the classroom.

**Activity: recitation and reciprocal teaching**

What are the different ways that teachers can encourage children's learning?

From your memories of being taught in primary and secondary school (and in higher education) can you recall any examples of:

- recitation teaching;
- reciprocal teaching?

Vygotsky's theory requires the teacher and students to play untraditional roles as they collaborate with one another. Instead of a teacher dictating her meaning to students for future recitation, she should collaborate with her students in order to create meaning in ways that students can make their own.

*Scaffolding* is another key Vygotskian term. Scaffolding is sometimes used to describe the assistance given that allows the child to successfully perform a task they would not have been able to do otherwise. It requires the teacher to provide students the opportunity to extend their current skills and knowledge – that is, to engage, simplify and motivate. Indeed, it allows the student to successfully perform a task he or she could not have accomplished otherwise. In addition, the teacher must look for discrepancies between the student's efforts and the solution, control for frustration and risk, and model an idealized version of the act.

Scaffolding can be utilized in a variety of subject areas. For example:

- in teaching science, the teacher may scaffold by first showing the children the simple experiment, then outline how to structure it, then ask them to set it up on their own;
- in teaching geography, the teacher first shows the children key school landmarks on a map, then outlines how to find out more about those landmarks, and then encourages the children to navigate their way to those landmarks;
- in teaching mathematics, counting may be demonstrated through the use of pennies, using a simple song to help with memory; the children are then encouraged to try the task in small groups, helping each other, utilizing the song as a prompt.

The physical environment is key to this type of teaching. The physical classroom, based on Vygotsky's theory, would provide clustered desks or tables and work space for instruction, peer collaboration and small group instruction, in order to allow these group activities to work well. Both scaffolding and reciprocal teaching are effective strategies to access the zone of proximal development.

## The zone of proximal development (ZPD)

In thinking of about traditional educational testing, Vygotsky recognized the importance of solitary skills, but he was even more interested in what children or others can do with assistance. The zone of proximal development is the difference between what a student can accomplish with help and what he or she can do alone without help. Vygotsky believed in learning through assisted performance such as 'look, do' teaching methods within the ZPD (Vygotsky 1978).

Classroom activities can be organized in the following ways.

- Instruction can be planned to provide practice in the ZPD for individual children or groups, for example hints or prompts.

- Cooperative learning activities can be planned with groups of children at different levels who can help one another learn.

- Scaffolding is a tactic for helping the child in his or her zone of proximal development in which adults provide the hints or prompts at different levels. The task is easier through the intervention of the teacher.

- For example, a teacher may work at an arithmetic problem in front of a child, repeating as necessary until the child can master the skill.

## Use of symbols in learning

Vygotsky (1986) believed that human and animal learning are fundamentally different. Speech makes symbols possible. Symbols allow the child to have 'quasi needs' and to form plans and strategies to accomplish a task. Vygotsky saw the symbolic life of the child as coming from the community, not from autonomous development. For example, in teaching Geography, a field trip may be taken or a newspaper created. In teaching History, props such as photographs, maps and excerpts from newspapers may be used.

---

### Activity: symbols and props

Think about the types of community symbols or props you could use to teach subjects such as:

- English;
- French;
- Mathematics;
- Art;
- Physical Education.

---

The idea is that the child is encouraged to relate out-of-school experiences to their school experiences.

## Children with special needs

Within his general theory of child development, Vygotsky (1986) created a comprehensive and practice-orientated paradigm. There is the notion of 'primary' defects, 'secondary' defects, and their interactions in the field of psychopathology and different disabilities. The primary defect can be described as an organic impairment due to biological causes, whereas the secondary defect refers to distortions of higher psychological functions due to social factors.

Vygotsky believed that organic impairment prevents mastering some or most social and/or cognitive skills, and from acquiring knowledge at a proper rate and in an acceptable form. He offered a view on a disability as a social abnormality of behaviour. A teacher needs to deal not so much with the disability but with the social consequences and conflicts arising from that disability within the education setting.

Vygotsky focused on the social implication of disability, and the use of psychological tools and mediated learning provided by adults. Vygotsky had the concept of the internalization of psychological tools as the main mechanism of development in the field of special education. The main goal of special education, according to Vygotsky, is not to compensate for primary defects through facilitation and strengthening of intact psychological functions, but to prevent, correct and rehabilitate secondary defects by psychological and pedagogical means.

Vygotsky's positive approach to disability was adopted 60 years later by the American Association on Mental Retardation (AAMD 1992). Vygotsky's idea that a disabled child's development is determined by the social impact of his organic impairment creates a new perspective for socialization, acculturation and cognitive development of children with special needs.

Vygotsky lived during the Russian Revolution, a time of great change in culture. He was certainly ahead of his time, particularly regarding his ideas in the field of special education. Vygotsky's assertion that biological and cognitive development does not occur in isolation was key. Modern society is also going through a culture of change due to the infusion of computer technology. This might give us some insight as to why Vygotsky's theory of social development is receiving increasing attention more than 70 years after its conception.

Vygotsky focused on the social construction of cognitive ability as opposed to cognition being innate. Models of cognitive ability, and in particular the theme of intelligence, have key prominence within the field of educational psychology and so it is important to look now at the idea of the 'intelligence quotient' (IQ). The first standpoint to be considered is intelligence as a predetermined entity, and how we might measure intellectual power.

## Key theme 3: intelligence

**Activity: thinking about intelligence**

Consider the following questions.

1. Is intelligence predetermined?
2. Are you able to influence your own intelligence?
3. Can we influence children's underlying intelligence?

One way of considering ideas around intelligence is to look at ways of measuring it. Conduct some research on intelligence testing.

4.   What do you think IQ tests are designed to do?
5.   What are the beliefs and values of the researchers who designed them?

In many ways, mystery remains over IQ tests and their inflated importance. The first IQ tests were designed by Binet and Simon (1905). These tests were based on the assumption that individuals differed in their mental abilities. The tests came with a practical purpose – to identify children who would have difficulty continuing highly academic schooling beyond the age of 11. School-like tasks were devised, such as measures of vocabulary, comprehension of facts and relationships, mathematics and verbal reasoning.

Terman (1916) and Terman and Merrill (1937) modified and extended many of these original tests, with six tests devised for each age. The intelligence quotient was therefore given by means of an equation: mental age (given by the number of questions correctly answered) divided by chronological age multiplied by 100. The result meant that an IQ score above 100 was given for children whose mental age was higher than their chronological age, whereas a score below 100 was given for children whose mental age was below their chronological age. This crude calculation is no longer used. Nowadays IQ scores from any type of test are calculated by direct comparison of a child's performance with those of a large group of other children of their own age.

The bell curve distribution, as seen in Figure 6.1, illustrates well the common grouping of the majority of children around the average IQ score of 100, with higher

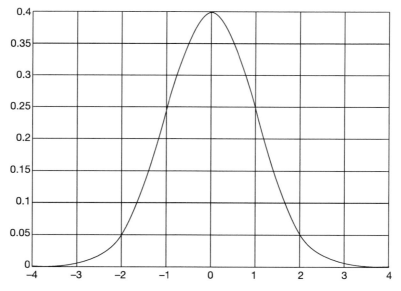

**Figure 6.1** Bell curve

or lower scores allowing IQ scores of above or below average performance. The extremes at each end of the bell curve are often described as learning difficulties at the lower end and gifted at the higher end.

---

**Activity: IQ testing**

Have you ever taken an IQ test? What was your score?
The following points will help to explain how IQ scores work.

- Most of the population cluster around the mean (average). Psychologists work out the mean and this is said to be the most 'normal'.
- The mean for IQ is 100.
- If your score is above the mean for a given population (100), then you have 'above average' intelligence.
- If your score is >140 then you are in the 'gifted' category for intelligence!

Consider the following questions.

1. Do you think IQ tests give us a clear indication of a person's intelligence?
2. What might IQ tests be able to predict?
3. What characteristics might IQ tests often fail to measure?
4. What limitations can you foresee with traditional IQ tests?
5. What factors might cause a child's IQ score to fluctuate?

*Note: Beware the vast number of web-based free IQ tests. Although many do have similar questions to validated IQ tests, they are developed with the agenda of getting you to sacrifice your valuable personal details! If you are keen to find out your IQ score, you would be better advised to sit one offered by an authentic organization such as MENSA (although there is usually a fee for this).*

---

Nowadays, the Wechsler Intelligence Scale for Children (WISC) is often used by psychologists. On the WISC, each child is tested with ten different types of problem, each ranging from very easy to very hard. The ten tests are divided into subgroups, verbal skills (vocabulary, general information) and performance tests (copying pattern, pictures to tell a story), which can indicate for psychologists whether a child has particular learning difficulties.

For most psychologists, the critical question is the stability of test scores. These are viewed as unrelated to later IQ and there is no widely used measurement to predict what a one year old's IQ score will be. Indeed there are wide fluctuations in test scores, particularly in younger children. As a rule of thumb, the older the child, the more stable the IQ score becomes. Stresses, such as parents' divorce or birth of a sibling, can have a considerable impact on IQ scores. Older children may have some fluctuation in scores as a response to major stresses but by around the age of ten, IQ scores are normally quite stable.

## What do IQ tests predict?

The correlation between IQ test scores and levels of school performance are quite consistent but not a perfect correlation. However, there are some variations. IQ scores can predict future marks as well as current scores. It is often suggested that preschoolers who have higher IQs do tend to perform better throughout their school lives.

The predictions for impoverished children may lead us to theorize that intelligence and resilience can allow such children to move out of poverty. For those children with higher IQs, self-confidence and personal competence can allow children to move out of poverty. In the same way, low intelligence has been linked to negative long-term outcomes. It is not always the case, but a low IQ can make a child more vulnerable. Low intelligence is associated with negative long-term outcomes such as adult illiteracy, delinquency in adolescence and criminal behaviour in adulthood.

## The limitations of traditional IQ tests

Certainly, the predictive power of traditional IQ tests can be impressive and many people find it interesting to find out their IQ score. However, what they measure is not a fixed underlying competence. These cannot be predicted at birth as IQ scores can shift particularly in response to stresses, as discussed. IQ tests do not measure many important skills such as social skills, insight, creativity, spatial awareness and relationships.

Gardner (1983) identifies six separate types of intelligence (linguistic, musical, logical – mathematical, spatial, bodily – kinaesthetic, and personal). Only two of these are measured on traditional IQ tests. Psychologists in the past decade have been struck by limits in traditional ways of thinking about intelligence.

## Moving beyond IQ tests

Intelligence, in classical psychological terms, is known as 'general intelligence', which is calculated as 'g' with the use of IQ tests, such as those developed by Wechsler (the most widely used measure of IQ). Knowing a person's IQ can be useful, for example in predicting academic performance (Petrides et al. 2004) and job execution (Schmidt and Hunter 1998). But we also accept that the testing of IQ and the application of an IQ score is problematic because their construction can hold issues of cultural and social bias (Murdoch 2007). Increasingly in education, it has been found to be more helpful to think of 'IQ' as just one domain of intelligence, which is a capacity to score well on particular tests that have a known focus on mathematical/logical/linguistic/spatial reasoning, set within the context of a particular culture and that culture's linguistic paradigm. And so, at this point in the chapter, we need to move away from the traditional conceptualizations of intelligence. We should now take some time to take a broader, modern perspective on what intelligence is, or can be perceived to be.

To broaden our understanding of intelligence we need to explore *interpretations* of intelligence. Think of the phrase, 'he is an intelligent child': what would be the assumed behaviour of this child? You could say that the child has certain *abilities*; that the child is equipped with knowledge and a cognitive capacity that enables him to make good sense of the word. In this case we can view intelligence *as 'a tool'* that the child possesses. However, the phrase is also loaded with assumptions from the person commenting – in other words, 'the child has achieved, met or exceeded my abilities'. There is also a judgement that the child is able to display cognitive abilities that are deemed necessary for success within the culture (i.e. it is an expectation within society). In this case we can view intelligence *as 'conformity'*. Intelligence can also be viewed as a commodity, where if others perceive you to have a high level of intelligence then you are generally valued and revered. It can provide a feeling of power for one individual over another. Further, there can also be an obvious, negative connotation to phrases such as, 'he lacks intelligence'. This is a deliberate act where power is wielded. In some cases, intelligence is even used as *a 'weapon'* by one person to suppress or damage the confidence and self-esteem of another.

What if we challenge you to consider 'general intelligence' to mean just that – a *general* intelligence where *all* human beings are viewed as intelligent rather than the top section of the population? We will now begin to look at the different ideas regarding intelligence, and to consider just how valuable it is as a construct. First, to look beyond the traditional view of intelligence requires equality and diversity at the core of your world-view, one that is devoid of the power differential and competition with others. There is also an alternative paradigm of intelligence; that intelligence is not something we should use to describe the *potential* of an individual, but regarded as *possibilities* that lie within all people.

This idea aligns with Abraham Maslow's (1962) theory of 'self-actualization' – the supreme expression of a human's life. This described the humanistic values of an individual's power to grow and change, which provoked a different perspective for the concept of intelligence. Whereas the traditional view of intelligence had a focus on innateness and permanence (Terman 1925), there was a shift to a conceptualization of what intelligence *could be* within the context of human life.

Project Zero, begun at Harvard in 1967, established itself as an intellectual home for a group of researchers who wished to challenge the ideas of Piaget, wanted to highlight the limitations of psychometric testing and had concerns with the classification of intelligence solely as an IQ rating. Howard Gardner (a co-director of Project Zero from 1972 to 2000) has a particular interest in defining intelligence as the abilities and possibilities believed to lie within us all. Gardner (1983) developed the 'Project on Human Potential' and this was the platform for the ideas of his theory of 'multiple intelligences'.

## Howard Gardner's theory of 'multiple intelligences'

**Key figure: Howard Gardner (1943–)**

Howard Gardner was born in Pennsylvania (USA), the son of refugees from Nazi Germany. Gardner trained as a developmental psychologist and later as a neuropsychologist, and is best known within education circles for his theory of multiple intelligences (MI theory). The seminal text for MI theory was *Frames of Mind: The Theory of Multiple Intelligences* (Gardner 1983), which was based on research he conducted with 'normal' and gifted children and with adults who suffered from brain damage. Gardner also directs the 'GoodWork' project, which concentrates on identifying attributes of excellence in work that is socially responsible and meaningful to its practitioners, to determine how best to increase the incidence of good work in society.

Gardner (1983, 1993) believed that there exists a multitude of intelligences, quite independent from one another. He wished to oppose the traditional, single-construct view of human intellect and the innate perspective that accompanies it. Gardner's view of intelligence was supported mainly by those who were looking to reject a view of intelligence centred around IQ tests, and also celebrated by many teachers and education policy-makers who saw traditional views of intelligence as problematic to the schooling of children (e.g. the early pigeonholing of children based on performance on IQ tests, disengagement of children with low interest or low capability in mathematical/logical/linguistic/spatial reasoning).

There were two important elements that underpinned Gardner's theory:

1. neuro-biological work relating to brain organization, including work with brain damaged patients and gifted children (he highlighted how there can be distinct abilities that can remain intact alongside partial cognitive impairment);
2. the relationship between intelligences and the different cultural contexts within which we can operate (individual experience and enrichment through opportunity or deprivation can impact on innate cognitive abilities).

'Multiple intelligence' theory (MI theory) was a way of looking at those cognitive processes not explained by 'g', for example creativity, musicality, proprioception (the ability to perceive and coordinate own movements) or socio-interpersonal skills (the skills we use to interact with, or relate to, others).

Gardner saw the individual differences we may have as humans as socially adaptive (i.e. that we can complement one another with our perceived strengths). This is good news for those of us who have a low 'musical intelligence'; it means that we are not denied music because of this because others with a high 'musical intelligence' can fill the world with music! Gardner was keen than we should appreciate variations in ability and relish uniqueness, and he supported a *constructive* tendency (where any strengths are used to the benefit of society). Gardner also advocated that we should seek to avoid the temptation to use a high intelligence in one's domain as a *destructive* force or in the pursuit of power.

But what is the implication of having a range of intelligences in an educational setting? If you are the professional needing to construct an educational programme that takes account of various intelligences, then your job is made much harder because you would be expected to take account of highly diverse learning needs. Also, as a teacher, if you need to address a number of possible intelligences within the individual then you would be faced with the potentially overwhelming task of enabling appropriate curriculum breadth that, if deployed, could detract from specific educational instruction focused on the one central skill that we associate with intellect (i.e. processing and analysing information), which has been shown to relate to higher achievement in education and better job prospects.

---

**Activity: reflecting on multiple intelligences**

Perhaps Gardner's view of intelligence makes intuitive sense to you. You may well have been able to identify your own unique blend of 'intelligences'.

- How might knowing your particular blend of 'intelligences' help you? Do they help you in your academic studies? Or do you view the intelligences as more practical life skills or as talents to develop?
- Do you see Gardner's intelligences as equivalent to traditional general intelligence?

---

There have been a number of critical discourses centred on the validity of multiple intelligences as a 'theory of intelligence' (Waterhouse 2006). It has also been suggested that Gardner uses the word intelligence where others would use 'ability' (Sternberg 1989) or 'virtues' (Scarr 1989). Another argument has been that MI theory outlines variation in cognitive *style*, and should not be confused with a stand-alone construct of intelligence (Morgan 1996). However, it would seem that the drive to set 'multiple' and 'unitary' intelligence against each other is futile as it is actually a matter of semantics (i.e. centred around meaning) and thus not necessarily appropriate for debate.

In our pursuit of understanding facets of intelligence, perhaps, one of the more constructive ideas of intelligence is one that enables us to move beyond a view of intelligence as a highly efficient cognitive function, to take into account how we *externalize* our cognitive function. Taking this stance, Robert Sternberg has provided us with an alternative conceptualization of intelligence with a focus on 'intelligent behaviour'.

## Intelligent behaviour

**Key figure: Robert Sternberg (1949–)**

Dr Robert J. Sternberg, born in New Jersey, USA, is a professor of psychology with a PhD (Psychology) from Stanford University. Sternberg is best known for his expertise in intelligence testing and his critical view of IQ tests, for his *Handbook of Human Intelligence* (1982) and the Sternberg Triarchic Abilities Test

(STAT). Sternberg's ground-breaking book, *The Triarchic Mind: A New Theory of Human Intelligence* (1989), identified a trio of mental abilities: analytical intelligence, creative intelligence and practical intelligence (the *Triarchic Theory of Human Intelligence*) as a challenge to traditional IQ tests.

Imagine for a moment that your brain is like the engine of a car . . . your engine is well built with good-quality parts (you have efficient cognitive structures and grey matter rich in brain cells plus fully connected and firing neurons) and there is engine oil added and the pistons are moving (the processes impacting on the efficiency of the structures). In much the same way you need both structures and processes for intellectual activity. Sternberg's way of viewing intelligence highlights the need to look beyond biological inheritance and development of cognitive facility, and takes account of ongoing contextual factors that regulate cognitive abilities. Therefore, we should recognize the *social context* within which intelligent behaviour occurs.

You will recall what it was like when you started your current course of study. Can you remember what strategies you used when you were faced with a new social context? How well we operate in novel situations can be interpreted to be 'intelligent behaviour'. Sternberg's theory of intelligence also identified how in novel situations we may (a) adapt to our present environment, (b) select a more optimal environment, or (c) reshape our current environment. Any of the three would be interpreted as an 'intelligent' choice! Which did you opt to do when you started studying in higher education?

To be intelligent, within Sternberg's conceptual framework, you would need to display an ability to make the most of strengths to counterbalance weaknesses (display metacognitive, performance and knowledge acquisition components), be able to adapt to novelty (apply prior experience to novel situations and apply new skills swiftly) and show adaptation to the environment (integrate into or shape present environment) or simply select a better one. It is important to recognize that Sternberg (1989) splits intelligence into three parts – analytical, creative and practical abilities to succeed within your socio-cultural context.

There are few critics of Sternberg's theory, but one issue that has been identified by Sternberg himself is that it should have a defined measure. The Sternberg Triarchic Abilities Test (STAT) has been developed, and studies carried out in different cultures have supported the validity of the STAT (Sternberg 1999; Sternberg et al. 2001; Zhang 2004; Sternberg and Grigorenko 2007). It has been found that STAT scores correlate to academic performance in domains other than those identified through a measurement of 'g' (Koke and Vernon 2003). Has the STAT identified an element of 'human potential' that is not captured in IQ tests?

Another psychologist, J.P. Guilford, also had an alternative perspective for what intelligence looks like in the context of everyday life. He felt that that previously there had been a focus on creativity arising only from a high intellect, but he believed that creativity should be viewed as being a discrete ability unrelated to intellect. In his later works, Guilford (1983) progresses his view of intelligence to focus on transformations (the ability to understand *changes* in information) and insight. This suggestion has enabled us to recognize that there are psychological processes that are regulating our thoughts and ideas at higher levels than the cognitive skills being tested in IQ tests. Guilford's ideas have been expanded and developed within the conceptual field of 'metacognition'. Metacognition is a key concept currently being explored in educational psychology; it concerns an individual and conscious process that serves the regulation of cognitive skills (Efklides 2008), our knowledge and beliefs about our own thinking, and the factors affecting thinking which then control the articulation of strategy and knowledge (Pressley et al. 1998). Conceptualizations of metacognition have provided us with a broader cognitive framework for understanding human intelligence. This has enabled the convergence of various perceptions of intelligence – innate intellectual ability, contextual variables and motivational influences.

An awareness of the role of metacognitive thoughts in general intelligence is important for when we consider contemporary perspectives on intelligence. One such contemporary perspective is '*social intelligence*'. Social intelligence is associated with the understanding of the states, strategies and intentions of others as they relate to everyday social interactions. One interpretation of social intelligence is that it is essential for the *expression* of innate cognitive ability in our social world. This means that social interactions enable attention to intelligent behaviour in individuals (i.e. intellect exists only when others are aware of it, and it arises out of social relations). However, there is also the alternative hypothesis forwarded for social intelligence, that it may have evolved as *an adaptation* to the complexities of social living (Humphrey 1976), in other words intellect is biologically determined and social cognition has evolved through necessity due to our need to coexist with other humans.

## Emotional intelligence

### Key figure: Daniel Goleman (1946–)

Daniel Goleman was born in California, USA. Goleman's doctoral research was on meditation as an intervention in stress arousal. His best-seller (*Emotional Intelligence*) in 1995 provided a platform for his view that that non-cognitive skills can matter as much as IQ. Goleman co-founded The Collaborative for Academic, Social and Emotional Learning at the Yale University Child Studies Center with a mission to introduce emotional literacy courses to schools. Goleman currently lectures internationally to business audiences, professional groups and on college campuses.

An important aspect of intelligence relating to metacognition is that of '*emotional intelligence*' (EI), where metacognitive processes have a role in a person's beliefs about their own mental state. This ability to perceive, integrate, understand and regulate emotions (Mayer and Salovey 1997) entwines with the ability to process information efficiently. An important aspect of emotional intelligence is that of emotional hijacking, or '*amygdala hijack*' (Goleman 1995). This is a state when an individual's cognitions are overpowered by their emotions; it is a physiological process in response to a stressful situation that influences the ability to think (process information effectively). Evidently, our current emotional state can wield a strong influence on our ability to perform cognitive operations well, and this challenges the view of intellectual ability as a static entity. Daniel Goleman is well regarded for his published work on emotional intelligence and his views are a popular challenge to the prioritization of 'g' as the single factor of human intelligence. His assertion is that the concept of intelligence should be dynamic, and it also should recognize the knowledge that the individual *seeks* to apply in their real-world context.

### Activity: is IQ enough to define intelligence?

Imagine a person with a high IQ score but

- without the ability to relate to others, or interpret behaviour in other people;
- without the ability to understand their own emotions, or regulate internal emotional states or external emotional expression.

Do you think these additional qualities are important characteristics of intelligence? Why?

Central to Goleman's model of emotional intelligence are his claim that scores for EI can be more meaningful as an indicator of human success than IQ scores. However, according to McCrae (2000), there are four main issues with Goleman's work: Goleman is referring to particular personality traits and he should not attempt to amalgamate them to form a unitary construct; Goleman has unclear distinction of the terms emotional literacy, emotional health, emotional skill, and emotional competency with the term 'emotional intelligence'; Goleman is misleading others when he suggests that we can override our emotional reactions; and the established measures to support the hypothesis by Goleman of an EQ quotient have not been validated. Nevertheless, Goleman's highly publicized work is a core contemporary view that merges factors of emotional regulation with the traditional definition of intelligence as a way of providing an integrated model for the human intellect.

When using psychological theory for the study of education, it is easy to assume that we have a comprehensive account of the human mind. In particular, models of intelligence are loaded with complexity, based on personal perspective and experience and, in many cases, come with an agenda. You may prefer to adhere to the traditional view of intelligence (which is useful for conceptualizing and measuring a defined cognitive process) or align with contemporary theories of intelligence (intelligence as a well-defined ability, as a social construct or facilitated by emotional regulation) but you need to recognize that your use of the term will be directed by your perception of your own intellect, which is a construct of your personal experience and circumstance.

What is clear is that any consideration of intelligent behaviour within an educational context is done to aid our assessment and planning for appropriate educational experiences. We know that it is not enough to have a high IQ (there are broader skills and abilities that support and drive the expression of this in the real world), but equally if a child has cognitive impairment characterized by a low IQ then we should not be envisaging that they will be able to achieve the same educational outcomes. However, it is this type of articulation that may have led some to assume that educational experiences should be limited for some children and enhanced for others. There is a complex moral debate that accompanies this. This is why any theory of intelligence must incorporate and give acclaim to the wide range of skills and attributes that a healthy society needs (sociability, creativity, music, arts) and the freedom to express and develop these. The Cambridge Primary Review (Alexander and Flutter 2009) has found this to be a specific weakness in the current Primary Curriculum in England.

Anyone who seeks to construct or use activities that measure intelligence to categorize children, without a focus on developing the individual potential in all children, should be viewed with suspicion. Psychological theories of intelligence are to inform a process to balance out educational input (our investments into children within society) and what we draw out (i.e. benefits for society). Classifications and uses of intelligence models should never be distorted by becoming reductionist ideas, steeped in self-interest within a competitive framework. This is likely to occur with an exclusion of its placement within a social context.

## Conclusion

This chapter has explored three key themes central to psychology as applied to education – *behaviour, learning* and *intelligence*. You should now have some understanding of the main ideas utilized by teachers, educational psychologists and other professionals working within education. Although there may be a temptation to use psychology theory to help deal with 'problems', 'issues' or 'disruption' in classroom behaviour or developmental concerns, what you need to do is focus on applying these ideas to aid your understanding about individuals (and their positive attributes) within an educational context. In doing so, you will better understand what might be driving their atypical learning, behaviour or development.

---

**Further research**

Consider the role of the educational psychologist outlined by the Children's Workforce Development Council – what does an educational psychologist do? See http://www. cwdcouncil.org. uk/educational-psychology/what

To what extent can the 'science' of psychology be used to inform and evaluate the 'art' of teaching?

## Key readings

### Books

Bentham, S. (2007) *Psychology and Education*. Abingdon: Routledge. A brilliant, concise book that gives you the 'bare bones' of psychology within education.

Long, M., Wood, C., Littleton, K., Passenger, T. and Sheehy, K. (2011) *The Psychology of Education* (2nd edn). London: Routledge. This is an invaluable text that gives you comprehensive information regarding psychology of education.

Walkup, V., Hughes, M. and Woolfolk, A.E. (2007) *Psychology in Education*. Harlow: Longman. A world-renowned textbook that utilizes international research well in an easy-to-read format.

### Websites

The British Psychological Society:

- (Division for Teachers and Researchers in Psychology) http://www.bps.org.uk/dtrp/dtrp_home.cfm
- (Division of Educational and Child Psychology) http://www.bps.org.uk/decp/decp_home.cfm

Association of Educational Psychologists: http://www.aep.org.uk/

Psychologist World: http://www.psychologistworld.com/

'Theory Into Practice' (TIP) database for theories, domains and concepts about learning: http://tip.psychology.org/index.html

### Journals

*British Journal of Educational Psychology*
*European Journal of Psychology of Education*
*Journal of Educational Psychology*

## References

Alexander, R.J. and Flutter, J. (2009) *Towards a New Primary Curriculum: A Report from the Cambridge Primary Review. Part 1: Past and Present*. Cambridge: University of Cambridge Faculty of Education.

American Association on Mental Retardation (1992) *Mental Retardation: Definition, Classification, and Systems of Supports*. Washington, DC: AAMD.

American Psychiatric Association (APA) (2009) *Diagnostic and Statistical Manual of Mental Disorders* (*DSM-IV*). Washington, DC: APA.

Bandura, A. (1974) Behavior theory and the models of man. *American Psychologist*, 29: 859–69.

Bandura, A. (1977) *Social Learning Theory*. New York: General Learning Press.

Bandura, A. (1986) *Social Foundations of Thought and Action: A Social Cognitive Theory*. Englewood Cliffs, NJ: Prentice-Hall.

Binet, A. and Simon, T. (1905) The Binet-Simon Scale. *L'Année Psychologique*, 12: 191–244.

Bruner, J. (1996) *The Culture of Education*. Cambridge, MA: Harvard University Press.

Efklides, A. (2008) Metacognition: defining its facets and levels of functioning in relation to self-regulation and co-regulation. *European Psychologist*, 13: 277–87.

Gardner, H. (1983) *Frames of Mind: The Theory of Multiple Intelligences*. New York: Basic Books.

Gardner, H. (1993) *Multiple Intelligences: The Theory in Practice*. New York: Basic Books.

Goleman, D.P. (1995) *Emotional Intelligence: Why it Can Matter More than IQ for Character, Health and Lifelong Achievement*. New York: Bantam Books.

Guilford, J.P. (1983) Transformation abilities or functions. *Journal of Creative Behavior*, 17: 75–83.

Humphrey, N. (1976) The social function of intellect. In P.P. Bateson and R.A. Hinde (eds) *Growing Points in Ethology*. Cambridge: Cambridge University Press.

Koke, L.C. and Vernon, P.A. (2003) The Sternberg Triarchic Abilities Test (STAT) as a measure of academic achievement and general intelligence. *Personality and Individual Differences*, 35: 1803–7.

Lave, J. and Wenger, E. (1990) *Situated Learning: Legitimate Peripheral Participation*. Cambridge: Cambridge University Press.

Maslow, A.H. (1962) *Toward a Psychology of Being*. Princeton, NJ: Van Nostrand.

Mayer, J.D. and Salovey, P. (1997) What is emotional intelligence? In P. Salovey and D. Sluyter (eds) *Emotional Development and Emotional Intelligence: Educational Implications*. New York: Basic Books.

McCrae, R.R. (2000) Emotional intelligence from the perspective of the five-factor model of personality. In R. Bar-On and J.D. Parker (eds) *The Handbook of Emotional Intelligence: Theory, Development, Assessment, and Application at Home, School, and in the Workplace*. San Francisco, CA: Jossey-Bass.

Morgan, H. (1996) An analysis of Gardner's theory of multiple intelligence. *Roeper Review*, 18: 263–9.

Murdoch, S. (2007) *IQ: The Brilliant Idea that Failed*. London: Duckworth.

Petrides, K.V., Frederickson, N. and Furnham, A. (2004) The role of trait emotional intelligence in academic performance and deviant behaviour at school. *Personality and Individual Differences*, 36: 277–93.

Piaget, J. (1972) *The Psychology of the Child*. New York: Basic Books.

Piaget, J. and Inhelder, B. (1966) *The Psychology of the Child*. New York: Basic Books.

Pressley, M., Van Etten, S., Yokoi, L., Freebern, G. and Van Meter, P. (1998) The metacognition of student scholarship: a grounded theory approach. In D.J. Hacker, J. Dunlosky and A.C. Graesser (eds) *Metacognition in Educational Theory and Practice*. Mahwah, NJ: Lawrence Earlbaum Associates.

Scarr, S. (1989) Protecting general intelligence: constructs and consequences for interventions. In R.L. Linn (ed.) *Intelligence: Measurement, Theory, and Public Policy*. Urbana, IL: University of Illinois Press.

Schmidt, F.L. and Hunter, J.E. (1998) The validity and utility of selection methods in personnel psychology: practical and theoretical implications of 85 years of research findings. *Psychological Bulletin*, 124: 262–74.

Sternberg, R.J. (1989) *The Triarchic Mind: A New Theory of Human Intelligence*. New York: Penguin.

Sternberg, R.J. (1999) Successful intelligence: finding a balance. *Trends in Cognitive Science*, 3: 436–42.

Sternberg, R.J. and Grigorenko, E.L. (2007) *Teaching for Successful Intelligence*. Thousand Oaks, CA: Corwin Press.

Sternberg, R.J. et al. (2001) The relationship between academic and practical intelligence: a case study in Kenya. *Intelligence*, 29: 401–18.

Terman, L.M. (1916) *The Measurement of Intelligence*. Boston, MA: Houghton Mifflin.

Terman, L.M. (ed.) (1925) *Volume I: Genetic Studies of Genius*. Stanford, CA: Stanford University Press.

Terman, L.M. and Merrill, M. (1937) *Measuring Intelligence: A Guide to the Administration of the New Revised Stanford-Binet Tests of Intelligence*. Boston, MA: Houghton Mifflin.

Vygotsky, L.S. (1978) *Mind in Society: The Development of Higher Psychological Processes*. Cambridge, MA: Harvard University Press.

Vygotsky, L.S. (1986) *Thought and Language*. Cambridge, MA: MIT Press.

Waterhouse, L. (2006) Inadequate evidence for multiple intelligences, Mozart effect, and emotional intelligence theories. *Educational Psychologist*, 41: 247–55.

Zhang, L.F. (2004) Revisiting the predictive power of thinking styles for academic performance. *Journal of Psychology*, 138: 351–70.

# 7

## DEBBIE LE PLAY
## Comparative Education

---

### Learning outcomes

By the end of this chapter you should be able to:

- explain what comparative education is as a field of inquiry, taking account of its complexity and multi-faceted nature;
- offer a brief history of comparative education, while acknowledging that it continues to develop and embrace new educational themes and topics;
- describe some key areas of inquiry from among a long list of possible topics;
- name some of the key organizations and centres involved in researching or in compiling data for purposes of comparative inquiry.

---

### Introduction

We live today in a fast-changing world, which has been made increasingly accessible through technological advances, not only in the way we travel and communicate, but also in the ways we both access and generate knowledge. If we are unable to experience different nations directly ourselves, the internet offers opportunities to discover how people live in other parts of the world. What are their societies like? What values do they hold? How do their institutions differ from or compare with what we know and have experience of ourselves? Most would agree that we live in an increasingly 'globalized' world, but the globalization debate is a fierce one. The globalists foresee the economic and political convergence of states into a new world order, the sceptics refute the strength of such transformational forces, and the transformationalists emphasize the shift of power across the world's major regions and continents (Hankin 2009).

Education is, regardless of its precise meaning or structure in individual nations, along with the challenges it involves, a common feature among most nation states.

Through the lens of formalized education structures, we can learn much about a nation's people, their history, their political structures and their institutions, their social norms and cultural values, and their economy. But we cannot fully appreciate a nation's education system without understanding the key principles that underpin that nation's culture, its political structures, its economy or its history.

Even when considering European nations whose education systems have many similarities with those of the UK, it is being able to understand and fully appreciate the sometimes very subtle but highly significant differences that are key to making rigorous and objective judgements, and that pose particular challenges for the comparativist scholar. Indeed, setting our own education system in this context enhances our understanding and appreciation of it. Comparing education systems 'challenges assumptions and stops people from being ethnocentric' (Wood 2004: 11); we can learn from others. However, while we might 'borrow' some aspects of policy and what is considered to be best practice, this should by no means be undertaken systematically and unreservedly. This chapter will reflect on what is meant by comparative studies in education, look briefly at its history as a discipline, and consider the key themes and organizations that are the focus of its endeavours.

> **Key centres: the Centre for International and Comparative Studies (ICS)**
>
> The Centre for International and Comparative Studies is located at the University of Bristol. The Centre builds on a body of comparative research and consultancy already well established in the Graduate School and its activity centres around three key areas: theory and methodology in the context of international and comparative research in education; educational policy, practice and outcomes; and educational development in small states. For further information see: http://www.bristol.ac.uk/education/reserach/centre/ics/
>
> The Education in Small States Research Group was established in 1994 and its work focuses on 'the study of education and human development in small states throughout the Commonwealth, in Europe and elsewhere'. The current Director of the Group is Michael Crossley, Professor of Comparative and International Education and Joint Co-ordinator of ICS. Professor Crossley's most recent works examine tertiary education and educational research in small states. He is Editor of the journal *Comparative Education,* and a member of the Editorial Boards for the journals *International Journal of Educational Development, Compare* and *Research in Post Compulsory Education*. For further information see: http://www.bristol.ac.uk/education/reserach/centres/ics/smallstates/

## Definitions

What is comparative education? Is it a field of inquiry or a discipline? And where does 'international education' fit within comparative education? The answers to these questions are not as obvious as they might seem. The distinction between the term international education and comparative education is not always obvious and, while sharing some conceptual territory (Thompson 2002) with comparative education, international education may be broader in its interpretation and include education in developing countries, the work of international organizations such as UNESCO, and international schools and their work (Phillips and Schweisfurth 2006). The way in which these terms have been and are still to an extent used, especially in the UK, mean that comparative education has been largely associated with education in western industrialized nations, whereas international education has referred more frequently to education in the developing world. However, recent scholars of comparative and international education have recognized the arbitrary nature of this distinction and generally seek to emphasize the complementary nature of both fields of study (Halls 1990; Epstein 1994; Phillips and Schweisfurth 2006).

The historical foundations for international *educational* relations are to be found in the Enlightenment of 18th-century Europe, and also the French and American Revolutions. Thus, curiosity with regard to how other nations, their governments and peoples are addressing educational and other issues is not new. That this should become a credible field of academic inquiry, however, is relatively recent. Anweiler (1977: 110–11) suggests that

> [t]he formation of an independent academic discipline which concerned itself with 'international' educational problems in a systematic way, and took on the name *comparative education* . . . followed relatively late: it is the result of an already existing real 'international infrastructure'.

In order to be considered a 'discipline', a field of study should have at its root a body of knowledge, seminal thinkers and texts, and a set of rules and methods. But what about fields of inquiry that draw on and are informed by several, complementary disciplines all offering their own view of the world? Education Studies is a field of academic inquiry informed by the history, sociology, philosophy, psychology and politics of education, and comparative education forms part of this rich plethora of educational inquiry.

Phillips and Schweisfurth (2006) suggest that comparative education is not a discipline in the conventional sense. They prefer to use the term 'quasi-discipline'. They argue that, while comparative education has many of the features of an academic discipline, there is not a common approach to the subject matter being investigated. In fact they go on to suggest that the use of many and sometimes opposing methodological and theoretical approaches should be considered a strength of comparative education rather than a weakness, since comparativists are not limited by disciplinary constraints and boundaries, often the case of more traditional academic disciplines. The implication is that the field is huge and covers many and varied topics, and what 'brings them together in a coherent way is the common attempt at comparison'.

But more than this is the centrality of *context* to comparative education (Broadfoot 1977). Without an understanding of how and why education in one part of the world has come to be as it is, we cannot really appreciate its differences (and similarities) or be truly critically evaluative. Comparative inquiry enhances our understanding. We learn about other ways of doing, and the information we glean from this and the conclusions we draw can help us to understand better our own provision or indeed improve on it. In a speech delivered in 1900 Michael Sadler (1861–1943), an English pioneer in comparative education, underlined the purpose of comparative study when he maintained that '[t]he practical value of studying, in a right spirit and with scholarly accuracy, the working of foreign systems of education is that it will result in our being better fitted to study and understand our own' (Higginson 1961: 291). But Noah (1983) warns of seeing things only through our own perspective and in relation to our own experience, as if that experience is in some way more valid. Certainly there is a tendency for some to see things almost exclusively through the lens of western industrialized nations.

In order for objective and unprejudiced conclusions to be drawn about a nation's education system, including our own, the collection, classification and analysis of data must be rigorous and systematic. The data may be obtained through both quantitative methods (e.g. surveys and questionnaires) and/or qualitative research (e.g. interviews and focus groups). International bodies such as UNESCO, the OECD and the European Union all provide a wealth of statistical and descriptive data for the purposes of comparative study. An informative discussion on the differences between and criticisms of the quantitative and qualitative research paradigms can be found in Bryman (2008).

**Key agencies: the United Nations Educational, Scientific and Cultural Organization (UNESCO)**

The United Nations Educational, Scientific and Cultural Organization was born in 1945, just after the Second World War had ended. Today UNESCO has 193 member states and has its headquarters in Paris. Its mission remains 'to contribute to the building of peace, the eradication of poverty, sustainable development and intercultural dialogue through education, the sciences, culture, communication and information'.

UNESCO plays a leading role in taking forward the global Education for All (EFA) initiative, and has a particular interest in the following areas:

- adult literacy;
- gender equality;
- youth;
- society's most vulnerable and marginalized groups;
- sustainable development.

It focuses its attention in particular on Africa, the least developed countries and small island developing states (SIDS). The objective of the international community is to achieve 'education for all' by 2015.

## A brief history of comparative education

Comparative education, in its broadest sense, has a very long history, dating back as far as the Ancient Greeks and Romans. In more modern times comparativists point to the wide-reaching influence of seminal educational texts such as *Émile* (1762) by Jean-Jacques Rousseau (1712–78), which made alternative and different views of education more widespread. It was however the early years of the 19th century, with increased travel and international communication, that saw the start of what Phillips and Schweisfurth (2006: 27) describe as 'the deliberate and systematic attempt to compare educational provision "elsewhere" with that "at home"'. They describe the historical development of comparative education in terms of 'emphases' and as an interactive process.

The early stages in the development of comparative education were characterized by observation and description, and came through travellers' tales (Noah and Eckstein 1969). Increasingly reliable statistical and quantifiable information was later used to support or refute politically motivated debate on education and educational reform. This was then further extended to enable a better understanding of how social phenomena and economic conditions were related. Certainly, the notion of 'policy borrowing', in other words policy informed by education policy and practice elsewhere, continues to an extent today.

By the beginning of the 20th century, European and American comparativists were strengthening their appreciation of their own education systems by comparing them with others and, if appropriate, looked to improve them through 'policy borrowing'. These same nations were equally intent on 'ameliorating' life for the 'natives' of the countries they were colonizing through western-style education provision. Such actions were, of course, a consequence of the attitudes and policies of the time. Today's comparativists view education as relative; relative to the historical, political, cultural, social and national factors that underpin it. Post-modern perspectives are critical of a view that sees the white, male, western viewpoint dominate aspects of social and cultural life, including education. The post-modern view is pluralistic and 'acknowledges and celebrates that individuals and groups of individuals have equally valid but different perspectives and an equal right to constitute knowledge' (Phillips and Schweisfurth 2006: 38).

In more recent times, international organizations have accumulated enormous amounts of information on different nation states, their institutions, societies and peoples, including education systems. This has enabled quite focused comparison of specific aspects of education provision, and outcomes such as performance and attainment across similar ages and levels. This has in turn led to certain countries being highlighted as 'performing' particularly well or badly by comparison, and to debates around common modern educational themes (e.g. starting age for formal education, approaches to literacy and numeracy, employability and so on).

---

**Activity: key themes**

Think about what other educational topics or themes might be of interest from a comparative perspective (and why) to the following groups:

- governments and policy-makers;
- educational practitioners (teachers, headteachers, lecturers, etc.);
- international development agencies.

Can you think of any others?

---

## Some key themes in comparative education

The following sections group under broad headings some of the key fields of inquiry and research in comparative education. These represent significant educational phenomena being investigated from an international perspective. However, the list is by no means exhaustive and new areas of investigation and exploration are appearing all the time. This is particularly true in the context of advances in technology and associated changes in pedagogy linked to technology-enhanced learning. Researchers in comparative education have a very wide and diverse range of educational topics to draw on and while this could be considered attractive to the prospective researcher, the field is complex. Researchers in comparative education must be mindful of methodological issues and, of course, issues of rigour and validity. For example, how does the researcher control assumptions that come from familiarity and experience of a phenomenon in one's own country when considering the same educational issue in another? The methods used and the theoretical frameworks chosen to analyse the findings will also be varied according to the purpose of the study or research.

---

**Key centres: the Centre for Comparative and International Education Research (Department of Education, University of Oxford)**

The Centre for Comparative and International Education Research focuses its work on 'the nature of educational systems, educational policy and learning and the curriculum'. Its Director is David Phillips, Professor of Comparative Education. Professor Phillips' particular areas of expertise are theoretical and methodological issues in comparative education and policy issues in historical context. He has published widely on education in Germany and on the phenomenon of 'policy borrowing' in education. He is also a member of the editorial board of *Comparative Education*. For further information see: http://www.education.ox.ac.uk/reserach/resgroup/cie/index.php

Professor Phillips has chaired the British Association for International and Comparative Education.

## Key theme 1: education and the developing world

Research into the relationship between education and development is, and has been for some time, a key area of focus for comparative education. Comparativists are interested in investigating and comparing not only how education systems begin and develop within their respective nation states, but also the potential impact of education on individuals and on the burgeoning economic health of the developing world. In so doing they may also gain further insights into the significance of education in the 'developed' world. However, it is important to bear in mind when considering this key focus the difficulty in defining the words 'development' and 'developing' world.

## What do we mean by the 'developing' world?

As Phillips and Schweisfurth (2006) point out, listing countries under one of the two headings of 'developing' or 'developed' is a false dichotomy since most nations in the world fall into a category that could be called 'middle-income' countries, and there may be more or less well developed areas in many parts of the world. An assumption that not only underpins a lot of research in this area, but also characterizes western societies' understanding of the relationship between education and the economy, suggests that the more developed and sophisticated the education system the more economically developed a country. Nevertheless, it is not always easy to determine whether economic progress accounts for improvement in the level of education of a country's workforce or whether it is the quality of the education provision that produces a better qualified and skilled worker.

Understanding educational provision only in economic terms does not take account of issues to do with sustainability, environmental concerns and questions of equity and equality. Since the 1990s, for instance, it has become increasingly apparent that global shifts in power, particularly economic power, are seeing young educated people from countries that were considered to be 'developing' in the 1960s and 1970s (e.g. the East Asian Tiger economies of Hong Kong, Taiwan, Singapore and South Korea) taking over jobs that would previously have been done by the educated from 'developed' countries, and that 'developed' and 'developing' countries alike are facing similar challenges to do with social exclusion, poverty (Little 2003) and fully understanding the impact of education on the economic and social health of a nation.

## Key theme 2: transition and post-conflict education

Transition and post-conflict education are areas of inquiry that are clearly rooted in both politics and education. Countries that can be said to be 'in transition' are those that are progressing from one set of conditions to another. An example would be the eastern European countries post-1989, after the fall of the Soviet Union. A key interest that comparativists have generally in investigating most, if not all, educational phenomena is in trying to achieve a theoretical understanding of those phenomena. In the case of transitional states, researchers are keen to determine a framework of common features of educational provision in those countries and in identifying and comparing elements of pre-transitional education systems considered to be successful and effective.

## Transition

Following research undertaken in 1995, McLeish et al. (cited in Phillips and Schweisfurth 2006) devised a model based on variable movement through the different stages that take countries from authoritarian to democratic forms of government, and they applied this model to the processes of educational transition in the relevant countries. One of their main findings in relation to the eastern bloc countries was that it was misleading to lump countries together in this way since each of the eastern bloc countries had approached the Soviet Union differently. Therefore the way it interpreted Marxism-Leninism in the context of education was different. For example, Hungary turned out to be far less conformist in its education provision than the German Democratic Republic and allowed uncensored western textbooks.

What was also interesting was that there appeared to be, by western standards, a number of praiseworthy features in the education provision that risked being abandoned post-communism. For instance, the seemingly egalitarian principles on which the systems were founded and an effective pre-school provision that, in turn, helped working mothers juggle employment and family commitments. Consideration had also to be given to the individual cultural and religious traditions, and linguistic and ethnic mix of each of these countries. McLeish et al. (1998) suggest as part of their theoretical framework that in the analysis of transition processes the areas of investigation or issues to be addressed can be grouped under four key headings, which are *reconstruction, transition, educational change* and *context*.

## Conflict

Comparativists are equally concerned to investigate the relationship between education and conflict. How do countries engaged in or coming out of conflict recover their sometimes lost educational infrastructure? Is it possible that education can exacerbate as well as prevent conflict? Recent research on education and conflict has questioned the basic assumption that education is 'a good thing' and necessarily decreases the propensity of individuals to engage in conflict in future (Tomlinson and Benefield 2005). Early work on education post-conflict focused on educational reconstruction after the Second World War, with particular regard to Germany and Japan (see Shibata 2005 for more recent research in this area).

Davies (2004) uses examples from a range of countries engaged in or recently engaged in conflict in more recent times, including Northern Ireland, Afghanistan, Bosnia and Rwanda. She argues that 'education indirectly does more to contribute to the underlying causes of conflict than it does to contribute to peace' (p. 203). Davies also acknowledges that analysis of education and conflict throws up many contradictions that arise from the cultural, social, political and historical peculiarities of individual nation states. She suggests that post-conflict societies would benefit from radical transformation of their schooling and education systems rather than from reconstruction of what went before (and which may have been part of the problem in the first place).

**Activity: understanding the context(s)**

Phillips and Schweisfurth (2006: 104) recommend that in the context of researching education and development it is important to take account of 'the voices of the less powerful' and not to underestimate the practical and ethical aspects of researching and conducting research in developing countries.

Consider the significance of historical and cultural contexts.

Discuss what the practical and ethical issues might be and whose 'voices' are being referred to.

---

**Key centres: the British Association for International and Comparative Education (BAICE)**

The British Association for International and Comparative Education (BAICE) began as the British Section of the Comparative Education Society in Europe (CESE) in the 1960s and underwent a number of name changes until it was relaunched in its current form in 1997. Its aims include: promoting teaching and cross-disciplinary research, supporting students and providing a resource to policy-makers.

Many leading scholars of comparative education have been associated with BAICE, including both Professor Brian Holmes and Professor Edmund King, founder members of the World Council of Comparative Education Societies. BAICE is responsible for producing the journal *Compare*. See http://www.baice.ac.uk

## Key theme 3: the European Union and European education systems

European education systems are attractive to comparativists in the western world because European nations face similar economic, social and educational challenges, and the study of alternative ways of rising to those challenges through different educational approaches may offer potential 'policy borrowing' and practice-sharing opportunities to governments and educational experts. However, the caveat is that geographical proximity does not mean necessarily that individual nations will share all the same cultural, political or historical imperatives. In fact, researchers should be far more wary of falling into the trap of making assumptions about other European countries' approaches to education and being 'blinded by the obvious'. Hence, automatic and systematic 'policy borrowing' should be avoided.

Of course there is much that Europeans share, nevertheless 'each country in Europe has its specific and dominant knowledge tradition which is intelligible throughout Europe because it is also part of a common European culture' (McLean 1996: 37). Therein lies the trap of taken for granted assumptions. Consider the traditions of knowledge on which education systems are built in Europe. The following list of divergent features in education systems across Europe is adapted from McLean (1996):

- different hierarchies of status between subjects;
- differing views as to what should be central or compulsory;
- specialization happens at different times and levels, and to different degrees;
- outcomes for different subject areas in terms of students' cognitive, moral and emotional development may differ;
- the learning environment and whole educational experience may differ enormously;
- the purpose and status of different educational trajectories may be more or less prized within society.

The English education system, for example, has its roots in Humanism, which is among the most powerful of intellectual forces in Europe. The key principles that underpin Humanism are *morality, individualism* and *specialization*.

If we take each of these principles in turn we can find examples of how these are or have been in recent times reflected in the English education system. In the Humanist tradition, knowledge was considered to be a means through which to achieve 'goodness' (principle of morality) and to develop moral capacities, the idea being that individual moral 'men' would make for a 'good' society (principle of individuality). English history and particularly English literature were at the top of the hierarchical pyramid in terms of subject status and whilst much literature, for example in the late 19th and early 20th centuries, described the plight of the working-class masses and the conditions of the poor, education still remained very much a privilege of the elite in English society. Rather than making education available to a broader section of society, it was the elite whose knowledge was broadened, especially through literature, by being made aware of the conditions and lives of the poor.

The Humanist philosophy of learning is intuitive. The learner responds individually to knowledge, and interaction between teacher and learner is highly regarded. Hence the development of a strong pastoral element within the teaching role in English education, and the importance of the 'tutorial' system typical of traditional university settings such as those associated with Oxford and Cambridge. Standardized, methodical and systematic learning, which we might associate with some elements of the English education system since the Education Reform Act of 1988 and the National Curriculum, are not wholly reconcilable with an intuitive, learner-centred view of education; and notwithstanding some quite radical changes to the English curriculum in recent times, it continues to be highly specialized post-14 and beyond in comparison to curricula in most other European countries. This feature of English education reveals its underlying Humanist thinking whereby an individual learner seeks depth of knowledge, and from this specialization general principles can then emerge. This is contrary to encyclopaedic thought, which contends that breadth of knowledge precedes depth of knowledge.

## The encyclopaedic tradition

Encyclopaedism is underpinned by principles that encourage breadth rather than depth of knowledge and that see rationality as the defining feature. Its three key principles are *rationality, utility* and *universality*.

The French education system clearly manifests aspects of the encyclopaedic tradition. Rationality is the criterion by which branches of knowledge, in other words different academic disciplines, are recognized to have value. Both mathematics and philosophy have significant positions within the French curriculum. Despite some changes in recent years, a *baccalauréat* (i.e. an end of secondary-level academic qualification) specializing in mathematics is still a huge advantage for access to the preparatory classes of the elite higher education establishments in France called *les grandes écoles*.

Rational knowledge is not only worthwhile in itself but also in the use it can be put to (utility). Utility has focused on the development of professional and specific technical skills through the specialist technical and professional colleges (*lycées professionnels* and *lycées techniques*) and in the clear distinction at higher education level between the generalist education offered by the universities and the advanced specialist training of top professionals, technicians and civil servants in the elite *grandes écoles*. Some critics refer to this system as two-tier and in contradiction with the third principle of universality. Nevertheless, a limited degree of equality is guaranteed through standardization of the broad core curriculum, if not the educational experience, at least up to the age of 15. The education systems of Spain, Portugal, Italy and Belgium also reflect elements of the encyclopaedic tradition.

## Challenges to European 'unity'

Nation states in Europe share a common heritage but preserve distinct national traditions, which are reflected in their institutions and not least in their education systems. But change is occurring and with it come new and more difficult challenges. According to Tulasiewicz and Brock (2000: 6) educational change in member states of the European Union is about the economic challenge that highlights the need for preparation for skilled work of school pupils and professionals through wide access to technological innovation, the socio-political skills of citizenship and the creation of opportunities for life-long learning. The consequent issues to be addressed and of interest to the comparative researcher are, among others:

- language competence, language awareness and issues associated with the supremacy of the native tongue;
- concerns over the sustainability of successful EU educational initiatives and projects such as ERASMUS (European student exchange/mobility scheme);
- enlargement, expansion and alignment (currently 28 member states) with implications for education and employment across Europe;
- implementation of the European Dimension in the curriculum, and the raising of awareness of Europe and its peoples;

- the apparent conflict between European educational objectives and current educational diversity (see *Bologna* below);
- the integration of 'new' Europeans (not of European cultural heritage) in European societies.

The EU maxim is 'unity in diversity'. An important question in this context will be whether education in its diverse forms can, or indeed should, take member states one day to economic convergence or convergence of a more radical nature.

---

### Activity: comparing approaches to religion in education

*Reflection*

Think about the ways in which religion and education have been and still are 'connected', and how religious needs are accommodated in your own country's education system.

*Research*

Find out about and compare the English and the French approaches to 'religion in education' using a variety of sources. The following questions might help you to put these approaches into context.

- Are both the English and French states secular? How do we know?
- What are the fundamental principles that underpin the education systems of each country?
- Where does 'religion' feature in the curriculum, if at all? How does 'religion' and 'religious diversity' manifest itself in schools and schooling?
- What, if any, connections are there between the underpinning principles of each state and the approach taken to 'religion' in education in France and England?
- What provision is there in each country for meeting diverse religious needs?

*Debate*

Consider the different approaches and different contexts described above, and debate the merits, drawbacks and obstacles of 'transferring' the French approach to the English context and vice-versa.

---

### Key agencies: the Organization for Economic Co-operation and Development (OECD)

The OECD was established in 1961 and brings together the most prosperous economies from around the world and who are committed to democracy and the market economy. Its key mission is to better the world economy by providing a global forum for the development of ideas to sustain economic growth, effective education systems and employment, and to support developing economies around the world. Its wealth of comparative statistical data, economic and social information, research and analysis allows governments to compare policy experiences, seek answers to common problems, identify good practice, and coordinate domestic and international policies. This is, of course, also a valuable source of data for comparativists.

Twenty countries originally signed the Convention on the Organization for Economic Cooperation and Development on 14 December 1960, including the UK on 2 May 1961. A further ten countries have since joined, the most recent being the Slovak Republic on 14 December 2000.

The OECD Annual Report 2009 describes recent projects undertaken in the context of comparing educational systems and learner attainment in member and partner countries. These include a study called *Improving School Leadership* (August 2008), which draws on comparative analysis of 22 countries and identifies a range of policy options to help governments in improving school leadership, and also a study known as the *Assessment of Higher Education Learning Outcomes* (AHELO), designed to assess the feasibility of comparing the learning outcomes of students enrolled in different types of institutions of higher education across different geographic, cultural and linguistic backgrounds. The study focuses on generic skills, economics and engineering.

## Key theme 4: policy perspectives

### Policy 'borrowing'

Transferring, or rather investigating the possibilities of transfer, of educational ideas and approaches is especially attractive to comparativists because, as we have already seen, one of the key reasons for comparative educational research is to learn from others and to explore how things are done elsewhere. Increasingly detailed statistical and other information about education systems elsewhere through mechanisms such as PISA (Programme for International Student Assessment) or the European Commission (*Eurostat*) leads policy-makers all too often into being seduced by educational successes in other countries with insufficient regard paid to the complex cultural, political and historical contexts involved in such successes. The desire to seek 'easy' solutions to educational difficulties from abroad was fuelled to an extent in the UK by the so-called Ruskin Speech of 1976 by the then Prime Minister, James Callaghan, which focused the debate around education and its link with the nation's economic competitiveness. Politicians and educationalists began to look abroad for solutions to the educational problems with which they were struggling. Green (1999: 56) describes policy borrowing as a 'by-product of governments facing common problems'.

A recent example would be a key principle of the education policy outlined in the Conservative manifesto in the run-up to the 2010 general election, which draws on the Swedish 'free schools' model of educational provision whereby 'independent' groups such as parents, charities or private companies would be able to set up and manage schools within the state sector, ostensibly to drive up standards and to improve discipline. However, 'transferring' a policy (in this case, of school choice) from one system to another, without taking due account of the social and cultural imperatives of its origins or in-depth research on its impact in the home nation, could potentially be fraught with difficulty.

Comparativists are interested in analysing the effects of 'borrowing' policy in this context. For example, why and how the ideas or approaches are adopted in the first place by a given country, and how effectively they are adapted to their 'new' environment. Ochs (2006) suggests that examples from abroad might be borrowed to simply influence policy discourse or debate without an intention to adopt them necessarily into the local context, but they might also be 'borrowed' in the more literal sense, in other words to inspire policy change where policy 'talk' becomes policy 'action'.

---

**Case study: improving achievement in Barking and Dagenham (Ochs 2006)**

*The case*

Between 2003 and 2004 a study was undertaken in the London Education Authority of Barking and Dagenham to investigate the 'borrowing' of ideas prevalent in Swiss education to improve primary mathematics teaching.

*The study*

The study used a variety of quantitative and qualitative research methods and data sources, and the analysis was undertaken principally with the aid of theoretical models developed by Ochs and Phillips (2004), which propose four stages of 'policy borrowing':

1.  cross-national attraction whereby a foreign approach to a local problem appears attractive;
2.  decision-making – why and how the 'new' information is to be used;
3.  implementation;
4.  internalization – 'internalization entails the "absorption of external features", "synthesis" and "evaluation"'.

*The findings*

The IPM programme (Improving Primary Mathematics) that began in 1996 was effective in raising standards in project schools. It was also behind many of the approaches adopted by the National Numeracy Strategy (1998).

There have been significant changes in the teaching of mathematics in primary education in the UK since this time and an updated version of IPM, called New IPM, is being devised to reflect changes in the *Primary Framework for Mathematics* (2006).

See the IPM website, http://www.ipmaths.co.uk/index.html, for full details about the programme.

Despite increasing instances of national policy being influenced by ideas and approaches from abroad, and the development of a familiar international discourse in European policy-making on education and training, Green et al. (1999: 235) argue that in many of the key areas of educational policy and practice different countries remain very different to one another. 'The direct jurisdiction of supranational bodies over national education systems [remains] relatively limited' (Green 1999: 56).

---

**Key initiatives: the Programme for International Student Assessment (PISA)**

PISA is an OECD programme for international student assessment and was developed jointly by participating countries to survey 15 year olds in schools every three years, hence its relevance and significance not only to the governments and educators in the relevant OECD member and partner countries, but also to researchers in comparative education. The survey is designed to assess the extent to which 15 year olds nearing the end of their compulsory schooling have acquired the knowledge and skills required to engage fully with everyday life. The assessment covers reading, mathematics and science. There have been three assessments so far, in 2000, 2003 and 2006, involving between 4500 and 10,000 students in each cycle. The results of the 2009 assessment, which focused on reading, show that Korea and Finland are the highest-performing OECD countries.

Grek (2009: 23) offers an interesting reading of the significance of PISA as a tool in our understanding of European education systems, and contends that PISA has become 'an indirect, but nonetheless influential tool of the new political technology of governing the European education space by numbers'.

---

## Key theme 5: higher education and the Bologna Agreement

The study of higher education and higher education policy as a field of inquiry in its own right has gathered momentum over recent years. The Society for Research in Higher Education (SRHE) is one academic body, for example, which unites scholars and researchers of higher education from the UK and abroad. The contribution of higher education to the economy in terms of preparing (young) people for employment, lifelong learning and responsible citizenship, has also become increasingly significant. Changes in higher education in some countries from an elite to a mass system also reflect changing economic as well as educational priorities. What is known as 'the Bologna process' is of relevance here. Since its very beginnings in 1999, the Bologna process has highlighted many of the issues and complexities involved in comparing different education systems. The way in which each European signatory to the Bologna Agreement is trying to implement its guiding principles provides a rich and interesting source of comparison for the comparative researcher.

## The Bologna process

When the Bologna Declaration was originally signed in 1999 by 29 European countries (including the UK), its signatories undertook to work towards a number of common objectives to establish the European Higher Education Area (EHEA) and the Europe of Knowledge. It recognized the significance of education and educational cooperation in the development and strengthening of peaceful and democratic societies, and emphasized the need to increase the international competitiveness of the European system of higher education. It sought to achieve within a decade of the third millennium (by 2010) the following:

- the adoption of a system of easily readable and comparable degrees;
- the adoption of a system essentially based on two main cycles, undergraduate and graduate;
- the establishment of a system of credits as a proper means of promoting the most widespread student mobility.

Today, 47 countries are committed to the creation of a European Higher Education Area, and the process involves organizations and agencies such as the European Commission, the Council of Europe, the UNESCO European Centre for Higher Education, European Students' Union and the European Association for Quality Assurance in Higher Education. Additional areas of interest now part of the process are: life-long learning (added at the Prague Summit in 2001), doctoral studies as a third cycle (agreed at the Berlin Summit in 2003), equality of opportunity in and access to higher education, and EHEA in a global setting.

## Challenges for the European Higher Education Area

The EHEA was officially launched when ministers responsible for higher education in the participating countries met in Budapest and Vienna on 11–12 March 2010. While recognizing some achievements, the Budapest–Vienna Declaration (12 March 2010) nevertheless acknowledges the immense challenges involved in taking the process forward.

It could be argued that successes of the process thus far include:

- the adoption of the Diploma Supplement, which gives the detail of a graduate's course and grades, and is a common tool used by all European signatories;
- the proliferation (but with varying success in terms of uptake by students) of ERASMUS exchange programmes between institutions;
- cooperation between researchers on European collaborative research projects.

This is quite some way from the original idealism of the 1999 Declaration, but this should not come as a big surprise, particularly to those involved in comparative education research.

Consider, for example, the particular challenges associated with student and staff mobility. Native English-speaking students and staff are far less likely to take up opportunities to study abroad through ERASMUS and other schemes than their European counterparts, not least because they often lack the language skills required to be mobile. Some might argue that this is due to the prevalence and importance of the English language for business and commerce globally, that English native speakers have become linguistically lazy (and culturally complacent) and no longer feel the need to master other languages or know other cultures. Some may point to the narrowness of the English National Curriculum. Cultural and political factors have certainly down-played second language competence over many years. Added to this is the (in)significance paid to the European Dimension in schools in the UK compared to other European countries such as Germany, for example.

In terms of the purpose of higher education and the status of undergraduate qualifications, Corbett (2005) points out further differences. The Bachelor/ Masters structure in higher education in the UK is well established, and 'the degree' is a well-known and generally well-respected qualification on the employment market. It is expected that about 50 per cent of students achieving an undergraduate qualification will leave university and go on to join the labour market. Whereas in Europe as a whole the expectation is that only 17 per cent will not stay on to take a higher qualification; in Germany the figure is 10 per cent, in Austria, Italy, Spain and Portugal this is 6–10 per cent and in France only 4 per cent. There is also inconsistency in terms of course length and associated credit points across the countries. Different nations have developed different quality systems, ranging from strong administrative intervention to the precise opposite, and those with an evaluative element and those without (Tomusk 2006). While universities across Europe are facing very similar challenges – increasing student numbers, cuts in funding, the relevance of higher education to the economy, public accountability and so on – it is difficult to see how such divergent systems, which have arisen out of distinct national cultural, political and historical imperatives, could one day converge in a meaningful way.

**Key centres: the Centre for Higher Education Policy Studies (CHEPS)**

CHEPS is an interdisciplinary research institute located at the School of Management and Governance of the University of Twente (Universiteit Twente) in the Netherlands. Its Director is Guy Neave, Professor of Comparative Higher Education Policy Studies. Professor Neave's areas of expertise are higher education policy in Europe and European integration. He has been Vice President of the Comparative Education Society in Europe, Vice President of the Society for Research into Higher Education (SRHE) and in 1999 became a member of the National Academy of Education of the USA. See http://www.utwente.nl/cheps/

## Key theme 6: migration, diaspora and identity

### What is diaspora?

Diaspora refers to the phenomenon of displacement and dispersion of people, their culture, language and associated practices. It derives from the Ancient Greek word for dispersal and denotes the experience of such cultural communities, for example communities of Arab and North African origin in France, Turkish migrant workers in Germany and Mexican migrant workers in the United States. Roth (2008: 891) describes diasporic identities as emerging from 'a process of cultural bricolage that leads to cultural métissage and therefore hybridity and heterogeneity'.

### The challenges of multi-culturalism and diaspora

Such movement of peoples presents challenges to national institutions and structures (such as education systems) since these are founded on and operate, in most cases, according to the dominant, indigenous culture and traditions. In the United States, recent migration of large numbers of Mexicans to 'New Latino Diaspora towns' has, for instance, been especially challenging not only for local civic life and structures but also for the communities themselves: indigenous populations, the local residents *and* the newcomers seeking to understand their place and identity in a new and unfamiliar context (Wortham et al. 2009).

In a paper that explores transcultural literacy in the context of current debates on literacy, multi-culturalism and diasporic identity, and looks specifically at Greek communities in Melbourne, Australia, Kostogriz and Tsolidis (2008: 132) describe diasporic people as 'people who struggle to come to terms with their ambivalent position'. They describe 'diasporic space' as a place where a 'new' set of cultural references and practices operate and which build on common histories and traditions, and where the sense is one of 'belonging to several socio-cultural places – and thus to no particular place' (p. 134). In France, for example, second-generation French of Arab descent often identify themselves through a language and culture (especially in music, but also in literature and cinema), that is particular to them and known popularly as *beur* (a derivation of the word 'arabe' in French 'back-slang'). They are French, having been born and still living in France, and yet they are North African by heritage and through family ties; they often feel rejected by both communities. The implications for education are clear. A narrow, polarized view of education that seeks to reproduce the dominant culture seems inappropriate and outdated. School populations in multi-cultural societies are characterized by diversity and heterogeneity. How different nation states address these challenges in a globalized world, through education in its broadest sense, is not only of interest to the comparativist but also of concern to policy-makers and educators.

---

**Activity: globalization and education**

1. Write down three key words that you associate with the idea of globalization.
2. How has society changed over the past 50 years?
3. How has our understanding of knowledge, education, and teaching and learning changed over the past 50 years?
4. Consider the following and discuss what might be the implications for education in the future:

| Digital educational communities | | Education for sustainable development |

5. Consider the following:

   The globalization of educational policy and practice is bringing about an almost exclusive dominance of a western paradigm of what constitutes good practice. (Lynch 1996)

   Explain and discuss the implications for comparative education research and its purpose.

---

## Key theme 7: global education, global learning and citizenship

Comparativists are particularly interested in investigating the different ways in which countries worldwide prepare their young people to become responsible, tolerant and peace-loving individuals in a globalized world. While the terms 'global education', 'global learning' and 'citizenship' have been linked in the above heading, global education and global learning are not synonymous, even if their ultimate objective is the same.

UNESCO (2000a) defines global education broadly in the following terms: 'Education for human rights, peace, international understanding, tolerance and non-violence, [and] all aspects of education relating to the principles of democracy and multicultural and intercultural education'.

The link with 'global' citizenship is evident and this objective has taken on special poignancy since the terrorist attacks of September 2001 in the United States, of March 2004 in Madrid and of July 2007 in London. Countries who subscribe to the UNESCO ideals attempt to embed the principles in their schools through programmes and initiatives that focus on 'citizenship'. Nevertheless, the ultimate aim is for these principles to be rooted in the curriculum as whole. Despite discrete and focused initiatives over a number of years in English schools, for example, designed to develop an awareness and understanding in young people of human rights, diversity and change, 'citizenship' as a distinct component of the English curriculum and a route through which to provide global education is, in comparative terms, a quite recent addition to the National Curriculum. It was introduced as a statutory subject for secondary schools only in 2002 (see Breslin and Dufour 2006).

France, on the other hand, has had a form of 'civics education' that addresses some of the concerns of responsible citizenship above since the Jules Ferry Laws of the late 19th century, albeit in the specific context of becoming a 'good French citizen'. In Danish schools there is considerable focus on participatory democracy and lessons in citizenship, and there is a long tradition of working with international topics in learning environments, particularly in history, geography and social studies, but also in the teaching of foreign languages. The importance of the international dimension is recognized in the *Folkeskole* Act of 1989 and in the 2006 Danish government strategy for enhanced internationalization of education. The latter specifies that teaching in schools should include a strong global perspective and encourage pupil participation in a minimum of two international projects during the compulsory schooling stage (Eurydice 2009).

Global learning, by contrast, has been described by Gibson et al. (2008: 11) as 'a student centred activity in which learners of different cultures use technology to improve their global perspectives while remaining in their home countries', and that should enable young people to develop and acquire the skills, knowledge and attitudes that are prerequisite to world citizenship. If new technologies feature so prominently as an (educational) vehicle to enable global citizenship, there are inevitably questions around accessibility, equity and opportunity. All young people may not have equal access to new technologies and new media. This may be true of certain sections of economically strong, industrialized societies, but it is even more so of (still) developing, post-colonial countries.

---

### Activity: rethinking globalization and its implications

Think about what is meant by 'developing, post-colonial countries' and which countries they might be.

Ake (1996, cited in Ojo 2009: 74) suggests that 'many Africanists contend that the current spate of global transformation is nothing but a re-colonization process that not only democratizes dis-empowerment but facilitates the sustenance of the status quo'.

Explain to a partner what you understand by this and how this might relate more broadly to current understandings and conceptions of education.

---

### Key initiatives: Dakar Framework for Action

*The Dakar Framework for Action, Education for All: Meeting Our Collective Commitments* was adopted at the World Education Forum (26–28 April 2000) in Dakar. It builds on the vision of the World Declaration on Education for All adopted in 1990 (Thailand) and is based on the EFA (Education For All) 2000 Assessment, which was an extensive evaluation of the state of education around the world. This assessment revealed that, in 2000, more than 113 million children had no access to primary education, that 880 million adults were illiterate, that gender discrimination continued to permeate education systems and that the quality of educational provision still differed markedly between societies (UNESCO 2000b). The international community thereby committed itself to a number of fundamental objectives that would demand political will, commitment and resources primarily at national level, with UNESCO taking on a co-ordinating role and maintaining the collaborative momentum.

---

### The Dakar Framework Education for All: Meeting Our Collective Commitments

The international community committed itself to the attainment of the following goals.

1. Expanding and improving comprehensive early childhood care and education.
2. Ensuring that all children, particularly girls, children in difficult circumstances and those belonging to ethnic minorities, have access to and complete, free and compulsory primary education of good quality.
3. Ensuring that the learning needs of all young people and adults are met through equitable access to appropriate learning and life skills programmes.
4. Achieving a 50 per cent improvement in levels of adult literacy, especially for women, and equitable access to basic and continuing education for all adults.
5. Eliminating gender disparities in primary and secondary education by 2005, and achieving gender equality in education by 2015.
6. Improving all aspects of the quality of education and ensuring excellence of all so that recognized and measurable learning outcomes are achieved by all, especially in literacy, numeracy and essential life skills.

(Adapted from UNESCO 2000b)

---

## Conclusion

This chapter has offered a definition of comparative education while acknowledging the complexities of comparing systems and practices across Europe and the world. It has focused on those areas of inquiry the author believes to be most pertinent to an understanding of what constitutes 'education' in a globalized world, but recognizes that the potential list is vast and that new areas for research will inevitably present themselves. Advances in technology have made the world that much smaller, and enable the sharing and comparing of ideas on a scale never before imagined. Changes in social structures and in the values that underpin them have also meant profound shifts in the way we interact with institutions and with one another. Yet the way young people are educated has in many ways remained unchanged over many years. As Broadfoot (2000: 370) suggests, 'it is the unique privilege of comparativists to straddle cultures and countries, perspectives and topics, theories and disciplines', and in this context comparative education research has a fundamental role to play. It has the potential to lay bare and take forward key debates about the nature of education in a globalized world and its relationship with society, the economy and the world order. Teachers, educationalists, politicians and all who are passionate about the value of education and its potential to enhance and empower have a responsibility to look outside national confines; comparativists have a duty to help facilitate this.

---

**Further research**

There are clearly many and various educational topics worthy of investigation by comparativists, and this chapter has mentioned only a few. Among others might be:

- teacher perspectives, for example initial teacher training, the role of the teacher (academic/pastoral);
- learner perspectives, for example the classroom context, the student experience, special educational needs;
- school perspectives, for example the curriculum, assessment, qualifications; the school environment; levels of schooling from early years through primary and secondary to post compulsory;
- technology-enhanced learning;
- education for sustainable development;
- comparative research methodology and methods.

---

## Key reading

### Books

Bignold, W. and Gayton, L. (2009) *Global Issues and Comparative Education*. Exeter: Learning Matters. Part of the *Perspectives in Education Studies* series edited by John Sharp, this book provides a comprehensive and accessible introduction to comparative education at undergraduate level. It offers a comparative analysis of education systems around the world by level/age.

Osborn, M. et al. (2003) *A World of Difference? Comparing Learners Across Europe*, Maidenhead: Open University Press. This book is based on a study (ENCOMPASS), which compares the experience of young learners in England, France and Denmark, and explores the relationship between national educational cultures, individual biographies and classroom practices. It investigates the effect of different policy-making on pupils by giving space to the voice of the young learners in the three different contexts.

Phillips, D. and Schweisfurth, M. (2006) *Comparative and International Education: An Introduction to Theory, Method and Practice*. London: Continuum. Phillips and Schweisfurth approach comparative education from theoretical, methodological and thematic perspectives, and in so doing provide an in-depth grounding in what it is/means to be a comparativist.

### Websites

- The European Union and European national profiles:

  http://europa.eu/index_en.htm

  http://epp.eurostat.ec.europa.eu/portal/page/portal/statistics/search_database

- Organization for Economic Co-operation and Development (OECD): http://www.oecd.org/statisticsdata/0,3381,en_2649_35845621_1_119656_1_1_1,00.html

- The United Nations Educational, Scientific and Cultural Organization (UNESCO) http://www.unesco.org/new/en/unesco/
http://www.unesco.org/en/efa/

- The official Bologna process website: http://www.ond.vlaanderen.be/hogeronderwijs/Bologna/

## Journals

Peer-reviewed journals (i.e. those that publish articles and research outcomes that have been scrutinized by fellow scholars and experts in the field, provide the most up-to-date information on a given topic).

- *Comparative Education* is an international journal of educational studies. Its editors include Professor Michael Crossley and Dr Michele Scweisfurth.

- *Compare* is the official journal of the British Association for International and Comparative Education (BAICE).

- *European Journal of Education* is an international, peer-reviewed journal of which the key focus is the study of European education within an international perspective. The first part of each issue focuses on a particular theme. For example, part one of the December 2010 issue looks at the last ten years of the Bologna process.

## References

Anweiler, O. (1977) Comparative education and the internationalization of education. *Comparative Education*, 13(2): 109–14.

Bologna Declaration (1999) available at http://www.ond.vlaanderen.be/hogeronderwijs/bologna/documents/MDC/Bologna_Declaration1.pdf

Breslin, T. and Dufour, B. (eds) (2006) *Developing Citizens: A Comprehensive Introduction to Effective Citizenship Education in the Secondary School*. London: Hodder Murray.

Broadfoot, P. (1977) The comparative contribution: a research perspective. *Comparative Education*, 13(2): 133–7.

Broadfoot, P. (2000) Comparative education for the 21st century: retrospect and prospect. *Comparative Education*, 36(3): 357–71.

Bryman, A. (2008) *Social Research Methods: Third Edition*. Oxford: Oxford University Press.

Budapest–Vienna Declaration (2010) available at http://www.ond.vlaanderen.be/hogeronderwijs/bologna/2010_conference/documents/Budapest-Vienna_Declaration.pdf

Corbett, A. (2005) *Universities and the Europe of Knowledge: Ideas, Institutions and Policy Entrepreneurship in European Union Higher Education Policy, 1955–2005*. Basingstoke: Palgrave Macmillan.

Davies, L. (2004) *Education and Conflict: Complexity and Chaos*. Abingdon: RoutledgeFalmer.

Epstein, E.H. (1994) Comparative and international education: overview and historical development. In T. Husén and T. Postlethwaite (eds) *The International Encyclopaedia of Education*. Oxford: Pergamon.

Eurydice (2009) *The Organization of the Education System in Denmark, 2008/9*. EACEA, available at http://eacea.ec.europa.eu/education/eurydice/index_en.php

Gibson, K.L., Rimmington, G.M. and Landwehr-Brown, M. (2008) Developing global awareness and responsible world citizenship with global learning. *Roeper Review*, 30: 11–23.

Green, A. (1999) Education and globalization in Europe and East Asia: convergent and divergent trends. *Journal of Education Policy*, 14: 55–71.

Green, A., Wolf, A. and Leney, T. (1999) *Convergence and Divergence in European Education and Training Systems*. London: Institute of Education, University of London.

Grek, S. (2009) Governing by numbers: the PISA 'effect' in Europe. *Journal of Education Policy*, 24(1): 23–37.

Halls, W.D. (ed.) (1990) *Comparative Education: Contemporary Issues and Trends*. London: Jessica Kingsley/UNESCO.

Hankin, L. (2009) Global citizenship and comparative education. In J. Sharp et al. (eds) *Education Studies: An Issues-based Approach*. Exeter: Learning Matters.

Higginson, J.H. (1961) The centenary of an English pioneer in comparative education: Sir Michael Sadler (1861–1943). *International Review of Education*, 7(3): 286–98.

Kostogriz, A. and Tsolidis, G. (2008) Transcultural literacy: between the global and the local. *Pedagogy, Culture and Society*, 16(2): 125–36.

Little, A. (2003) Development studies and comparative education: context, content, comparison and contributors. In E.R. Beauchamp (ed.) *Comparative Education Reader*. New York: RoutledgeFalmer.

Lynch, J. (1996) Learning and teaching: the international transfer of dysfunctional paradigms. Paper presented at the 'International issues in teaching and learning' conference, Bristol, January.

McLean, M. (1996) School knowledge traditions. In J. Ahier, B. Cosin and M. Hales (eds) *Diversity and Change: Education, Policy and Selection*. London: Open University.

Mcleish, E.A. and Phillips, D. (eds) (1998) *Processes of Transition in Education Systems*. Oxford: Symposium Books.

Noah, H.J. (1983) *The Use and Abuse of Comparative Education*. New York: Teachers College.

Noah, H.J and Eckstein, MA (1969) *Toward a Science of Comparative Education*. London: Macmillan.

Ochs, K. (2006) Cross-national policy borrowing and educational innovation: improving achievement in the London Borough of Barking and Dagenham. *Oxford Review of Education*, 32(5): 599–618.

Ochs, K. and Phillips, D. (2004) Processes of educational borrowing in historical context. In D. Phillips and K. Ochs (eds) *Educational Policy Borrowing: Historical Perspectives*. Oxford: Symposium Books.

Ojo, B.A. (2009) E-learning and the global divide: the challenges facing distance education in Africa. *Turkish On-line Journal of Distance Education*, 10(3): 68–79.

Phillips, D. and Schweisfurth, M. (2006) *Comparative and International Education: An Introduction to Theory, Method and Practice*. London: Continuum.

Roth, W.M. (2008) Bricolage, métissage, hybridity, heterogeneity, diaspora: concepts for thinking science education in the 21st century. *Cultural Studies of Science Education*, 3: 891–916.

Shibata, M. (2005) *Japan and Germany under the US Occupation: A Comparative Analysis of the Post-war Education Reform*. Oxford: Lexington Books.

Thompson, J. (2002) International education: towards a shared understanding. *Journal of Research in International Education*, 1(1): 508.

Tomlinson, K. and Benefield, P. (2005) *Education and Conflict: Research and Research Possibilities*. Draft report, January: National Foundation for Educational Research.

Tomusk, V. (ed.) (2006) *Creating the European Area of Higher Education: Voices from the Periphery*. Dordrecht: Springer.

Tulasiewicz, W. and Brock, C. (2000) The place of education in a united Europe. In C. Brock and W. Tulasiewicz (eds) *Education in a Single Europe*. London: Routledge.

UNESCO (United Nations Educational Scientific and Cultural Organization) (2000a) *Fifth Session of the Advisory Committee on Education for Peace, Human Rights, Democracy, International Understanding and Tolerance: Final Report*. Paris: UNESCO.

UNESCO (United Nations Educational Scientific and Cultural Organization) (2000b) *The Dakar Framework Education for All: Meeting Our Collective Commitments*. Paris: UNESCO.

Wood, K. (2004) International perspectives: the USA and the Pacific Rim. In S. Ward (ed.) *Education Studies: A Student's Guide*. Abingdon: RoutledgeFalmer.

Wortham, S., Mortimer, K. and Allard, E. (2009) Mexicans as model minorities in the New Latino diaspora. *Anthropology and Education Quarterly*, 40(4): 388–404.

# APPENDIX: Governments and secretaries of state for education

**Table A.1** Post-war administrations 1945–2010

| Party | Date formed | Prime Minister |
|---|---|---|
| Labour | July 1945 | Clement Attlee |
| Labour | February 1950 | Clement Attlee |
| Conservative | October 1951 | Winston Churchill |
| Conservative | May 1955 | Sir Anthony Eden |
| Conservative | January 1957 | Harold Macmillan |
| Conservative | October 1959 | Harold Macmillan |
| Conservative | October 1963 | Sir Alec Douglas-Home |
| Labour | October 1964 | Harold Wilson |
| Labour | March 1966 | Harold Wilson |
| Conservative | June 1970 | Edward Heath |
| Labour | February 1974 | Harold Wilson |
| Labour | October 1974 | Harold Wilson |
| Labour | April 1976 | James Callaghan |
| Conservative | May 1979 | Margaret Thatcher |
| Conservative | June 1983 | Margaret Thatcher |
| Conservative | June 1987 | Margaret Thatcher |
| Conservative | November 1990 | John Major |
| Conservative | April 1992 | John Major |
| Labour (1) | May 1997 | Tony Blair |
| Labour (2) | June 2001 | Tony Blair |
| Labour (3) | May 2005 | Tony Blair |
| Labour (4) | June 2007 | Gordon Brown |
| Conservative/Liberal-Democrats | May 2010 | David Cameron |

**Table A.2** Ministers of Education 1945–64

| | |
|---|---|
| Ellen Wilkinson | July 1945–February 1947 |
| George Tomlinson | February 1947–November 1951 |
| Florence Horsbrugh | November 1951–October 1954 |
| Sir David Eccles | October 1954–January 1957 |
| Viscount Hailsham | January 1957–September 1957 |
| Geoffrey Lloyd | September 1957–October 1959 |
| Sir David Eccles | October 1959–July 1962 |
| Sir Edward Boyle | July 1962–March 1964 |

In 1964, the Education Minister became known as the Secretary of State for Education and Science when the Ministry of Education was reorganized as the Department of Education and Science.

**Table A.3** Secretaries of State 1964–2010

| | |
|---|---|
| Quintin Hogg | April 1964–October 1964 |
| Michael Stewart | October 1964–January 1965 |
| Anthony Crosland | January 1965–August 1967 |
| Patrick Gordon-Walker | August 1967–April 1968 |
| Edward Short | April 1968–June 1970 |
| Margaret Thatcher | June 1970–March 1974 |
| Reginald Prentice | March 1974–June 1975 |
| Fred Mulley | June 1975–September 1976 |
| Shirley Williams | September 1976–May 1979 |
| Mark Carlisle | May 1979–September 1981 |
| Sir Keith Joseph | September 1981–May 1986 |
| Kenneth Baker | May 1986–July 1989 |
| John MacGregor | July 1989–November 1990 |
| Kenneth Clarke | November 1990–April 1992 |
| John Patten | April 1992–July 1994 |
| Gillian Shephard | July 1994–May 1997 |

**Table A.4** New Labour

| | |
|---|---|
| David Blunkett | May 1997–June 2001 |
| Estelle Morris | June 2001–October 2002 |
| Charles Clarke | October 2002–December 2004 |
| Ruth Kelly | December 2004–May 2006 |
| Alan Johnson | May 2006–June 2007 |

In June 2007 the Education Secretary became the Secretary of State for Children, Schools and Families.

| Ed Balls | June 2007–May 2010 |
|---|---|

Conservative–Liberal coalition government

| Michael Gove | May 2010– |
|---|---|

In May 2010, Michael Gove became the Education Secretary at the Department for Education.

# Index

The index entries appear in word-by-word alphabetical order.

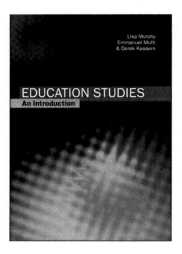

**EDUCATION STUDIES**
**An Introduction**

Lisa Murphy, Emmanuel Mufti
& Derek Kassem

978-0-33522-351-0 (Paperback)
2008

This book is an essential guide for all education studies students, providing you with a clear overview of the key issues within your first year. It is an introductory text that encourages critical engagement, to enable you to develop a detailed understanding of the power and importance of education.

**Key features:**

- Introductions to each chapter to link the themes discussed in each section
- A summary of the key issues in each chapter for reflection
- Examples and case studies
- Links to key readings

www.openup.co.uk

OPEN UNIVERSITY PRESS
McGraw - Hill Education